2897877

1/

828,912

Bloom's Modern Critical Views

Bloom's Modern Critical Views

Bloom's Modern Critical Views

G.K. CHESTERTON

Edited and with an introduction by
Harold Bloom
Sterling Professor of the Humanities
Yale University

CHELSEA HOUSE
PUBLISHERS
An imprint of Infobase Publishing

Bloom's Modern Critical Views: G.K. Chesterton

Chelsea House
An imprint of Infobase Publishing
132 West 31st Street
New York NY 10001

Library of Congress Cataloging-in-Publication Data

Bloom, Harold.
 G.K. Chesterton / Harold Bloom.
    p. cm. — (Bloom's modern critical views)
 Includes bibliographical references and index.
 ISBN 0-7910-8131-1
 1. Chesterton, G. K. (Gilbert Keith), 1874-1936—Criticism and interpretation. I. Title. II. Series.
 PR4453.C4Z6457 2005
 828'.91209—dc22   2005030084

Chelsea House books are available at special discounts when purchased in bulk quantities for businesses, associations, institutions, or sales promotions. Please call our Special Sales Department in New York at (212) 967-8800 or (800) 322-8755.

You can find Chelsea House on the World Wide Web at http://www.chelseahouse.com

Contributing Editor: Jerry Napoli
Cover design by Keith Trego

Printed in the United States of America

Bang EJB 10 9 8 7 6 5 4 3 2 1

This book is printed on acid-free paper.

All links and web addresses were checked and verified to be correct at the time of publication. Because of the dynamic nature of the web, some addresses and links may have changed since publication and may no longer be valid.

Contents

Editor's Note

My introduction, unhappily ambivalent, celebrates Chesterton's marvelous fantasy narrative *The Man Who Was Thursday*, but also surveys the virulent representations of "The Jews" throughout Chesterton's career.

Hugh Kenner, the late High Priest of what once was called Literary Modernism, exalts Chesterton's "perceptivity", which he audaciously compares to the mythmaking faculty of William Blake and of James Joyce.

More realistically, Garry Wills give us a carefully limited defense of Chesterton-as-poet, particularly in *The Ballad of the White Horse*.

In a careful study of Chestertonian allegory, Lynette Hunter leads us through the work of 1904–1907: *The Napoleon of Notting Hill*, *The Ball and the Cross*, and *The Man Who Was Thursday*.

John Coats usefully traces the mingled influence of Robert Browning, Charles Dickens, and Victor Hugo upon Chesterton's conception of the Grotesque in literature, which Chesterton consciously opposed to the Aestheticism of Walter Pater.

Browning's version of the Grotesque is shrewdly judged by John Pfordresher to be peculiarly central to Chesterton, who defended it from the attack of Walter Bagehot, while employing John Ruskin as a critical armory in the defense.

The Sublime and Terrible, both allied to the Grotesque, are emphasized in Elmar Schenkel's account of the Father Brown stories, where Chesterton fights to reconcile his dread of chaos with the Christian arguments for discovering an order in reality.

Orthodoxy, Chesterton's major idea of order, is analyzed by Ed Block, Jr. as an antidote to nihilism, always a temptation for the tumultuous Chesterton.

Chaucer, Chesterton's crown as a literary critic, is seen by John McCabe as a celebration of Chaucerian piety, which I find to be a simplification of a critical study that warns us to be wary of Chaucer's ironies. As Chesterton wisely remarked, they sometimes are too large to be seen.

Marian E. Crowe gracefully reminds us of Chesterton's esteem for Jane Austen, whose *Pride and Prejudice* is then read as an allegory of Chestertonian Orthodoxy, reconciling opposites in a creative tension.

In this volume's splendid final essay, Robert Caserio illuminates *The Man Who Was Thursday* by contrasting its identification of Modernism and Anarchist-terrorism with similar insights of Don DeLillo in *Mao II*, and of Joseph Conrad's *The Secret Agent* and *Under Western Eyes*. But Caserio adds his own apprehension of Chesterton's central touch of paradox: terrorism is ultimately sanctioned by the God of orthodoxy, who works his own ends, beyond our comprehension.

HAROLD BLOOM

Introduction

Chesterton goes on puzzling me, because I find his critical sensibility far more congenial to me than that of T.S. Eliot, and yet his anti-Semitism is at least as ugly as Eliot's. Borges, anything but anti-Jewish, praised the Father Brown stories while overlooking their rabid vilification of Jewry, and Auden, whose Christianity purified itself of any prejudice, told me that he blamed Chesterton's dislike of Jews upon the malign influence of Hilaire Belloc. Auden, alas, was mistaken, as anyone can learn by reading Bryan Cheyette's *Constructions of "The Jew" in English Literature and Society, 1875–1945* (Cambridge, 1993). Cheyette demonstrates rather fully that even Chesterton's early fiction and journalism abound in obsessive portraits of the "cosmopolitan Jew" as the dreaded enemy of Christian virtue and orthodoxy.

Dying in 1936, Chesterton did not experience the Second World War and the eventual exposure of Hitler's Holocaust. Whether he would have reacted as Eliot did, with indifference, I am unable to surmise. But Chesterton's nervous breakdown of 1914 evidently was caused by his brother Cecil's loss of a case for criminal libel brought against him by the brother of Rufus Isaacs, the Lord Chief Justice. So far as I can tell, G.K. Chesterton thereafter unceasingly associated his own fear of madness with the menacing figure of "the Jew." In *The Everlasting Man* (1925), Christianity is referred to as "wholly European" in opposition to those "inhuman" religions, Judaism and Islam. Chesterton went beyond this in *The New Jerusalem* (1920), which calls upon England to pass a law requiring that all Jews must be dressed like Arabs. One could admit that would have been more colorful than making them wear yellow Stars of David.

I would like to conjure up the great and good Borges in a séance to ask how he could tolerate the story "The Resurrection of Father Brown" (*circa*

1925). In this lively tale, two Latin-American Jewish terrorists, Mendoza and Alvarez, plot to discredit all Catholic miracles, from Jesus to Chesterton. Indeed, Father Brown, in other stories, is one of the pioneers in discovering vast international plots that bring together Jewish Communists and Jewish finance capitalists.

By 1930, Chesterton was praising Mussolini, and he went on later to blame the Jews for Hitler's ascension to power. I remember saying to Auden that anti-Semitism was indistinguishable both from Chesterton's Roman Catholicism and from Eliot's Anglo-Catholicism, an observation Auden found unacceptable. He had retorted to Belloc that: "Every Christian is, of course, both Pilate and Caiaphas," which is an observation in the spirit of Kierkegaard, who equated the political triumph of Christianity with its abolishment. But then, neither Chesterton nor Eliot was at all Kierkegaardian.

2

As a Jewish literary critic, nevertheless I turn to *The Man Who Was Thursday* (1908) because it remains the best of all Chesterton's dozens of books, and the most genial, composed in his prime at thirty-three or -four. His obsessions and his breakdown are far in the Unapparent, and his exuberance is extraordinary, even for him. Six of seven Anarchist archons turn out to be detectives-in-disguise, and Sunday, whom they pursue vainly at the close, is the Sabbath or Peace of God, and so the Chestertonian God Himself. Paradoxes tumble over one another, and an ecstasy of total reconciliation happily ensues. A day before his death in 1936, Chesterton printed an odd little note asserting that Sunday was *not* "a serious description of Deity," but an "elemental imp," though on the right side, that is, optimism. But that was only another paradox: I like best the hint that God was rather like Chesterton, and not the other way around.

Of course, just as Jesus Christ was an Englishman (for Chesterton, as he is an American, for George W. Bush) so Sunday is altogether a British eccentric. But why should he not be? In 2006, Chesterton cannot be cleansed of his Fascist leanings, but few will care in a United States that now fuses plutocracy with Evangelical theocracy. As a poet, Chesterton blended Swinburne with Kipling, but his stories and fantasy-narratives are his own. Except for *The Man Who Was Thursday*, the best of Chesterton, for me, is in his biographical criticism of Chaucer and of Dickens. On Shakespeare, he had the wisdom to temper his quest for a fellow-Catholic with the fine observation that the protagonists of the major tragedies were "great spirits in chains." Chesterton's book on Browning preludes D.H. Lawrence's *Study of*

Thomas Hardy: both Chesterton and Lawrence happily wrote about themselves and not their rugged precursors criticism, Oscar Wilde rewarded, is the only civilized forum of autobiography.

HUGH KENNER

The Word and the World

The essential Chesterton is the man with the extraordinarily comprehensive intuition of being the implications of which we have been exploring. There is a sense in which his enormous literary production is a by-product; what must be praised in Chesterton is not the writing but the seeing. The reader who has followed the preceding chapters is well on the way to realizing this fact; if he has seen that Chesterton's wildest parallels and metaphors are not excogitated illustrations of the vision but ingredients of it he has gotten nearly all a commentary can give him. Our final task is to examine the nature and quality of Chesterton's writing, defining as we do so a third kind of paradox which may be labelled the aesthetic. It is essential to consider him as an artist, however inartistic he may be, because his vision is after all manifested in language, and his every excursion into language brings him up against certain problems of the artist.

We must first of all enforce a distinction that was made in the opening pages of this book, between art as making in general and art as a significant expansion of sensibility. This may be most directly done by determining exactly what kind of merit can be claimed for Chesterton's poetry. Like most poets he is praised to-day by his admirers for the wrong reasons. Charity would suggest leaving the uncritical Chestertonian to his illusions, but

---

From *Paradox in Chesterton.* © 1948 by Sheed and Ward, Ltd.

prudence insists that the bubble must be pricked, because of the curiously exclusive nature of misguided praise. If a man is praised for the wrong reasons he will almost certainly not be praised for the right reasons. This is attested in the present instance by the abject refusal of Chestertonians to see that interest in their idol as a significant figure must centre not on his cleverness or heartiness but on his perceptivity.

Consider, for example, the opening of one of the best of Chesterton's poems, *Gloria in Profundis*:

> There has fallen on earth for a token
> A god too great for the sky.
> He has burst out of all things and broken
> The bounds of eternity:
> Into time and the terminal land
> He has strayed like a thief or a lover,
> For the wine of the world brims over,
> Its splendour is spilt on the sand.[1]

The paradoxes here are perhaps more directly and explicitly rooted in the Incarnation than any considered in the last chapter, and a little thought will justify any of them. Our concern here is with the mode of their poetic realization, and the judgment must be that the realization is not poetic at all, but intellectual. The alliteration (via Swinburne) and the hearty rhythmic thump (via Kipling) exert a hypnotic influence in their own right and direct attention away from the intellectual content. There is no development of imagery: one must pause, shutting one's ears to the sound, to think out the aptness of the thief, the lover, and the wine-cup as analogues for Christ; and each image exists in isolation, without connections before and after. The latter is also true of each stanza; the four stanzas of the poem may be arranged, without serious confusion, in any one of twenty-four possible orders. In sum, the reader is confronted with a cluster of epigrams while a brass band drums at his ears.

The reader who will compare this poem, or any Chesterton poem he likes, with, say, the fourth part of T.S. Eliot's "East Coker" (in *Four Quartets*) will have no difficulty perceiving the radical difference. Eliot, for example, writes, in a passage equally replete with paradox:

> The whole earth is our hospital
> Endowed by the ruined millionaire,
> Wherein, if we do well, we shall

Die of the absolute paternal care
    That will not leave us, but prevents us everywhere.[2]

Here the operative word is "die," finely enforced by its initial position in the line. Expectancy of the rhyme with "hospital" slows down the reading of "we shall"—a process accentuated by the parenthetical interruption "if we do well"—and further isolates the key-word "die," enforcing the paradoxical contrast with "doing well"; which contrast in turn suddenly expands the convalescent associations of "if we do well" to a moral well-doing implicated in the moral irony of the nature of man. These hints on the way one word in the stanza is made to function could be carried on indefinitely to involve all the rest of the poem, although written analysis is at best a clumsy demonstrative instrument. Enough has been said, however, to show that in the Eliot stanza all the poetic devices are enlisted behind, and not at cross-purposes with, the "meaning"; which meaning is not a detachable intellectual thing but consists in one's total response to the entire stanza.

This radical difference in the mode of working of the two poets cannot be brushed aside by calling the demonstrable differences merely finicky or ascribing Eliot's superiority to more laborious craftsmanship. Indeed the latter argument tells exactly the other way. Chesterton is simply uninterested in the job a serious poet undertakes. The merit that can be claimed for his verse, once the careful reader has shut his ears to the sound-effects and deciphered the relevance of the array of images, is simply the merit owing to any triumphal celebration. Read in this way, as celebrations of cosmic fact, his poems take on their full meaning; but it is a philosophical, not a poetical meaning, and a noisy rather than a perceptive celebration.

That he should write in this way is the inevitable consequence of the way he perceived. The conflicts reflected in the language are not in his mind but out in front of him, in the things; he admires them, he does not feel involved in them. His analogical vision was both total and in an odd way painless. It unfits him for poetry; it equips him admirably and beyond question for philosophy and exposition.

The next thing to be said about Chesterton as an artist is that his poetic failure carries with it no moral imputation. He fails because he is so constituted that certain gears will never mesh: not because he misconceives the moral basis of making. In a moral sense, in fact, and within the limits of a "less intense definition that includes under "art" all making, even the making of expositions, he is unsurpassed in his time. He never fumbles to reach a position, because he never needs to reach a position. He occupies a central position all the time. And he never fumbles in stating some truth drawn from contemplation of the nature of things, because his statements are so intimately bound up with his perceptions that the central clarity of the latter induces an authoritative finality in the former. It cannot be too often repeated that his gifts and habits were such as to fit him pre-eminently for philosophical discourse. In a better age, with greater incentive for scholarship and less pressure for immediate, continuous, and dissipating journalistic action, he might have been a principal ornament of the mediaeval Sorbonne. It is doing him the fullest possible homage to call him a splendid anachronism: the operative word is splendid.

Yet he was by no means an anachronism in any moral or political sense. Indeed it is curious to compare his continual centrality with the centre to which the most recent of the intelligent socially conscious are turning. The comparison emphasizes even further Chesterton's firm roots in a timeless philosophy. For the post-war world is cluttered with the hulks of disillusioned Marxists, and some few of them are suddenly and earnestly discovering the kind of cultural conditions and the kind of conception of man which Chesterton had been celebrating since the turn of the century.

From a September, 1946 speech by André Malraux, for example, I extract the following numbed recognition that the nineteenth-century progressive dream that nourished Marxism is at last pragmatically dead:

> At the end of the Nineteenth Century the voice of Nietzsche took up the classical refrain, "God is dead," and gave it a new and tragic sense. Everyone knew that the death of the deity meant the liberation and deification of man.
>
> The question which faces us all to-day on this old European earth is whether not God but man is dead....
>
> Europe, ravaged and bloody, is not more ravaged and bloody than the picture of mankind which in the pre-war days it hoped to create.[3]

It is with pardonable satisfaction that one now turns to *Heretics*:

> The modern man says, "Let us leave all these arbitrary standards and embrace liberty." This is, logically rendered, "Let us not decide what is good, but let it be considered good not to decide it." He says, "Away with your old moral formulae; I am for progress." This, logically stated, means, "Let us not settle what is good, but let us settle whether we are getting more of it." ...

Never perhaps since the beginning of the world has there been an age that had less right to use the word "progress" than we.[4]

Malraux is lamenting the passing on an ideal in which he had for a long time invested everything. Chesterton did not need to have any such ideal beaten out of his head by two bloody wars. *Heretics* was published in 1905.

The April, 1946 issue of *Politics*, to take another example, contains some 10,000 anxious words of socialist self-searching under the general title, "The Root is Man." The author is a sincere man, and a responsible one. Yet to follow him in his valiant, hesitant, fumbling approach to the Chestertonian position ("All I attempt here is to explain, as coherently as possible, why the Marxian approach to socialism no longer satisfies me, and to indicate the general direction in which I think a more fruitful approach may be made") is to realize most forcibly, while applauding a new political hopefulness, the fact that Mr. Dwight Macdonald is merely groping after the most elementary principles of *What's Wrong With the World*, which Chesterton dashed off in 1912. This is not to wish that Chesterton had been listened to long ago: too facile a mass conversion would have been unearned and subject to relapse. It is rather to wish that there had been, contemporary with him, twenty men of his unique gifts.

Such comparison of his spontaneity with the hampered and stammering effort of other men emphasizes the easy inevitability of phrase and analogue which made his vast output possible, and which is usually wrongly accounted for. What, to take a concrete instance, is the exact explanation of that Chestertonian habit which has so distressed so many sensitive reviewers, the habit of allowing a categorical conclusion to issue from a play upon words? Mr. Maurice Evans, for example, is concerned with

The illegitimate use to which Chesterton frequently puts his admirable command of word and image, so that proof appears, where, in fact, none exists. Analogy is obviously a very dangerous weapon in this respect, for what begins as an illustration may, after sufficient development, be accepted as proof.... For example, he observes that the American mentality is child-like and laves "to watch the wheels go round" (*Generally Speaking*). Then taking the metaphor literally, he argues from it: "watching the wheels go round" implies that they will return back to the same place, or if they move on, they will move in a rut. Therefore, Americans are conservative. This may be the case, but there is no logical connection in the argument.[5]

This may be the case, one must reply, but there is in fact no argument present. Mr. Evans does not realize that he has been told a parable.

The parable, as Belloc had the sagacity to observe, is Chesterton's chosen form:

> His unique, his capital genius for illustration by parallel, by example, is his peculiar mark.... No one whatsoever that I can recall in the whole course of English letters had his amazing—I would almost say superhuman—capacity for parallelism.
>
> Now parallelism is a gift or method of vast effect in the conveyance of truth.
>
> Parallelism consists in the illustration of some unperceived truth by its exact consonance with the reflection of a truth already known and perceived....
>
> Thus if some ass propounds that a difference of application destroys the validity of a doctrine, or that particulars are the enemies of universals, Chesterton will answer: "It is as though you were to say that I cannot be an Englishman because I am a Londoner." ... Always, in whatever manner he launched the parallelism, he produced the shock of illumination. He *taught*.
>
> He made men see what they had not seen before. He made them *know*. He was an architect of certitude, whenever he practised this art in which he excelled.
>
> The example of the parable in Holy Writ will at once occur to the reader. It is of the same origin and of similar value. The "parable" of the Gospels differs only from pure parallelism in the artifice of introducing a story in order to capture the reader's mind. But in essence a parable is the same thing as a parallelism.
>
> Let us remark in conclusion that parallelism is of particular value in a society such as ours which has lost the habit of thinking. It illustrates and thereby fixes a truth or experience as a picture fixes a face or landscape in the mind.[6]

When Christ says, "Salt is good; but if the salt have lost his saltness, wherewith will ye season it? Have salt in yourselves, and have peace one with another," no one accuses Him of a *non sequitur*. The parable is obviously a parallelism, the illumination of the unknown by its exact consonance with a truth previously perceived. There is no attempt to argue from an observation about salt to an injunction about peace, which is the kind of argument Mr. Evans and other critics accuse Chesterton of attempting. Yet they never so accuse Christ: not merely; it may be suspected, because it is patently not the job of Divinity to argue. One reason Christ is sacrosanct is probably to be found in a popular tradition that He is solemn: as if He had never produced the wine for a feast. If Christ had playfully turned the lost sheep of the parable of the ninety and nine into a stray from a herd of kangaroos, it would have been all up with Him as a theologian. Apropos of solemnity Chesterton observes:

> If you say that two sheep added to two sheep make four sheep, your audience will accept it patiently—like sheep. But if you say it of two monkeys, or two kangaroos, or two sea-green griffins, people will refuse to believe that two and two make four. They seem to imagine that you have made up the arithmetic, just as you have made up the illustration of the arithmetic. And though they would actually know that what you say is sense, if they thought about it sensibly, they cannot believe that anything decorated by an incidental joke can be sensible.[7]

The joke and the parable are not so far apart as they seem; for properly speaking even the statement, "two sheep and two sheep make four sheep" is a parable; a common corporeal phenomenon corresponding exactly to the unfamiliar, almost mystical idea that two and two make four. Sheep as a parallel to an abstract idea are fascinating and fantastic enough to make one wonder why the solemn critic should boggle at kangaroos. It is still more important, however, to recognize the almost irresponsible fantasy by which the word "two," either as a set of wriggly marks on paper or as a man-made noise at once abrupt and cooing, is made to correspond to that same abstract idea, the idea of twoness. The word is certainly not the reality; it is only something analogous to the reality. Apropos of allegorical painting, Chesterton asks:

> But what does the word "hope" represent? It represents only a broken instantaneous glimpse of something that is immeasurably older and wilder than language, that is immeasurably older and wilder than man: a mystery to saints and a reality to wolves. To suppose that such a thing is dealt with by the word "hope," any more than America is represented by a distant view of Cape Horn, would indeed be ridiculous. It is not merely true that the word itself is, like any other word, arbitrary; that it might as well be "pig" or "parasol"; but it is true that the philosophical meaning

of the word, in the conscious mind of man, is merely a part of something immensely larger in the unconscious mind, that the gusty light of language only falls for a moment on a fragment, and that obviously a semi-detached, unfinished fragment of a certain definite pattern on the dark tapestries of reality. It is vain and worse than vain to declaim against the allegoric for the very word "hope" is an allegory and the very word "allegory" is an allegory.[8]

Language is not thought, and thought is not reality, any more than figures in a ledger are money, or money is human wealth. Yet one must always use language and thought, as the book-keeper must always use figures and coins. One can never, in short, escape parallelism; and we never speak but in parables.

"I doubt whether any truth can be told except in parable," Chesterton makes one of his characters say; and the proposition is accompanied by its Chestertonian corollary: "I doubt whether any of our actions is really anything but an allegory."[9] That these observations were self-evident to him in the light of his metaphysical intuition of being may be guessed from the central lines of the poem *Ubi Ecclesia*:

Where things are not what they seem,
But what they mean.[10]

One who saw the world as a vast inter-reflecting organism saw language implicated in that reality along with every other ingredient. When Chesterton writes, in short, the very words he uses are part of the vision he exploits; his facility in word and image derives from a real analogical relation, of which he was keenly aware, between language and the other parts of reality. To tax him with verbalism is to deny the existence of analogy, to deny that anything is like any other thing, to deny therefore that connecting things by thinking has any metaphysical meaning: all that. It is rank nominalism.

He was a sturdy realist; and his vision of things showed him very clearly what he could most readily do. His favorite logical device was the *reductio ad absurdum*, because that line of argument springs most readily, with the least possible degree of abstractness, from a direct metaphysical perception. When you see that something is absurd, you are in touch with reality.

It is true for the same reason, though insufficient, to say that he was more concerned with stating cases than proving them. It is still more accurate to say that he strove above all else to *show* men what he saw, on the principle that a thing once seen is its own proof.

> False religion ... is always trying to express concrete facts as abstract; it calls sex affinity; it calls wine alcohol; it calls brute starvation the economic problem. The test of true religion is that its energy drives exactly the other way; it is always trying to make men feel truths as facts; always trying to make abstract things as plain and solid as concrete things; always trying to make men, not merely admit the truth, but see, smell, handle, hear, and devour the truth.[11]

Hence Chesterton's purple patches, his parallelisms, his vivid word-play. Hence his perpetual reiteration of concrete imagery, concrete argument: his avoidance of language which unhappily no longer keenly indicates reality, having been abstracted to death. In *Orthodoxy* he says

> If you say, "The social utility of the indeterminate sentence is recognized by all criminologists as a part of our sociological evolution towards a more humane and scientific view of punishment," you can go on talking like that for hours with hardly a movement of the grey matter inside your skull. But if you say, "I wish Jones to go to gaol and Brown to say when Jones shall come out," you will discover, with a thrill of horror, that you are obliged to think. The long words are not the hard words, it is the short words that are hard. There is much more metaphysical subtlety in the word "damn" than in the word "degeneration."[12]

On these principles, in the kind of argument we have caught Mr. Evans deploring, Chesterton translates the jargon of a Swiss professor about the conscience into short words which force men to think, and then reproduces the pattern of absurdity presented by those naked words with a corresponding pattern secured by putting for the word "conscience" the word "nose." He does not argue, he need not argue, that the statement about conscience is as absurd as the statement about noses. It was always absurd. One does not even need to know the meaning of the word "conscience" to see the absurdity. The law of logic has been transgressed, and it is a logical, not a factual, flaw that is being exposed. Unfortunately, logic is a strangely unfamiliar tool: equally unfortunately, no one has ever seen a conscience, though all men have seen noses. Hence it is that nonsense talked about the conscience has a fair chance of passing muster, though corresponding talk about noses fairly shrieks its own falsity.

Having grasped all this, the reader of the following passage will not accuse Chesterton of irresponsible play:

> The first argument is that man has no *conscience* because some men are quite mad, and therefore not particularly *conscientious*. The second argument is that man has no conscience because some men are more conscientious than others. And the third is that man has no conscience because conscientious men in different countries and quite different circumstances often do very different things. Professor Forel applies these arguments eloquently to the question of human consciences; and I really cannot see why I should not apply them to the question of human noses. Man has no nose because now and then a man has no nose—I believe Sir William Davenant, the poet, had none. Man has no nose because some noses are longer than others, or can smell better than others. Man has no nose because not only are noses of different shapes, but (oh, piercing sword of scepticism!) some men use their noses and find the smell of incense nice, while some use their noses and find it nasty. Science therefore declares that man is normally noseless; and will take this for granted in the next four or five hundred pages, and will treat all the alleged noses of history as the quaint legends of a credulous age.[13]

The nose-pattern repeating the conscience-pattern is the type of all Chesterton's writing. The truths with which he deals are not those of a rarefied kind which the normal mind can only discover at the further end of a wearisome logical process; they are mostly elementary truisms which have only to be *seen*. "It is the paradox of human language," he says of the fundamental convictions, "that though these truths are in a manner past all parallel hard and clear, yet any attempt to talk about them always has the appearance of being hazy and elusive.[14] The best that language can do is indicate them, and the best language for the purpose is that which indicates most sharply. It follows that Chesterton's concern throughout his writing will be to frame paragraphs which first, correspond with the reality whereon he has fixed his eye, and second, shout for attention. "We try," he says, "to make our sermons and speeches more or less amusing.... for the very simple and even modest reason that we do not see why the audience should listen unless it is more or less amused."[15]

Chesterton's humility here underrates his achievement. We have discussed in Chapter III the rhetorical function served by much of his paradox; equally important is the way word, image, and epigram cooperate to do superbly something that could not otherwise be done at all, when, as too rarely, he disciplines them rigidly in the service of metaphysical statement. The example of the nose and the conscience cited above is really excessively simple; as an instance of the precision and flexibility Chesterton was capable of when he chose, it is worth while examining the working of the paragraph, already quoted on page 76, which develops the comparison between the mystical mind and the dandy's dressing-room. As usual, he opens with a specific example, the wooden post:

> When (our contemporary mystics) said that a wooden post was wonderful, they meant that they could make something wonderful out of it by thinking about it. "Dream; there is no truth," said Mr. Yeats, "but in your heart."

The quotation from Yeats recalls to the reader any number of similar statements, and so places Chesterton's simplification in relation to the entire tradition he is attacking. With the next sentence the controlling image is introduced:

> The modern mystic looked for the post, not outside in the garden, but inside, in the mirror of his own mind. But the mind of the mystic, like a dandy's dressing-room, was entirely made of mirrors. That glass repeated glass like doors opening inwards for ever; till one could hardly see that inmost chamber of unreality where the post made its last appearance.

The word "dandy" reflects on "mystic" as much as on "dressing-room"; and at the same time the stock image of the mirror of the mind is subtly transmuted into a vivid, pejorative image of a room lined with mirrors. "Dressing-room" brings to mind the triptych mirrors at tailors', where everyone has had experience of infinite multiple reflections; and the additional comparison of doors opening inwards for ever gives additional concrete force to the idea. In the final clause, "inmost chamber of unreality" gives new precision to the comparison of the mystic's mind to a room: and the sequence ends where it began, at a deeper level of penetration. In the next sentence, mirrors return, with a difference:

And as the mirrors of the modern mystic's mind are most of them
curved and many of them cracked, the post in its ultimate
reflection looked like all sorts of things ... etc.

It is perhaps unnecessary to point out that "cracked," applied to the
mirror and to the mind, has double force. Another functional pun turns up
immediately afterwards:

But I was never interested in mirrors; that is, I was never
interested in my own reflection—or reflections.

"Reflection" is of course supplied by the mirror-imagery, with an
overtone of vanity vs. humility; Chesterton is never far from the moral
implications of metaphysics. And the pun introduced by "reflections"
brilliantly refocuses the entire enquiry on the operations of the mind,
preparing for a statement of the positive conclusions:

I am interested in wooden posts, which do startle me like
miracles. I am interested in the post that stands waiting outside
my door, to hit me over the head, like a giant's club in a fairy tale.

The giant's club recalls the episode of bumping into a post which was
the initial stimulus of the essay; but it here functions locally as a physical
image of the metaphysical surprise evoked in "posts which do startle me like
miracles." In the next sentence the door outside which the post stands
introduces a transition to the doors of the senses which open on that mental
room with which the preceding passage has been concerned: and the
peroration after so much preparation carries enormous force:

All my mental doors open outwards into a world I have not made.
My last door of liberty opens upon a world of sun and solid things,
of objective adventures. The post in the garden; the thing I could
neither create nor expect; strong plain daylight on stiff upstanding
wood; it is the Lord's doing and it is marvellous in our eyes.

Careful study along these lines of the way in which the transition from
image to image is made in similar passages will reinforce the constant theme
of this chapter: that Chesterton's writing at its best is concerned with fixing
exactly a statement of a metaphysical vision, by indicating relationships of
word and example within that vision. He is. not inventing illustrations, he is

perceiving them. The conventional patristic divine, Jeremy Taylor, summarizes the kind of analogical perception that this writing is exploring:

> Thus when (God) made the beauteous frame of heaven and earth, he rejoyced in it, and glorified himself, because it was a glasse in which he beheld his wisdom, and Almighty power: ... For if God is glorified in the Sunne and Moon, in the rare fabric of the honeycombs, in the discipline of Bees, in the economy of Pismires, in the little houses of birds, in the curiosity of an eye, God being pleased to delight in those little images and reflexes of himself from those pretty mirrours, which like a crevice in a wall thorow a narrow perspective transmit the species of a vast excellency: much rather shall God be pleased to behold himself in the glasses of our obedience....[16]

Gerard Manley Hopkins puts it more succinctly: "This world then is word, expression, news of God."[17] Chesterton would interpret that news. Perception of this fact reduces to a simple manifestation of humility his claim to be a journalist rather than an artist.[18] If he was not a creative artist, he was, when he took the pains, an extremely competent workman, framing intricate analogies to interpret the supreme analogy which he saw all around him. He was in this sense an artist because he was the highest kind of journalist, having as his object truth.

He suggests in *William Blake* the way in which the analogist's art must be called in to present truth:

> In the modern intellectual world we can see flags of many colours, deeds of manifold interest; the one thing we cannot see is the map. We cannot see the simplified statement which tells us what is the origin of all the trouble. How shall we manage to state in an obvious and alphabetical manner the ultimate query, the primordial point on which the whole modern argument turns? It cannot be done in long rationalistic words; they convey by their very sound the suggestion of something subtle. One must try to think of something in the way of a plain street metaphor or an obvious analogy. For the thing is not too hard for human speech; it is actually too obvious for human speech.[19]

The plain street metaphor or the obvious analogy are for Chesterton the simple key to the problem of conveying reality, short-circuiting as they

do the fore-doomed attempt to trace the contradictory labyrinth of being
with any continuous rational thread. "Long rationalistic words ... convey by
their very sound the suggestion of something subtle"; and being is the
reverse of subtle. It is simple, though the principle of analogy shows it to be
paradoxically complicated as well. A locomotive is both simple, in essence
and complicated in detail; one would scarcely call a locomotive subtle. And
one should beware of trying to describe a locomotive to the uninitiated by
rationalistically describing its workings, beginning with the vaporization of
heated water, lest its puffing power come to seem very subtle indeed. One
does better to call it an iron horse.

No one who has finally grasped these points will press the question,
why Chesterton's prose is so intricate. Too wise to try to explain the obvious,
he drew pictures of it; and his pictures, like those of God with whom the
artist is often audaciously compared, took on life; a life of their own; a life of
alliteration and epigram, of sudden unexpected correspondences, of
accidental patterns writhing and weaving with all the crawling energy of the
Gothic architecture which was his craftsman's ideal.[20]

We have shown in analysing the mirror-passage how Chesterton in his
best work manipulates his images functionally, to control the reader's
response towards a total meaning which cannot itself be briefly and exactly
stated. We have stated further Chesterton's explicit view that brief and exact
statement of an analogical reality is in fact *a priori* impossible. These
principles may be tidied up in a new statement of the ubiquitous necessity of
paradox: for in paradox is the practitioner of art, even expository art,
perpetually landed. The reason is that the thing, the work of art, that he is
constructing must both hang together itself and be consistent with the reality
on which his eye is fixed. Insofar as it hangs together itself, insofar as it obeys
its own artistic laws, it will have being, which is analogical. Its statements, to
put it another way, will in only a relative sense be logically interdependent.
Insofar as it is consistent with that other being whose shadow it is, it will not
only tend to be twisted out of coherent shape, but it will partake of the
paradoxicality of its prototype. The law that all being is intrinsically
analogical operates here with a double vengeance. Things are paradoxical,
and art performed in homage to those things is doubly so. If I say, for
example, that there is a pinkish man in the room, my exact transcript of
reality lands me in a paradox of language: it is customary to speak of a white
man. If I say that there is a white man in the room, I obey the laws of
language, but only by convention the laws of fact: a genuine white man
would be monstrous. The relationship between statement and fact is
analogical: you have paradox, whatever you do.

The artist, especially the artist like Chesterton with his eye on a ready reception, must be constantly in this way adjusting the strain between inner and outer consistency; constantly striving after words that will say something and at the same time say the right thing. And the more adequately his words proclaim both the unity of speech and that of being, both the contradictions of art and those of being, the more he will forge a chain of paradoxes. There is scarcely a great mystical poem in the language that is not, at the merely literal level, stark nonsense. Hence—and it is their most triumphant justification—hence the paradoxes of Gilbert Chesterton.

It is illuminating to notice how thoroughly paradox enters into the workmanship of that most conscious aesthetician among modern writers, James Joyce. The method of Joyce's masterwork, *Finnegans Wake*, concealed as it is by the use of some dozen different languages, is simply to fold paradoxes back upon themselves in such a way as to utter both contrasting halves simultaneously. When Joyce writes "phoenish," he is telescoping alpha and omega, the end and the beginning, *finish* and *phoenix*. When he writes, "For nought that is has bane," he says simultaneously, "Nothing that exists is evil," and "The appearances of evil have no permanence; they were not and they shall not be"; simultaneously posing and resolving the problem of pain.

The oddly esoteric vocabulary of *Finnegans Wake* represents a final straining attempt to overcome the basic paradox of art and make the Thing identical, beyond any possibility of separation, with its verbal vehicle. It utterly defeats paraphrase. It is not a little startling to see how this audacious, almost blasphemous attempt to re-utter the world-generating Word, to achieve a totality corresponding to the totality which is of God, achieves its object—insofar as it does achieve it—by virtue of multi-layered paradoxes whereby a river is all rivers, riverdom, woman, all of life, and but half of life; and a stone is an innkeeper, a dreamer, the fount of life, quite dead, and both food and feeder at his own funeral feast.

Joyce, as we shall see, has other affinities with Chesterton as a myth-maker. It is surely a demonstration of the contemporary critical muddle to find the most advanced experimenter of his time building upon the same first principles, and exploiting the same kind of analogical perception, as the man whom avant-garde critics decry as the very type of hearty Toryism.

Indeed it is the analogical perception which makes it possible for *Finnegans Wake* to be taken seriously; though Joyce, who, it is true, offers far more temptation to the inept than does Chesterton, has suffered from essentially the same charge of verbalism. Chesterton's insistence that the artist keep his eye on the object finds in the career of Joyce a particularly ironic vindication.

We have shown that Chesterton's eye never wandered from the object, from an especially intricate simultaneous perception. It is helpful to remember that he elevated this principle into a positive prescription. It is, to begin with, scarcely necessary to point out that keeping one's eye on the object does not mean copying the externals of the object. Rather it means knowing what the object is, knowing from the inside. This interior knowledge when it can be obtained is a guarantee against the errors introduced by falsely-framed concepts. The surest way to find out that the "economic man" doesn't exist is to try to draw a picture of him. It was the attempt to draw pictures of things that existed only as concepts that vitiated the later poetry of Blake; it took his art into that unreal otherworld of doubts and riddles that has for the past thirty years been the playground of a certain kind of critic. On the failure of Blake Chesterton commented,

> No pure mystic ever loved pure mystery. The mystic does not bring doubts and riddles: the doubts and riddles exist already.... The mystic is not the man who makes mysteries, but the man who destroys them. The mystic is one who offers an explanation which may be true or false but is always comprehensible. The man whose meaning remains mysterious fails, I think, as a mystic.[21]

The early Blake, he says, like every great mystic, was also a great rationalist.[22] In this sense, another great rationalist is Chesterton's own Father Brown. It is startling to count the Father Brown stories which turn on the war of reason with mystification. Father Brown, the professional supernaturalist, is constantly at war with the sham supernatural. In "The Arrow of Heaven" there is talk of a curse, misdirecting attention from a simple stabbing. In "The Perishing of the Pendragons" a family doom and a supernaturally flaming tower are reduced to mere arson and shipwreck. In "The Doom of the Darnaways" an ancient interdiction boils down to a very modern murder-plot.[23] These stories are repeated parables of the true function of the artist and seer; their wildly paradoxical solutions are true; the straightforward, frequently supernatural explanation is falsification. The cloak of evil, Chesterton seems to be saying, is the false paradox; the trap of truth is the incomplete paradox.

Equally the trap of truth is the word written in the void, the writer's eye not firmly fixed on the object. A parable of this principle is presented in the contrasting peasants of the following passage:

Knowing nine hundred words is not always more important than knowing what some of them mean. It is strictly and soberly true that any peasant, in a mud cabin in County Clare, when he names his child Michael, may really have a sense of the presence that smote down Satan, the arms and plumage of the paladin of paradise. I doubt whether it is so overwhelmingly probable that any clerk in any villa on Clapham Common, when he names his son John, has a vision of the holy eagle of the Apocalypse, or even of the mystical cup of the disciple whom Jesus loved. In the face of that simple fact, I have no doubt about which is the more educated man; and even a knowledge of the *Daily Mail* does not redress the balance. It is often said, and possibly truly, that the peasant named Michael cannot write his own name. But it is quite equally true that the clerk named John cannot read his own name. He cannot read it because it is in a foreign language, and he has never been made to realize what it stands for. He does not know that John means John, as the other man does know that Michael means Michael.[24]

Chesterton's acute awareness of this danger was one of the things that led him to prefer journalism to a more cloistered if less distracting life among the "pure artists." For it is patently true that for one such genius as Eliot, "the most conscious point in his age," there are a hundred poseurs of Bloomsbury with their eyes turned inward upon their egos. In exoneration of his trade he wrote,

A poet writing his name upon a score of little pages in the silence of his study may or may not have an intellectual right to despise the journalist: but I greatly doubt whether he would not morally be the better if he saw the great lights burning on through darkness into dawn, and heard the roar of the printing wheels weaving the destinies of another day. Here at least is a school of labour and of some rough humility, the largest work ever published anonymously since the great Christian cathedrals.[25]

He preferred journalism because it kept him constantly in touch with real work and real problems. What troubled him about the efforts of the emptier modern artists was that they had their eyes on no object: they meant nothing. The heresy of Realism, which celebrates things for what they seem and not for what they mean, he presents under the parable of a gigantic Gothic cathedral revisited by a priest who has lost his memory:

> He saw piled in front of him frogs and elephants, monkeys and giraffes, toadstools and sharks, all the ugly things of the universe which he had collected to do honour to God. But he forgot why he had collected them. He could not remember the design or the object. He piled them all wildly into one heap fifty feet high; and when he had done it all the rich and influential went into a passion of applause and cried, "This is real art! This is Realism! This is things as they really are!" ...
>
> The finest lengths of the Elgin marbles consist of splendid horses going to the temple of a virgin. Christianity, with its gargoyles and grotesques, really amounted to saying this: that a donkey could go before all the horses in the world when it was really going to the temple. Realism means a lost donkey going nowhere.[26]

He closes this essay "On Gargoyles" with an illuminating reference to his own work:

> These monsters are meant for the gargoyles of a definite cathedral. I have to carve the gargoyles, because I can carve nothing else; I leave to others the angels and the arches and the spires. But I am very sure of the style of the architecture and of the consecration of the church.[27]

Journalist or no, gargoyle-carver or no, he nevertheless knew what his words meant, and the contradictions into which language leads; he knew what being meant, and the contradictions implicit in it; and he did not shrink from the baffling task of making the latter visible through the former.

Keeping in mind all the criteria we have considered: Chesterton's insistence that art be responsible to truth and rooted in the perceptions of the artist; the scope and explicitness of Chesterton's metaphysical perception, within which he moved so freely; yet disabling both, his patent incapacity to realize particular conflicts seriously enough to produce significant poetry: keeping all this in mind, what are we to make of his output of novels and stories? What kind of relevance have they to his lifelong moral and metaphysical concern?

The novel that is not simply documentation owes its vitality to the epigram at its heart: it works by expansion.

Chesterton's novels expand his elsewhere concisely developed perceptions, function in the same way, and have the same kind of value: but with (as Belloc said of the scriptural parable) a story to capture the interest of the reader. The reader who has followed the analysis above of the richly allusive passage on the mirrors of the mystic's mind, with its shifts of imagery and expanding and contracting symbolism, can see that the movement of ideas is exactly like that of a Chestertonian story; and the experienced reader can readily imagine the story Chesterton might have made of it. The reader familiar with the Father Brown collection will know the story he did make of it: *The Man in the Passage*.

Like a paragraph of vintage Chestertonian exposition, the Chestertonian novel or story constructs a web of analogies. Its value is ultimately moral: the value of any parable. His novels, like his poems, are the products of a born philosopher, not of a born dramatist. The Father Brown stories, for example, with all their machinery of murder and repentance, and all the genuine moral interest in the fact of human sin that makes them unique among detective stories, are patently devoid of the intense dramatic life of *Crime and Punishment*. This is not to say that they exist, like the ordinary mechanical detective story, only as neat constructions: rather they exist as ingenious analogues of psychological facts. Chesterton knew perfectly well, and repeatedly asserted, that as human documents they are trifling; he took them seriously enough to write them because they reflect, like everything else he wrote, the unique metaphysical intuition it has been the purpose of this book to explore.

To say that the characters exist as abstractions, that the life of the stories is conferred entirely by the continual local brilliance of the writing; and that they function ultimately as expansions of the philosophic conflicts in his paragraphs of moral and metaphysical paradoxes, is to say that Chesterton's fiction is not drama but parable; on a large scale, as in *The Man Who Was Thursday*, it is allegory: myth. It is unnecessary to recall the tradition of Christian allegory in which they are rooted: *Pilgrim's Progress* may be cited as a late example, springing from the tradition that had flowered in the morality plays. It is more fruitful and suggestive to point to two men whose perceptions tended to be, like Chesterton's, of a detached and philosophical kind, and much of whose output is explicitly on the level of myth: William Blake and James Joyce.

Much of the recent re-emphasis on Blake is based on the appetite of a collapsing civilization for sustaining myths, and to a current belief that the artist fulfilling his supreme function assumes a sort of priestly character and becomes myth-maker. That the myth tends to become dehumanized is counted no demerit by the modern taste for the abstract. At best, the myth-maker erects a pantheon and brings it to life; and so bringing the universe to life, he presents that life under the figure of something living: a man: hence the approach of the most ambitious philosophical speculation to the ancient conception of the macrocosm: the gigantic man who is all things. This conception is everywhere present in Christian thought: to say that in Adam all die and in Christ all are made alive is literally to think in terms of the fall of one all-subsuming human form and the redemption effected by an all-sustaining human God.

Men capable of thinking with any comfort in terms of such magnitude have been few; one is William Blake, another is James Joyce; a third is Gilbert Chesterton. Blake in the nineteenth century and Joyce in the twentieth represented the pattern of the cosmos by the figure of a gigantic man, or by the eternal recurrence of a gigantic circle or wheel; or contemplating the persistence of the unfallen state as an eternal reality lying behind the fallen, by both together.

Such figures were Chesterton's, and they were the logical fruit of his talent for metaphysical perception dramatized on a large scale. One of his themes, developed in *The Man Who Was Thursday*, is the figure of fallen and scattered men conceived as parts broken off the whole and perfect man, free according to their limited being to recapture some analogical image of that former wholeness by pushing to the limit such virtues as now lie within their powers: an image of the isolation of soul from soul. It is in this sense that he sees the supernatural goodness of saint after saint arising to union with God and yet intrinsically imperfect because its emphasis is on goodness of one kind. It is in obedience to this principle that "St. Francis, in praising all good, could be a more shouting optimist than Walt Whitman; St. Jerome, in denouncing all evil, could paint the world blacker than Schopenhauer."[28] Saints may contradict one another's virtues and be right, because saints live in a fallen world. The best man develops only a corner of his potential virtue; he is but a fragment of the unfallen Adam.

Following from and completing this idea is the corollary conception of good men everywhere seemingly at odds, breaking each other's heads in the name of good, yet ultimately fighting all on the same side, the warring members of the cosmic man.

At the end of *The Napoleon of Notting Hill* there stands a passage pushing this idea to the utmost of which Chesterton was capable, a passage pointing back to the celestial wars of Blake and forward to the cosmic paradoxes, as yet unuttered, of Joyce. There comes out of the silence and darkness that followed the settling of the dust upon the last battlefield of Notting Hill a chill voice saying:

> "So ends the Empire of Notting Hill. As it began in blood, so it ended in blood, and all things are always the same."

And another voice replies out of the ruins,

> "If all things are always the same, it is because *all* things are always heroic. If all things are always the same, it is because they are always new. To each man one soul only is given; to each soul only is given a little power—the power at some moments to outgrow and swallow up the stars. If age after age that power comes upon men, whatever gives it to them is great.... We who do the old things are fed by nature with a perpetual infancy. No man who is in love thinks that anyone has been in love before. No woman who has a child thinks that there have been such things as children.... Yes, oh, dark voice, the world is always the same, for it is always unexpected."

... Wherein the experienced reader will hear the soft Irish voice of James Joyce: "Teems of times and happy returns. The seim anew." Then the first voice retorts again that all is dust and nothingness, and again the second voice carries forward its theme:

> "Men live, as I say, rejoicing from age to age in something fresher than progress—in the fact that with every baby a new sun and a new moon are made. If our ancient humanity were a single man, it might perhaps be that he would break down under the memory of so many loyalties, under the burden of so many diverse heroisms, under the load and terror of all the goodness of men. But it has pleased God so to isolate the individual human soul that it can only learn of all other souls by hearsay, and to each one goodness and happiness come with the youth and violence of lightning, as momentary and as pure. And the doom of failure that lies on all human systems does not in fact affect them any more than the worms of an inevitable grave affect a children's game in the meadow. Notting Hill has fallen; Notting Hill has

died. But that is not the tremendous issue. Notting Hill has
lived."

But the first voice laughs on, scoffing at Notting Hill as vanity. Then
they know one another: Auberon Quin, who gave Notting Hill its charter for
a joke, and Adam Wayne, who fought for that charter as a creed. And Wayne
finishes:

> "The equal and eternal human being will alter (our)
> antagonism, for the human being sees no antagonism between
> laughter and respect, the human being, the common man, whom
> mere geniuses like you and me can only worship like a god. When
> dark and dreary days come, you and I are necessary, the pure
> fanatic, the pure satirist. We have between us remedied a great
> wrong. We have lifted the modern cities into that poetry which
> everyone who knows mankind knows to be immeasurably more
> common than the commonplace. But in healthy people there is
> no war between us. We are but the two lobes in the brain of a
> ploughman. Laughter and love are everywhere. The cathedrals,
> built in the ages that loved God, are full of blasphemous
> grotesques. The mother laughs continually at the child, the lover
> laughs continually at the lover, the wife at the husband, the friend
> at the friend.... Let us go out together.... Let us start our
> wanderings over the world. For we are its two essentials. Come,
> it is already day."[29]

That, as the conclusion and summation of his earliest novel, shows
clearly the abstract and mythological conception on which it is based. The
"equal and eternal human being" was to become Sunday, the fantastic
anarchist whose face in the last wild chase of *The Man Who Was Thursday* is
concealed from sight, and who turns out finally to be the chief of police:
Sunday, "huge, boisterous, full of vanity, dancing with a hundred legs, bright
with the glare of the sun, and at first, somewhat regardless of us and our
desires;" Sunday—"Nature as distinct from God."[30]

The reconciliation of that antagonism between him who scoffs and him
who worships is accomplished in *The Man Who Was Thursday*; for the
antagonist of them both turns out to be the leader of them both. He is like
the cosmic man of so much quasi-mystical speculation: the stupendous figure
through whose limbs circle the stars. In him is transcended the isolation of
soul from soul, which begets both loneliness and its blood-brother courage.

The cosmos has the pattern of a man, which is one of its two traditional ultimate patterns; the other being the wheel, the unending cycle, the serpent with its tail in its mouth, which Chesterton also perceived and abominated, summing it up through countless scattered passages in the restless, formless patterns of Turkish carpets, the restless, pointless cycle of Nirvana, and the annihilistic self-contemplation of the East.[31] The cosmos has become a man, a man of will and energy and fantastic beauty, a man and therefore a cross.[32] And when, in the final sentences of *The Man Who Was Thursday*, the last mask is torn off the face of Nature, there is displayed the older face of God: "Can ye drink of the cup that I drink of?"

The restless brother-battle consequent on the Fall and resolved in a transcendental resurrection was a myth that Chesterton arrived at early in life: saw, embodied in a hasty novel subtitled "A Nightmare," and passed over. He said, with acute self-penetration, that he was a journalist because he could not help being a controversialist, and hence never a novelist.[33] Had he been a novelist he might well have lingered with that single vision, and elaborated it as it deserved to be elaborated, for his largest talents lay towards myth and allegory, and that vision, or rather the perception underlying that vision, underlay everything that he was later to write, in however scattered or fragmentary a form. Only twice in English letters has that vision been perceived and elaborated towards its perfection: in the Apocalyptic vision of *Jerusalem* and in that other nightmare of the dreamer of *Finnegans Wake*. Sunday is the gigantic Albion of Blake, the nameless panheroic HCE of Joyce. The Two Voices disputing amid the failing firelight of Notting Hill are the rebellious Orc and the sunlit Los of Chesterton's great predecessor, the scoffing Shem and the conserving Shaun of his great contemporary. Had he given himself to his art as did these men, he might have been received into their trilogy. It was as well that he did not. Myths tend to be sterile; Blake's reputation, after the flurry of symbolic interpretation has died down, will probably rest on his early dramatic lyrics, and Joyce's on the inevitable discovery that his myth is vitalized by an intense personal conflict. That Chesterton's potentiality, had he chosen to be an artist, lay in the direction not of drama but of myth, is another way of saying that with his secure metaphysical perception he would have found his true fulfilment as a great philosopher. The times, however, and his sense of immediate duty, were against him; that he preferred instead to be a practical mystic whose vast moral vision was to be placed at the daily service of immediate political and educational ends, is matter both for gratitude and regret. That he preferred loosing a thousand lightning-strokes to achieving the calm sunlight of a single perfect work is in the simplest sense a true summary of his career; and he would have justified it by his faith in the final paradox of *The Everlasting Man*: "The lightning made eternal as the light."

NOTES

1. *Gloria in Profundis* (chorus from an unfinished play), Faber and Faber, London, 1927. Not included in any collection.

2. T.S. Eliot, *Four Quartets*, Faber and Faber, London, 1944, p. 21.

3. Andre Malraux, "Is Europe Dead?," *New Leader*, Jan. 18, 1947, p. 11.

4. *Heretics*, p. 33.

5. Evans, pp. 147–149.

6. Belloc, pp. 36–40.

7. *Autobiography*, p. 169.

8. *George Frederick Watts*, pp. 94–95

9. *The Poet and the Lunatics*, p. 130. Cf. *George Frederick Watts*, p. 122. which at an early stage of Chesterton's realization mentions tentatively "the existence of genuine correspondences between art and moral beauty, the existence, that is to say, of genuine allegories."

10. *Ubi Ecclesia*, Faber and Faber, London, 1929. Not included in any collection.

11. *Alarms and Discursions*, p. 59.

12. *Orthodoxy*, p. 229.

13. *The Uses of Diversity*, pp. 93–94.

14. *Fancies Versus Fads*, p. 43.

15. *The Well and the Shallows*, p. 18.

16. Quoted in *Gerard Manley Hopkins*, by The Kenyon Critics, New Directions, New York, 1945, p. 19.

17. Quoted by G.F. Lahey, S.J., *Life of Gerard Manley Hopkins*, p. 124.

18. *Autobiography*, p. 288.

19. *William Blake*. The entire passage (pp. 196 sq.) repays study.

20. Cf. *Alarms and Discursions*, pp. 14–15.

21. *William Blake*, p. 131.

22. Ibid, p. 83.

23. *The Incredulity of Father Brown*, pp. 31–70; *The Wisdom of Father Brown*, pp. 185–215; *The Incredulity of Father Brown*, pp. 225–265.

24. *Irish Impressions*, pp. 52–53.

25. "A Word for the Mere Journalist." *Darlington North Star*, Feb. 3, 1902. Quoted in Ward, p. 156.

26. *Alarms and Discursions*, p. 14.

27. Ibid, p. 15.

28. *Orthodoxy*, p. 167.

29. *The Napoleon of Notting Hill*, Bk. V, ch. iii, pp. 193–200.

30. Quoted in Ward, p. 193, from an interview given by Chesterton to explain certain phases of the book, nearly twenty years after it was written.

31. Cf. *St. Thomas Aquinas*, pp. 135–136: "He who will not climb the mountain of Christ falls into the abyss of Buddha.... Most other alternatives of heathen humanity ... are sucked back into that whirlpool of recurrence which all the ancients knew"; *The Everlasting*

Man, Bk. II, ch. v, where "The Wheel of Asia" is taken as the antithesis of Christianity; also the story, "The Wrong Shape," in *The Innocence of Father Brown*, where the priest-detective says of the crooked knife, "'It's the wrong shape in the abstract. Don't you ever feel that about Eastern Art? The colours are intoxicatingly lovely; but the shapes are mean and bad—deliberately mean and bad. I have seen wicked things in a Turkey carpet.... They are letters and symbols in a language I do not know; but I know they stand for evil words.... The lines grow wrong on purpose—like serpents doubling to escape.'"

32. *The Man Who Was Thursday*, p. 329.

33. *Autobiography*, p. 289.

GARRY WILLS

Rhyme and Reason

Chesterton's favorite reading from childhood was the poets—Isaias and
Job and the psalms, Shakespeare and Browning and Swinburne. His taste was
catholic, including Pope as well as Shelley, though he was always faintly
irritated by Milton's inhuman epic. Very soon he had begun his own
versifying, interspersing ballads modeled on Scott with his first romances
and fairy tales. The next two stages of his work have already been
mentioned—the sprawling monologues in *The Debater* and the attempt to
put the Notebook's aphorisms into rhymed form. The poems of his first
volume of importance, *The Wild Knight*, arose from that effort, and they
mark the end of his specifically poetic ambitions. After this first volume of
such promise, he became a jester in verse as in prose.

The Wild Knight includes poems like "The Fish," which Chesterton had
been working on since the Slade days. "By a Babe Unborn," which the
Autobiography relates to his struggle to burst out of his own mind, is a
concentration into verse of the story he had variously recast, then published,
as "A Crazy Tale." The binding theme of the volume is Chesterton's
universal theme of praise for existence, but the nightmare—separation from
the world of reality is still vividly remembered. In eight poems we find the
fate of the outcast depicted, becoming at its most intense moments the final
loneliness of an unregarded death;[1] while in two poems solipsism is directly

From *Chesterton: Man and Mask*. © 1961 by Sheed and Ward, Inc.

described.[2] To Kenner's thesis it might, therefore, be objected that Chesterton *was* writing from his own experience, and of things he had intensely felt. But this response is too pat. The threat Chesterton felt was of madness, and the response is intellectually defiant, that is, argumentative. Argument rarely leads to good poetry; it would finally divert Chesterton from the course of the poet. But in this first volume, the intention and the workmanship are a poet's.

Diffusion, a Swinburnian laxity and facility, were the faults Chesterton had inherited from his early work; but we can see here his conscious opposition to this drift. He strives for a tight and pregnant simplicity, and often achieves it:

THE SKELETON

> Chattering finch and water-fly
> Are not merrier than I;
> Here among the flowers I lie
> Laughing everlastingly.
> No; I may not tell the best;
> Surely, friends, I might have guessed
> Death was but the good King's jest,
>   It was hid so carefully.

The entire volume shows an attempt at verbal asceticism which did not last. Swinburne's influence is still here, but in a very short flower of the sea; Browning's, too, but in a very short monologue. The greatest resemblance, strangely enough, did not arise from direct imitation. These poems, like Blake's, are very fierce auguries of innocence, their rhetoric patterned after that of the prophets, as in the poem whose first two lines are a paraphrase of Isaias' opening distich:

> To teach the grey earth like a child,
> To bid the heavens repent.

If the lion does not exactly lie down with the lamb, "The Donkey" moves surprisingly like the Tyger, and "The Fish" and "The Skeleton" are also of this company. Another brief poem traces the world's vitality into the narrow chamber of a seed, and discovers there

God almighty, and with him
Cherubim and Seraphim,
Filling all eternity—
Adonai Elohim.

Even more important than these stylistic considerations is the fact that
many of these poems achieve insight without argument—an attainment
difficult enough to one of his critical cast of mind, and one which he never
made his own during the many years after this first book appeared. The
poem to St. Joseph is an example:

If the stars fell; night's nameless dreams
    Of bliss and blasphemy came true,
If skies were green and snow were gold,
    And you loved me as I love you;

O long light hands and curled brown hair
    And eyes where sits a naked soul;
Dare I even then draw near and burn
    My fingers in the aureole?

Yes, in the one wise foolish hour
    God gives this strange strength to a man.
He can demand, though not deserve,
    Where ask he cannot, seize he can.

But once the blood's wild wedding o'er,
    Were not dread his, half dark desire,
To see the Christ-child in the cot,
    The Virgin Mary by the fire?

The poem does not hinge on intellectual paradox, but on a real emotional
ambivalence: Chesterton sees rather than understands man's conflicting
instincts—that sex is fruition and expenditure, that virginity is barren yet has
in itself some holiness. The poem's structure is perfect, rising to one climax,
then reaching a deeper climax and mystery. The symbols are theological, as
in Blake's work, but the reality is analogously physical and moral and mystical
and mad.

METAPHYSICAL MINSTRELSY

But other poems in the book, especially the exercises in political rhetoric, show that paradox was driving out the autonomy of direct emotional vision. This is not to say, as Kenner does, that philosophy was driving out poetry. It may have been poetry that was receding, but the new element was not philosophy. "Paradox" is constructed of the same symbolic stuff in Chesterton's verse as in his novels, and it must be judged by the same norms. Chesterton ceased to be a poet, in the conventional sense, but he became a rhyming jester. His later volumes, except for one poem which was in itself a book, were mere collections of his occasional verse written for the newspaper or for his friends. They are haphazard collections, and include things which are merely topical and things which are worthless. Three things Chesterton could write, those three which Shaw could not[3]—a love song, a war song, a drinking song. They are songs rather than poems, spontaneous as some feudal bard's "journalism." It is extraordinary how completely Chesterton's talents did express themselves in the manner of a jongleur. His drinking songs have less argument in them than any of his later verses; they arose from a deep enjoyment of his role as a truly festive Feste; for only the metaphysical jester can escape the melancholy of all other clowns. If we add two more genres to the list, both entirely in keeping with the minstrel's repertoire, it will be complete—satire and carols.

Haste and extravagance are marks of the jester's style—for it is not a mere lack of style. Even in *The Wild Knight* we can see this new mode of song coming to birth. One of the solipsist poems, in which the poet tries to escape a horrible world wherein everyone bears his own recurrent countenance, ends with these lines:

> Then my dream snapped: and with a heart that leapt
> I saw across the tavern where I slept,
> The sight of all my life most full of grace,
> A gin-damned drunkard's wan half-witted face.

There is a jolting bathos in the revelation of the poem's scene—as if the nightmare had been caused only by whisky fumes; but Chesterton had to admit this setting in order to make a drunkard the vision of grace, as Orm had been in another context. There is in the relishing of this extreme contrast a humor that is answered by the vivid, even gaudy, violence of the last verse. This is not poetry, but it is artistic in its aim; it is a metaphysical joke. The minstrel is laughing, and especially laughing at himself.

Chesterton's ability to play with pictures brightly picked out was simply another aspect of his central rhetoric of jest. Yet if it be granted that Chesterton was that kind of wild and logical symbolist which I have called a metaphysical jester, many objections to this kind of writing remain: for instance, the claim that it is merely philosophy in disguise. But we have already considered this claim in the case of Chesterton's novels, and found it baseless. A more serious charge is that such a rhetoric of ideas is "propaganda" in the modern sense of intellectual seduction.

Propaganda is not art; neither is it education of an honest sort. Propaganda is that bastard form of art and instruction which sugars a doctrine with colors and forms not integral to it or to the artifact used for this indoctrination. But Chesterton did not build an argument, then stick it all over with figures of speech. The symbols came first to him, as his real form of expression. These are always apt symbols, carrying their own meaning; there is no previously formulated expression of the ideas to which they must be fitted. They are the expression. We have seen this in the case of colors, which had a symbolic urgency which was activated in many ways, but always from within. Chesterton felt the symbol's vitality before he knew what it signified. Even persons and events—Joan of Arc, Lepanto—were symbols to him before he understood what they might symbolize. The figure of the white horse, too, had haunted him in various guises long before he thought of it primarily as Alfred's horse. If anyone thinks he is a mere propagandist, let him say what explicit concept or course of argument that white shape is meant to promote. An honest mind will soon disappear into the depths of that richest of Chesterton's symbols.

Chesterton's verses are those of the court fool, who does not pretend to make things as sane men do. The characters in his novels are not symbols of men, like Hamlet, but of ideas, like Zarathustra. Such a jester stands outside propaganda, the illegitimate use of art *ab extra*, in the same way that the satirist does. Oblique comment is the jester's mode, as syllogisms are the technique of the logician. A propagandist can use attractive but fallacious syllogisms, as he uses appealing but inept symbols. But this does not mean that the real logician or satirist or jester is a propagandist.

The proof that Chesterton was not a propagandist is that he ceased trying to write poetry and fiction of the conventional type. He forswore the quiet stories and self-contained nonsense verses which he had first excelled in. His first slim publication, *Greybeards at Play*, distorted the form of nonsense verses by inserting satire on decadent artists and philosophers.[4] He had the good sense not to attempt this again, and I think he grew to dislike his one essay into "pure" nonsense.[5] His work from that time on has a uniformity of texture which Chesterton sustained so well that men forgot it was artificial. It is reasonable to say that his artifact is worthless, but it is simply absurd to claim that it is not an artifact.

But if the verse be called a metaphysical minstrelsy—neither philosophy nor propaganda—other criticisms can still be adduced. For instance, an *a priori* argument against such verse is that its blatant and over-vivid coloring forbids all subtlety and makes delicate insight impossible. But jugglery is entirely a matter of delicate balance; and, as Chesterton frequently insisted in his comments on pantomime, even an exaggerated phrase or gesture can "act out" what is shadowy or deep-hidden. The poem in which Christ's double role is described—he is Zeus; he is Prometheus—is projected as a whirling pantomime of the eagle and the vulture, cornfields and chasms, daylight and fires in the night.[6] Yet the concept is a delicate one, nowhere else in Chesterton, nor in any other writer, given this uniquely illuminating expression. One cannot make the eagle and vulture mere trappings for the statement that God is both order and act. Such abstract words, or any multiplication of them, do not express what Chesterton says. There is no other way of saying it: God is Zeus, God is Prometheus. Similarly, there is no other way of saying what he says of the Virgin in "The White Witch"—that Mary is an anti-witch, who drives out all the evil phantasms which the image of Hecate—of that deepest of human perversions, the woman of evil—has spread in the imagination of men since the dawn of time.[7]

Even single lines have this ability to say much in a simple and direct stroke. The entire map of Europe is sketched in *Lepanto*, so that a single brush-stroke fixes, in this heraldry, France:

The shadow of the Valois was yawning at the Mass.

The cobwebby assonance is overdone, as the slumbering heaviness of "Sloth" is overdone in a mediaeval carving; but the exaggeration touches depths that careful statement often does not reach.

Mediaeval art is aptly brought in here—heraldry and the windows and the stiff chasubles and the gold everywhere. We have long since overcome the misconception, held for centuries, that only chiaroscuro can achieve subtlety and open man's soul. The density and richness of a window are complicated by the very brilliance and multiplicity of colors. Every Gothic cathedral wore motley. That dazzling multiplicity is what we have noticed already in Chesterton's tales—the jostling suspension of all colors in the scheme. The same technique is used in the poems. All the issues of liberty and Europe's fate are traced in the whirl of *Lepanto*'s colors, and then the whole thing is set in a comic frame which deepens the significance and interrelation of the historical sections of the poem. Chesterton looks backward from Quixote, using the comic knight as a means of understanding the hopeless, victorious knight of Austria.

Another objection, tangential to those just considered, is that such obvious and crude rhetoric as Chesterton used is easily reeled off by anyone with a modicum of talent. The fallacy at work here should be recognized. The juggler's art may not be worthy of exalted attention, but it is not easy. No one ever juggled by accident. It is an art, and it takes practice. The same is true of Chesterton's symbolic juggling of words and colors. Even in its simplest form this is a difficult thing. It may be a waste of time to write drinking songs; but when good ones are written, they are written only by skilled artificers, like Horace and Shakespeare. Where are the swarms of men succeeding in this easy pastime?

Chesterton certainly considered facility a part of his task as a minstrel; not simply a temptation, as it is for most poets. It is a mistake to think there is no asceticism in the immediate volley, as in the six years' chiseling. The asceticism lies in the difficulties undertaken, the willingness to accept any challenge. Look through the collected poems and notice the variety of forms Chesterton used: sonnets, triolets, ballades, odes, blank verse, couplets. His ballad forms are often deceptively simple in appearance. He tried one difficult metre in his first volume, with little success. It was used in a poem devoted to the praise of Woman. Many years later he used the rhythm again in a fine tribute of the Virgin:

> And a dwarfed and dwindled race in the dark red deserts
>   Stumbled and strayed,
> While one in the mortal shape that was once for immortals
>   Made, was remade.[8]

His early ballad of Gibeon, otherwise worthless, is a panting obstacle course of feminine rhymes. He frequently used the rhyme-scheme of *In Memoriam*. All this is tour de force, admittedly; but tour de force is by definition that which is not easy. And, like another master of tour de force, Chesterton as he ends the refrain thrusts home, not only in symbolic poems like "Lepanto" and "The Monster," but in the acerb verses on F.E. Smith and the Bishop who called St. Francis flea-bitten, in the brilliant translations of Dante, Du Bellay, Guérin.

THE BALLAD OF THE WHITE HORSE

Because Chesterton was a true balladeer, he could use certain traditional forms with a spontaneity and sense of the form's genius which is denied most poets by their very acuteness and personal accent. This was true not only of the drinking song but of the Christmas carol. Because of this, it was possible that Chesterton could write one kind of poem which would not be only jest or tour de force. He could retain his loose and rapid spontaneity, yet work to a larger plan, polishing and reshaping its parts. He could stitch together the ballad stanzas as the original singers had done at the dawn of epic, when the stories of Robin Hood and Roland were fashioned from the old, sporadic material to a new and larger pattern.

Chesterton's instincts led him to this form, and they did not fail him in the choice or execution. This was his most serious artistic endeavor, and he made the attempt but once. For at least four years that we know of he worked on *The Ballad of the White Horse*, the only example in his career of such extended labor and delayed publication. More than this, he used symbols, stanza forms, and words which he had been collecting in his mind for years. The white horse had been his private symbol of chivalry since the time when he owned a hobbyhorse of that color; an inn sign, a canvassing trip in Wiltshire, a honeymoon memory—these and many other experiences had been stored in the symbol's energy.[9] The first two lines of the finished poem were the inspired opening of a boyhood poem on Moses. One of Alfred's prayers had come to Chesterton in his sleep, and was copied down, in the first person, many years before the ballad appeared.[10] We can see the changes made in one section of the ballad by comparing it to the "Fragment of a Ballad of Alfred" published in the *Albany* for 1907, four years before publication of *The White Horse*.[11]

Chesterton's fascination with the ballad form dated from his school days, from the time when first he read Scott and Macaulay. A paper he delivered to the J.D.C. shows that he soon went to the original English ballads.[12] Discussing them in this paper, he praises especially their vigor of epithet and "signature phrase" which can bring a character to life at one stroke. Many of the figures in *The White Horse* are picked out in this vivid manner: the deserted king, for instance, is "Alfred of the lonely spear." One of his own first ballads, sung by the minstrel in a story written at the St. Paul's School, resembles the strain of the melancholy minstrel, Elf:

Softly and silently
Sail the fair Valkyrs,

Spirit-receiving ones
Whispering to warsmiths ...
Bending their bright course
Laden with thane-spirits
Up to high halls
Where with the wise Woden
Baldur the beautiful
Reigneth for Right.

Whenever Chesterton's ballad is brought up, the inevitable comparison is with Coleridge's "Rime." Maurice Baring, in his review of *The White Horse*, remarked that Chesterton told a vivid story as well as Coleridge but did not let the tale alone carry the theme.[13] He thought Chesterton's ballad was, for this reason, less "authentic." But this is the one point on which the more recent poem has an unquestionable superiority. Coleridge's theme is not more complex and exalted than Chesterton's, but it is less "popular." Chesterton works from popular sentiment, as the ballad must; his poem is full of patriotism and the spirit of a single landscape:

He sang of war in the warm wet shires
    Where rain nor fruitage fails,
Where England of the motley states
Deepens like a garden to the gates
    In the purple walls of Wales.

Coleridge filled the English ballad with Oriental horrors, but *The White Horse*

Seems like the tales a whole tribe feigns,
    Too English to be true.

Chesterton recaptures, moreover, that moment when the primitive ballads were woven together to become national epic. His poem is the record of a war from the heroic age; epic boasts and similes, a national hero, the hushed eve of battle and the screaming day that follows, make *The White Horse* echo the tales of Roland and Henry V as well as of Robin Hood. Coleridge's ballad, on the other hand, is a weird voyage into the self, its introversion making the "authentic" heroic note impossible.

The local scene and fiery patriotism do not limit *The White Horse*. The vale of Alfred is England, and England is Christendom, in the poem. The "triple symbol" mentioned in the prose introduction is an interpretation of the elements in the English greatness—Saxon, Celtic, Roman. But they are also symbols of that complexus, which Chesterton described in *Blake* as the formula of Western man—pagan poetry, Roman order, and Christian religion. Chesterton always insisted that Christianity did not drive out pagan things but subsumed them even in growing from them. There is a real conflict between poetry and reason, faith and doubt, the supernatural and nature, but this dialectic is life-giving, not destructive. This is the meaning of Colan, Eldred, and Marcus, united by Alfred, in the van of the English armies. In *The Everlasting Man* Chesterton would again describe a triple dialectic, considering three stages of history—not chronological stages, simply, but co-existent levels of human reality. First there is "minimal man"—child, savage, artist, god among the beasts. Then there is civilized man, giving law to the nations and searching the heavens. Finally, completing and ordinating the former elements, without banishing them, there is Christian man, exiled citizen of the City of God.

Against this Christian balance and complexity come the barbarian forces of simplification and destruction. The Danish heroes are merely the Christian thanes simplified, isolated from the balancing discipline which Christianity imposes on man's nature. Saxon Eldred typifies the love of life, of wine, of "slow moons and certain things"; his farm has become, by vow and charity, a haven of the poor and a storehouse of earth's good things. Danish Harold is the same type of man, but one whose vigor and blood have flamed into a destructive sensualism. Gaelic Colan is a mystic whose gods must be harnessed by the new God from Rome; but Danish Elf is the poet whose gods are free, and who spread their beautiful barrenness everywhere. Marcus is the lover of order for its own sake, of force and process subjected to a constructive asceticism; whereas "Ogier of the stone and sling" loves destruction for its own sake, and expresses the nihilist mystique in clear-etched lines which reveal the depths Chesterton's verse could reach:

> There lives one moment for a man
>   When the door at his shoulder shakes,
> When the taut rope parts under the pull,
> And the barest branch is beautiful
>   One moment, while it breaks.

Guthrum rises over his warriors as Alfred towers among the thanes. The pagan leader is a "clerk," whose weary sentences have the beauty of lyrics from some Greek tragedy:

Do we not know, have we not heard,
The soul is like a lost bird,
   The body a broken shell?
And a man hopes, being ignorant,
   Till in white woods apart
He finds at last the lost bird dead;
And a man may still lift up his head,
   But never more his heart.

This love of life is Horatian, strong within narrow limits, but desolate when the man lifts his eyes to the horizon and the encircling dark:

The little brooks are very sweet,
   Like a girl's ribbons curled,
But the great sea is bitter
   That washes all the world.

Even Guthrum, therefore, must try to forget his philosophy in the drunkenness of war. All the Danes' joy and wisdom leads to sterility and destruction. Marcus builds as a pagan, but he slowly changes into Ogier unless Christianity intervenes, "because it is only Christian men Guard even heathen things." Creation is loved with permanence only by men who believe in the Creator. The simple love of the Danes, uncomplicated by the mysteries of faith and humility, shifts with every mood, and brings ruin with its shiftings—fire on Ely fen, molten lead on Glastonbury, Roman colonnades left like "the spectre of a street," and the great hieroglyphic Horse fading, unkempt, to an undecipherable smudge on the hills. The Christians, on the other hand, keep arch and book, sing a hymn of the crafts at the height of battle, and tend the strange white sign stamped on their native earth. Alfred sees God as a laborer who fills the vines and tends the fields, and Marcus calls him "God that is a craftsman good."[14]

"LIKE A GOOD CHILD AT PLAY"

Alfred becomes the central Christian warrior by undergoing defeat, by "hardening his heart with hope" when there is no earthly hope. Only then is the vision given to him:

In the river island of Athelney
   With the river running past

> In colours of such simple creed
> All things sprang at him, sun and weed,
> Till the grass grew to be grass indeed,
> And the tree was a tree at last.

He is granted that carelessness about the world which alone reveals the world. The pagan must cling to the tree finally—making of it a god, a portent, an end—or destroy it in his rage. But the Christian recognizes the endangered and divine world as a picture wrought by the Artist who "saw that it was good."

Yet Alfred still asks for a pagan wisdom, for prevision and some power over destiny: will he win, or again be sent reeling? The Virgin answers that the Christian clarity of wisdom goes with an ignorance of such evil reckoning of the odds. The tree is a tree at last because it cannot be twisted into a magic instrument of power. It is a simple tool in the toy world of nature which reflects, in time, the City of God. Faith, like Christian hope, is based on a certain ignorance; it recognizes simple facts like trees. On this ignorance true knowledge can be built. Only Christianity has made men content with such knowledge, justifying the wisdom which grows from ignorance by making it correspond to the created reality which came from nothingness. The pagan does not believe in this radical creation of the world from nothing, nor in the formation of wisdom from innocence. He seeks always to know why he knows what he knows. He cannot begin at the beginning—his own beginning and the world's—because this involves a preliminary self-annihilation through humility, a humility which re-enacts one's passage out of the abyss of nonexistence. But Alfred, stripped of all pretensions in defeat, accepts that state of ignorance in which man can be taught, as by one's mother:

> And he saw in a little picture,
> Tiny and far away,
> His mother sitting in Egbert's hall,
> And a book she showed him, very small,
> Where a sapphire Mary sat in stall
> With a golden Christ at play.

This is the argument of *Orthodoxy* carried to its completion. In *Orthodoxy* Chesterton traced the folly of self-sufficient wisdom and claimed that the Church alone preserved knowledge—until we pulled the mitre from pontifical man and saw his head come off with it. But the approach was negative in that book; the pure intellect destroyed itself, and poetry was referred to as a sane counterbalance to such intellection. Here Chesterton looks at the *positive* wisdom of Christian innocence, the vision of trees as trees, the childlike hope and love which make Alfred follow a pillar not of fire but of darkness:

> The men of the East may spell the stars,
>   And times and triumphs mark,
> But the men signed of the cross of Christ
>   Go gaily in the dark.

Christianity saves even heathen things, but this "pragmatic" value of the Faith is only made possible by a deepest state of complete innocence which does not seek to use or to reject the world. The figure of the White Horse on the hill is a sacrament meant to reveal Alfred's love of his native earth in all its autonomy. But he does not fight, ultimately, to save the White Horse, or his kingdom, or the churches. He fights as Joan of Arc did, gravely and in ignorance of the reasons for which heaven bade her go forth, ready for victory or defeat, to defend that strange thing, scrawled on the earth of Europe, which we call France. Alfred is ready to lose all or win all with the same cheerfulness of faith, knowing that his home is here and yet not here.

The specifically Christian "detachment" and mysticism are articulated with precision in this attitude of Alfred. Christian asceticism does not arise from the simple opposition of matter to spirit, of time to eternity, of this life to some other. This cannot be the Christian's mind on these issues, for God not only made this world, His being supports and pervades and continues to activate it. He is in Orm and in Guthrum. He "labors" to

> Build this pavilion of the pines,
> And herd the fowls and fill the vines,
> And labour and pass and leave no signs
>   Save mercy and mystery.

Yet God constructs no lasting city here; it is a world of mystery and adventure, where His champions must go gaily in the dark, prepared to see their wisdom and planning collapse as ludicrously as the Council's did in *Thursday*. Around Alfred gather all these reflections on existence as something immeasurably valuable, yet something won by a carelessness and self-forgetfulness which only real faith in God has ever given men.

Of course, Alfred's vision at Athelney is only the beginning of the revelation, in and through him, of this Christian mysticism. The poem builds to a higher vision at its climax, the center of calm light in which a child plays—an odd, idyllic interlude placed dramatically in a setting of war and slaughter. It is this white light which fires the motley colors of battle and heroism and victory. Every line of the poem leads to that vision or follows from it. Alfred expresses a new facet of it in each episode. In his call to the warriors he repeats the Virgin's summons to the wise ignorance of faith:

> I call the muster of Wessex men
> From grassy hamlet or ditch or den,
> To break and be broken, God knows when,
>   But I have seen for whom.

In the Danish camp he scorns the pagan desires, shouting his joy at defeat against their weariness of triumph. In the forest he takes as his ensign of royalty a blow from a peasant woman; and when humility lights him through and through, laughter follows:

> The giant laughter of Christian men
>   That roars through a thousand tales,
> Where greed is an ape and pride is an ass,
> And Jack's away with his master's lass,
> And the miser is banged with all his brass,
>   The farmer with all his flails.

> Tales that tumble and tales that trick,
>   Yet end not all in scorning
> Of kings and clowns in a merry plight,
> And the clock gone wrong and the world gone right
> That the mummers sing upon Christmas night
>   And Christmas Day in the morning.

Laughter is very near that childlike innocence which the Virgin brought to Alfred, as we see in the laughing Madonna and Child of mediaeval art. Chesterton has fitted a separate "discovery" of his youth—laughter as a medium of knowledge and sanity—into the total Christian reality.

Before the battle, the pagan Harold delivers the ritual epic boast, but Colan makes real in this context St. Paul's "boast in the Lord":

Oh, truly we be broken hearts;
    For that cause, it is said,
We light our candles to that Lord
    That broke Himself for bread.[15]

When Colan flings his sword at Harold, Alfred sees this act as a parable of the whole campaign's meaning. Christian men are given victory because they surrender it, they are given the world as a gift only when they recognize that it is *God*'s gift and possession: "Man shall not taste of victory / Till he throws his sword away":

For this is the manner of Christian men,
Whether of steel or priestly pen,
That they cast their hearts out of their ken
    To get their heart's desire.

Then the champions fight according to their character—Eldred straightforwardly, by mere mass; Marcus in order, stemming the retreat when superstition begins to dissolve the Wessex line; Colan fighting, by some unworldly energy, longer than the others, only to fall like them at last:

As to the Haut King came at morn
Dead Roland on a doubtful horn,
Seemed unto Alfred lightly borne
    The last cry of the Gael.

These thanes are not only dead; they have been forgotten. They fought as Christians, but without the crystalline innocence of Alfred. "The spirit of the child" which Christ recommended is seen playing on the shore, along the line which God laid to sunder earth and sea. The child builds a tower, and the sea destroys it, and the child builds it up again. So does Alfred fight, "gravely, As a good child at play." Again defeated, his brave allies dead, he continues to obey the Virgin's call to battle with as simple trust as if the day had been his:

Came ruin and the rain that burns,
Returning as a wheel returns,
And crouching in the furze and ferns
    He began his life once more.

Then comes the last hopeless charge, the vision of Mary over the field, the impossible victory, the baptism of Guthrum, the peace of Wessex instituted under Alfred. But in time the sea washes in on the tower again, and Alfred in his age must buckle on armor and fight, calmly as the child rebuilds in sand.[16] Alfred now disappears from the poem; only echoes and dusty visions return from his campaign. We are left watching the grass grow around the Horse, news returning only at intervals of the grey horse that carries Alfred in his new battles. So the king disappears into the smoke and dust of history which had been stirred up in the first few lines of the poem. The bright vision breaks up and fades, and the White Horse is seen only through a blur of green.

NOTES

1. *Collected Poems*, pp. 307, 310-1, 321-2, 329-30, 332, 363-5, 365-6.

2. *Ibid.*, pp. 312-3, 327-8.

3. *Shaw*, p. 228.

4. Cf. Chesterton's own distinction between nonsense and satire in *The Defendant* ("Defence of Farce"), and his criticism of Barrie for neglecting "the congruity of nonsense" (*Nation*, Nov. 18, 1911).

5. Cf. Ward, p. 125. In the *Autobiography*, Chesterton overlooks his first book and calls *The Wild Knight* "my introduction into literature" (p. 91).

6. *Collected Poems*, pp. 3-6,"The Monster."

7. *The Queen of Seven Swords*, p. 2.

8. *Ibid.*, p. 5, "The Return of Eve."

9. *Autobiography*, pp. 30, 31, 127.

10. Ward, p. 164.

11. *E.g.*, "Her face was like a spoken word" became "an open word." "Under the old night's starry hood" became "nodding hood." "Under clean Christian grass to lie" became "warm Westland grass." "Their eyes were sadder than the sea" became "Their souls were drifting as the sea." "Gods of an empty will" became "of a wandering will." There are no changes in rhyme; Chesterton's facility made it unnecessary for him to write for a rhyme. The metric changes are all in the direction of irregularity, to keep the ballad's loose and vigorous form. A number of false touches are eliminated, including these stanzas:

> His spear was broken in his hand
> But his belt bore a sword;
> His heart was broken in his breast
> But he cried unto Our Lord.

> He cried to Our Lady and Our Lord
> Seven times in the sun
> And the boar and the black wolf answered him
> And the tears began to run.

False naïveté of this sort does not appear in the finished poem, whose refrains and slight archaisms are perfectly modulated. Chesterton avoided the great obstacle of this form, the "ye olde" style of which even Coleridge could not thoroughly purge the "Rime," what Chesterton called "a swagger of antiquity, like the needless outrage of calling the Mariner a Marinere" (*Ill. Lond. News*, Aug. 4, 1934, reprinted in *As I Was Saying as* "About S.T.C.")

12. *Debater*, I. 15–16 has a report on the paper, which is in one of the extant notebooks.

13. *Eye Witness*, Sept. 7, 1911.

14. Chesterton had long admired Kipling's line, "Then cometh God, the master of every trade" (*Debater*, 3.57).

15. The last line is a fine example of the compression and depth in these simple stanzas. The first mystery of the Sacrament is that bread becomes God; but a further mystery links this banquet table to the sacrificial altar. Calvary and the Last Supper meet by necessity in the Mass, for the Eucharist is both Sacrament and Sacrifice. Christ must die to feed us—"break Himself for bread."

16. Here Chesterton imitates the conclusion of "The Song of Roland," which he praised in an introduction to a 1919 edition of "Roland" (reprinted in *The Common Man*): "That high note of the forlorn hope, of a host at bay and a battle against odds without end, is the note on which the great French epic ends. I know nothing more moving in poetry than that strange and unexpected end, that splendidly inconclusive conclusion. Charlemagne, the great Christian emperor, has at last established his empire in quiet, has done justice almost in the manner of the day of judgment, and sleeps as it were upon his throne with a peace almost like that of Paradise. And there appears to him the angel of God crying aloud that his arms are needed in a new and distant land, and that he must take up again the endless march of his days. And the great king tears his long white beard and cries out against his restless life. The poem ends, as it were, with a vision and vista of wars against the barbarians; and the vision is true. For that war is never ended which defends the sanity of the world against all the stark anarchies and rending negations which rage against it for ever."

LYNETTE HUNTER

Mapping the Artistic Terrain:
1904–1907

The poem 'The Wild Knight' contained a radical divergence between Chesterton's style and the apparent meaning of his story. The style indicated a conflict between the conscious control of the writer through emblem, and the unconscious control that allowed, for spontaneity within metaphor. However, the content of the poem implied that spontaneity had to be destroyed completely in order to avoid the danger of anarchy and chaos. At the root of this division lay an inability to differentiate between a personal spontaneity, advocated by Lord Orm, and an externally inspired spontaneity, as found in the Wild Knight. The author recognised the positive value of the Wild Knight, and the decision to destroy him contradicts this awareness. Yet the conflict in the style indicates an intuitive knowledge that something is unbalanced.

The early criticism shows Chesterton asking the artist to walk on a thin line between control and spontaneity. The identification of personal and external inspiration as one left the artist in constant danger of slipping either into arbitrary impression or rational argument. The main discovery of the subsequent criticism was that control and inspiration were impossible to balance; human judgement alone could not do it. Once the critic begins to recognise an external authority he takes his first step towards the destination of his style, which is allegory; he realises that impressions may not be

From *G.K. Chesterton: Explorations in Allegory.* © 1979 by Lynette Hunter.

inspired, they may be personal only. Similarly didacticism may become personal despotism. The existence of a self-centred basis of non-inspired work provided him with a partial solution. Previously the artist had verged on the blasphemy of being God if he tended either to impressionism or rationalism. Chesterton now states that while art is still an absolute necessity for a human being, it is only valuable if consciously inspired by God. The artist's recognition of the presence of God in the work will effect the balance between spontaneity and control and the corresponding connection between essence and form. The idea is reached primarily in *Robert Browning*. One of the important conclusions of that work was that the style was instrumental in the necessary expression of the presence of God. *Robert Browning* becomes a landmark in Chesterton's work not only because it recognises a necessity for the presence of God, but also because it initiates the search for an adequate style to fulfil that need.

Following close on *Robert Browning* is Chesterton's first novel, *The Napoleon of Notting Hill*. Here the search for style is translated into a confrontation between the artist of the self and the artist of external inspiration. The message conveyed is that the conscious and unconscious control, the exercise in emblem and metaphor respectively, and can co-exist. Not only can they co-exist but also if they do co-exist, they create the ultimate form for human expression. Because emblem is personally based it may always lose the balance between form and essence. Yet despite the value of metaphor with its ability to communicate external inspiration through experience, Chesterton does not entirely trust it because of its experiential character which is open to misinterpretation. Emblem is more closely allied to explanation. It is shown to provide the conscious control metaphor lacks, and metaphor the external basis that emblem does not have. However, in practice the two together do not make an adequate form. The author himself senses this and opts for conscious emblematic control over the whole novel, with the exception of a few sections which attempt to incorporate metaphor. He thinks that although metaphor is a more valuable form of expression, it is also more dangerous if it fails. The novelist's expression is further stabilised by the extensive use of explanation to prevent misinterpretation of either form.

The novel takes place 80 years in the future when London is governed by a huge bureaucracy headed by a randomly selected despot. The action begins with the selection of a new despot, the artist Auberon Quin. He proceeds to enforce a personal joke on the town by re-instituting the old medieval boroughs, with all their customs and costumes. The bureaucracy is annoyed by this intervention, but because the joke does not interfere with the actual functioning of London they tolerate its existence. Ten years later, however, a young man called Adam Wayne appears who takes the joke seriously. As provost of Notting Hill, he refuses to let the other London boroughs run a road through the centre of his territory. He objects because of a patriotic dedication to Notting Hill and is prepared to live up to the conditions of Quin's joke by fighting for the territory's freedom. Such seriousness infects the other provosts and a war breaks out, resulting in the victory of Wayne and the Empire of Notting Hill.

Chesterton's tight control renders the story highly schematic. The characters have obvious and clearly defined emblematic roles. Auberon Quin is the personal artist, the aesthete working from his own impressions and consciously controlling them. Adam Wayne is the artist dependent on external inspiration and unconscious control through metaphor. The bureaucratic masses are represented by Barker, the non-artist, the man who cannot perceive any connection between expression and meaning. As an impressionist, the forms Quin thinks up are related only to himself. He does not believe in value that is not generated by his own ideas. Hence he sees no connection between form and essence. In fact he denies the existence of essence outside of his own perspective. The method of this art is to create emblems, or forms that stand for an object, and impose them on surroundings things. The mode is really a form of nonsense logic in that the intent is always to shatter the existence of 'normal' logic; and it has the same effects. The first effect is that it disorients one's usual response to the object; and the second is that it defines the response in the terms imposed by the artist.

The novelist indicates both the positive and negative value in these effects. After Quin is made King, he receives Barker in an audience. Immediately, he asks for Barker's hat which Barker hands over. Quin then sits on the hat saying that it is a 'quaint old custom'. Barker can see no logic in the nonsense. He cannot understand why Quin would want to create a 'custom' and is soon reduced to frantic walking back and forth. The unrelated forms Quin creates have the parodic function of nonsense. They strip away convention in order to reveal essence, only to reveal that there is no essence. Yet if the people cannot appreciate the intent, the disorientation of nonsense becomes purely arbitrary and unrelated, and is therefore dismissed as chaotic, and the imposition of his definitions is objected to as dogmatic.

The disorientation by nonsense through emblem is intended by Quin to destroy convention. It assumes that there is no essence to be revealed, and that there is no absolute meaning. As a result the emblem is easily misunderstood and reduced to didacticism and impressionism. If, however, the emblems do stand for an essence, which Quin does not believe, the disorientation reveals new aspects of meaning; and the imposed definitions become constructive forms within which to live. Adam Wayne takes the red uniform of Notting Hill seriously. He is not aware of the destructive satiric function of Quin's joke. The emblems become metaphors for him; they are inseparable from the inspiration of his life. He says 'I would paint the Red Lion on my shield if I had only my blood'.

The author calls Wayne a 'dumb poet', a man who normally expresses his inspiration in action. But Wayne has been born into a world where the form for expressing his inspiration exists in the medieval emblems of Quin; and through them he can communicate his inspiration to other people. Wayne employs the emblems as metaphors by insisting that they are at one with the object for which they stand. Metaphorical form recreates experience by fusing the actual with inspired expression. It cannot be simply dismissed as arbitrary definition since it claims to contain essence within it, and it demands involvement in the experience on the audience's part. The positive aspects of his expression are that he creates an experience of essence and causes an individual reassessment of meaning. But this depends upon the success of communication. If the connection between form and essence is not understood, his expression will appear to lack inspiration and relapse into the dangers of rationalism and impressionism. The negative effect of Wayne's metaphors which necessitate involvement are far more serious than Quin's arbitrary emblems that can be dismissed as chaotic. The experiencing of something unknown is frightening and terrible, and the negative aspects of metaphor exist in this potential for creating fear that destroys all sense of order.

Wayne manages to communicate momentarily his inspiration to Quin. The full force of essence beyond his emblems at first disorients Quin, just as his emblems disoriented Barker. He calls Wayne a mad man, just as he has been called mad. When he fully understands he is almost convinced of a view 'so desperate—so responsible'. Yet he will not allow himself to experience Wayne's essence. To do so would destroy his attempt at total personal control.

Quin, Wayne and Barker are portrayed emblematically by the novelist in that he does not change their basic nature. He himself curtails the negative effects of emblem by employing extensive explanations. The terms he uses do not ask for experience; the characters are presented to stand for modes of expression. Barker's 'bleak blue eyes', and his favourite expression 'speaking in the interests of the public', are constants throughout the book. When he is described 'flinging up his fingers with a feverish American movement' or walking with 'his frock-coat flapping like the black wings of a bird', the observations do not create an experience of Barker. Rather, they indicate the attitude of the novelist to the character; they are subtle explanations on his part. Quin is portrayed in a quietly satirical vein. The reader's reaction is an appreciation of the author's humour, of the point the author is making on Quin's external communication; he does not react to Quin himself. Similarly the chapter devoted to the 'Mental Condition of Adam Wayne' carefully builds up an explanation for his perceptions, actions and reactions. The novelist presents his characters so they cannot be radically misunderstood, and he makes sure that they continue to stand for the values with which he imbues them.

The conscious control extends to the tight structural movement of the book. The opening chapter establishes the 'cheat the prophet' action which underlies the serial progression of the chapters. The novelist's contemporaries have dared to try to predict the future; and he ridicules this as impossible. The book presents a sequence of the three static modes of expression each succeeding the other. The five sections of the book each contain three chapters that examine a point of view, show it in action, and lead to its change. The sequence leads finally to the last chapter which is quite different in tone. It contains the union of Wayne and Quin, and elevates them from the dual pattern of meaning the novel has followed. The author recognises the inadequacy of the child vision in the central novel; by itself it is closely connected with the childish joke of Quin. Yet the adult vision of the first chapter of purely rational prophets predicting static futures, is also inadequate. The control makes clear the recognition of the three static characters, the sequential structure culminating in union, and the significant difference in the function of the last chapter. However, a full appreciation of the value of the novel is dependent on the individual response the reader gives to the metaphorical skill of the author.

In *G.F. Watts* Chesterton says that style is at its best when it is shown to correspond with internal meaning. Unless it is purely a technical exercise there must be some connection between form and essence. Although the novelist recognises the dangers of metaphor, he also realises that it is necessary because it connects form and essence. At a few significant points he creates a metaphorical depth to the characters which yields a carefully confined transcendent meaning for the book. There are few consistent metaphors that become symbols, but there are metaphorically created actions and events. These are concentrated in the parts where the modes of expression of the characters come into contact.

An initial example is the introduction of Quin as he walks to work behind two men in frock-coats. The transformation of the coats into dragons indicates the ease with which Quin's mind separates the actual from the perceived, and helps the reader understand the importance to Quin of personal control. The event is partly metaphorical to ensure our experience of Quin's mind, but it is constantly controlled by the author's explanations. A more extended instance occurs when Barker becomes involved in Wayne's war, and all his perceptions become disoriented. The reader is allowed to experience the event through the rhythmic metaphors of Barker's story, but again only against careful authorial control which distances the emotions and fears expressed.

The technique is most clearly demonstrated at the moment when Quin finds his lunch interrupted by the first skirmish of the war. After building up a series of metaphors around the red uniform of Wayne's men, the narrator says:

> Then something happened which he was never able afterwards to describe, and which we cannot describe for him. (119)

After this disclaimer the author proceeds to describe. Wayne is then created as a vision of symbolic strength counterpointed against the grammatical control of the paragraphs and the uncertain note of Quin seeing him 'he knew not how'. But Quin and the reader are swept into an experience of Wayne as a symbol, and of his symbolic expression. But while the experience is necessary for both the character and reader because fundamental questions of self-expression are being evaluated, the danger of chaos inherent in the many interpretations possible from metaphor, is controlled by a careful use of explanation to ensure a defined comprehension. The relationship between Quin and Wayne is clarified by the experience and we feel with Quin that Wayne's communication is the more valuable. But the judgement is made with constant authorial guidance.

In many places, especially during the account of the war, the novelist's emphasis on explanation is too great. It slows the movement and dulls the response to the chapters. In contrast the final chapter of the novel is an earnest attempt to create experience without too much control; and it generates a feeling that defines and gives value to the story. The chapter begins in the darkness before sun-rise with two voices speaking, and the voices carry on a dialogue concerning the value of Notting Hill. As the night begins to lift, the men continue to give their opinions and explain their positions; and when the first silver of a new day becomes visible, the two humans are revealed as Wayne and Quin. The constant references to the growing light counterpoint the growing understanding between the two men as Quin reveals his joke and Wayne his acceptance of it. Their explanation of each other and of themselves concludes with Quin's statement that 'nothing can alter the antagonism—the fact that I laughed at these things and you adored them'. But Wayne's inspiration, that found its form for communication in Quin's joke, recognises the essential need for unity between the two men. The revelation comes to him simultaneously with the dawn; and in the now 'blank white light', Quin agrees. The two join together and go off to meet the world.

The explanation of the differing positions of Quin and Wayne is placed against the rising sun. The dawn is carefully integrated with each step in the growing knowledge of the two men, even though the metaphor is never allowed complete rein. In restricting the amount of explanation and closely integrating it with metaphor, Chesterton completely changes the tone of the chapter. No other part of the book stands out quite so sharply; no other part is so open to the reader's own involvement and interpretation. The reader not only sees the intellectual value of a balance between the conscious and unconscious control, but also experiences a personal value in it through the metaphor of the rising sun.

But it cannot be forgotten that Chesterton does not trust metaphor. He allows it to exist only in tandem with explanation, which however necessary to the meaning, curtails the potential experience. The fact that the style is heavily weighted towards emblem indicates the extent of the author's anxiety. Chesterton seems intuitively to acknowledge that perfect human expression, as proposed in the novel, is impossible in actual life. Small hints of another potential mode occur in the actions of an incidental character, the President of Nicaragua. He pins the yellow of a mustard advertisement to his shirt, and stabs his hand to provide the red colour of blood, yellow and red being his national colours. The action is not emblematic, it does not stand for anything. It is not metaphorical, for it does not recreate experience. It seems more directly connected to pure inspiration, yet is a definite, unmistakeable expression of patriotism. But the implications of his actions are not pursued.

Chesterton has tried to make a case for the balance between external and personal inspiration, to show the spontaneous inspiration receiving consciously controlled form. But he only succeeds in demonstrating that human expression is severely limited. In *G.F. Watts*, which was also written in 1904, the critic indicated a similar division between conscious and unconscious or spontaneous form. There he also implied that the unconscious divine inspiration alone communicated value. We have seen in the previous chapter that in *Heretics* Chesterton was beginning to think that opinions are only valuable when they indicate a conscious belief in an external. This idea, as well as the suggestion that ritual may be the best form for expressing the external, are both found in his next novel.

The Ball and the Cross was partially written in the same year as *Heretics*, and probably completed by 1906. In it Chesterton studies two men who both believe in something. One, Turnbull, has a reasonable basis for belief, centred finally in man and bounded by the limits of human understanding. The other, McIan, believes because of inspiration from an external divine source. Both are presented as necessary aspects of human belief but neither has an adequate form of expression to provide a unity between them. Turnbull is a journalist; he concentrates on the material facets of expression and is always in danger of losing the essence of the object. McIan uses symbol to communicate and is in danger of slipping too far from the actuality of the object. In either case imbalance results in communication centred in self. While they appear to be the same basic duo as that in *The Napoleon of Notting Hill* they are not. McIan is the externally inspired artist and Turnbull the personal dogmatist like Shaw. In *Heretics* it was the lack of Shaw's indication of external inspiration that made questionable his dogma; and this novel can be seen as an examination of the necessary fusion of the two aspects to gain precise communication. Further, there is a brief and not wholly successful study of a third character, Michael, and his mode of expression.

The style of *The Ball and the Cross* and the message about modes of communication, still run on different tracks. Here, however, the internal meaning does illuminate and, to an extent, confirms the author's form. There is a total explanatory control exerted over the complete work until the end of the book. The end provides neither explanation nor experience, but uses a different mode that only partially succeeds, and needs the content to be fully understood.

The conflict between the two main characters lies at the root of the meaning. It expresses itself most clearly in the dreams that the two men have when at the end of the book, they find themselves in an insane asylum. The atheist and individualist Turnbull is shown the result of discarding all external authority. The revolutionaries of his dream establish their freedom at the expense of other people's freedom. The ability of their minds to perceive limits collapses into a recognition of personal limits as the only definitions. In contrast McIan's dream shows authority taken to extremes and invalidating individual effort. In terms of perception, the external authority overwhelms the actual existence of the object, and sees only essence as important.

It is significant that both dreams occur in an asylum which harbours lunatics who believe themselves perfect. The denial of human limitation is the root of madness. The visions of Turnbull and McIan are their beliefs taken to extremes; they are thought of as perfect. And in both cases their modes of expression are revealed as inadequate. Yet while the novel gives the impression that there is a constant see-saw of discussion between McIan and Turnbull, which neither one wins, the argument is unbalanced; McIan is far more sympathetic. The basic parallels between the story and the framework equate McIan with the monk Michael and the cross, and Turnbull with Lucifer and the ball. Although Turnbull is a materialist, he does believe in actual identities; but this positive aspect is neglected. Further, the final revelation concerns the existence of an external authority. Initially Turnbull does not even believe in the external, let alone try to find a form to express it, so McIan has the edge from the start. The cross and the ball sum up the confusion. The central story of the novel attempts to show them in an equal balance with each other. Yet from the beginning the cross is more valuable, and at the end McIan says 'the great terrestrial globe will go quite lop-sided, and only the cross will stand upright'. The discrepancy not only results in a failure of the symmetrical structure of the novel, but also represents a serious confusion of ideas in Chesterton's thought. While supposedly admiring equally the opinions of the self and those of an absolute, he intuitively favours the latter.

The problem is compounded by the recognition that McIan's opinions although favoured are expressed in an demonstrably inadequate form. Chesterton felt that metaphor was too experiential to express absolute inspiration in *The Napoleon of Notting Hill*. The fear of didacticism and impressionism that result from the weakness led to a careful including of the explanatory in the experiential events. While McIan's symbolism is definitely shown to be the more powerful mode of expression, it is counteracted with an unwavering, conscious control by the author. No event of potential feeling or experience is expressed through metaphor which could potentially become arbitrary and impressionist. The main artistic technique used in the novel is emblem, and the function of emblem as 'standing for' something else, is painstakingly spelled out in the initial discussion between Michael and Lucifer about the meaning of the ball and the cross.

But just as McIan and Turnbull recognise their inadequacy when they reach the garden of human perfection and of madness, the novelist here too comes to terms with the inadequacy of his style. A mere balance between the two characters would leave open the potential dangers of each, but the monk Michael provides one answer for both. His miraculous walk through the flames of the burning asylum is a solid, acceptable fact to Turnbull even though it is not purely materialist; to McIan it is an actual representation of the power of God. Material and inspired expression fuse in this action. It is one form combining the two and delivering them from the dangers of balance.

The style of the final chapters is similar to that of Michael's walk through the flames. The garden and the asylum no longer stand for something, they are the actual. The dreams of Turnbull and McIan are unexplained but clear. They do not provide experience but indicate meaning alone. In the same way events surrounding their imprisonment are not explained. Intellectual reasons could be found for the details but they would not be adequate, and experiencing the imprisonment leaves the universal implications of the events enigmatic. The style, like Michael's walk, is an actual event; in other words not emblematic or symbolic. It contains rational meaning and indicates an experience. Yet the full expression implies more than these aspects; it points to a meaning that we cannot fully understand, but that we can know: the existence of an external and absolute authority.

The indication of essence is Chesterton's definition of the process of ritual. However in a novel it must be transformed into its verbal mode of allegory which aims to indicate with little or no interference by the author personally. But Michael is not a strong enough figure to carry the meaning. The author has constructed the novel as Michael's vision by beginning and ending the story with him. His character is established at the start. Although the reader recognises Michael in the conclusion, he is not sufficiently connected to a deeply-rooted meaning. The previously discussed confusion in Chesterton's use of the ball and the cross weakens Michael's effectiveness. The cross is the one external figure with which he is allied, and it loses its strength by being allied to the supposed balance between McIan and Turnbull that is shown to be an inevitable imbalance. Yet Michael's role in the story clarifies his function in the style. Although neither he, nor the form he presents, completely succeed, the character is important as an initial attempt at a mode that Chesterton will develop and refine to his own expressive needs as he matures.

II

In the search for form Chesterton has examined nonsense, emblem, symbol and material description. Behind these modes exists a growing recognition of ritual in the actions of the President of Nicaragua and the monk Michael. In *The Ball and the Cross* Michael has a unique expression of ritual that brings together the actual and the essence. In 1906 the critic further defines his idea through the appreciation of folklore in *Charles Dickens*. The folklore is based on the ritualisation of aspects of people by exaggeration which transcends the separation of essence and form. The critic condemns the realism of the later novels although it is better art, because it tries to imitate where folklore does not. The control of folklore admits the limits of the artist because it indicates meaning beyond him; yet the control of realism implies a confidence in self that denies limits. Folklore is ritual and externally based; whereas realism is centred in the self and open to misinterpretation. These different criteria and the modes they generate become the central theme of Chesterton's next novel.

The Man Who Was Thursday was written in 1907, the year of an increasing confidence in the essays. There is a force to the book not felt in the earlier work. It is not a joke, nor a disputation, but a clear expression of Chesterton's inspiration. The novel explores many modes of expression and shows them all failing. At the end ritual takes over to justify and provide meaning for the events. All other modes communicate essence as far as the human can see it, but are ultimately inadequate. However, the author states that despite their brilliant technique, they are not 'better art', that any mode leading to potential anarchy and despotism is not only immoral but also inartistic. The novelist finally differentiates between morality and ethics. He refuses to accept that the artist can avoid moral responsibility and depend on a self-centred code of conduct.

The artist now has two essential roles: those of artist and critic that Chesterton looked at in *Charles Dickens* when comparing himself to the novelist. He must function critically in perceiving the essence of the thing, and creatively in expressing that essence. The division must not be confused with that between the impressionist and inspirational, or didactic and dogmatic separations of the earlier novels. The two roles are not antagonistic, in conflict or in balance. They are both part of the same process in one man. The emphasis of the book is on both interpretation and representation of essence by the artist; and is far more mature in its recognition of the complexity of the issues. The dual role of the artist seems to put Chesterton at ease. It necessitates admission of human limitation, yet allows for creation. The conclusion of both the content and the style is that ritual is the only form which satisfies both conditions, and that allegory is the artistic mode that expresses ritual.

The novel begins in a London suburb. The resident poet Gregory, presents himself as an anarchist, and is in the middle of holding forth when a poet of order, Gabriel Syme, turns up. After an argument, Gregory takes Syme with him to a meeting of the English anarchists who are just about to elect him to their European Council. Syme first has to promise not to reveal anything to the police. Then he in turn makes Gregory promise not to reveal him to the anarchists, for he is a police detective. Putting this mutual secrecy to use Syme gets himself elected to the Council instead of Gregory. He becomes Thursday, the day of the week allotted to the English member. The European Council meets the next day under their president, Sunday. After the unexpected exposure of Tuesday as a policeman, the remaining anarchists plot the death of the czar who is visiting France, and then break up. Throughout the central section of the novel Syme is involved in tracking down the individual members of the Council to try to halt the plot. One by one they are revealed as police detectives.

First he meets Friday, Professor Worms; together they expose Saturday, Dr Bull, and all leave for France. When they reveal Wednesday or Ratcliffe, they find that Monday, the one remaining anarchist has got an army together to destroy them. They escape to the edge of the sea where Monday tries to arrest them in the name of the law, for he too is a policeman. Confused but relieved they return to England to find out who Sunday is. There is an absurd chase through London and the countryside which leads them to Sunday's house where they are looked after and feasted. The book ends with them asking why it all happened. Then Sunday disappears and Syme wakes up to find himself walking along a road talking to Gregory.

Sunday is the key to the meaning of Syme's experience. He is also the guide to the overall meaning of the book. Sunday is introduced first as the leader of the anarchists: a powerful, intelligent man, commanding respect. It should be noted that at the beginning of the central section a similar figure is introduced as the head of the police force. He is unseen, always living in a dark room. Sunday, by contrast, is almost 'too large to see'. As Syme approaches him he is overcome by a sense of 'spiritual evil' that grows with the face of Sunday. The sense gets stronger, and Syme is afraid that the face will grow so large it will be impossible to see, and he is reminded of seeing the face of Memnon as a child at the British Museum. Sunday's position as an anarchist is weakened in the central section of the novel when he himself begins the break-up of the Council by exposing Tuesday. When all the policemen are revealed, the third action begins and the reader meets Sunday once more. Syme asks him who he is. His only answer is that they can never know, only that he was also the policeman in the dark room. Each member tries to define him in his own terms, and each relates him in a different way to life. Sunday is seen as the two sides of man, the animal and the god. Finally he becomes a fusion of the two initial images of the seen and the unseen men:

the great face grew to an awful size, grew larger than the colossal mask of Memnon, which had made him scream as a child. It grew larger and larger, filling the whole sky; then everything went black. (191)

The answer to who he is lies in his last words, 'Can ye drink of the cup that I drink of?' It is both enigmatic yet satisfying.

The shifting definition of Sunday parallels Syme's state of mind. In the first section of three chapters he is sure that he is a poet of the law. He knows the difference between anarchy and order; between Sunday and the man in the dark room. Sunday, however, begins the process that exposes the policemen, exposes order. Paradoxically, Syme, in continuing these exposures, becomes an anarchist. At he moment of becoming an anarchist he is revealed as a policeman. Throughout the central section he attempts to make sense of the situation, and when all the men are exposed it seems that the meaning of things should be clear, but it is not. Without Sunday being defined, none of the members can be properly defined. The dual role of Sunday which the final three chapters slowly clarifies, helps Syme understand why he had to become an anarchist. At the end he realises that he will never completely understand Sunday or himself; but he can know of Sunday's existence and that it justifies his own.

Sunday's definition also parallels the style of the novel. The first section is filled with explanation on both the author's and the poet's part. There are many carefully placed images with isolated and detached significance. The whole is constructed to set up the opposing sides of order and anarchy, and the rigid division reinforces the definiteness of Syme's attitude to law, and Sunday's initial duality. In common with the confusion of the central section, the style transposes impressionism and clarity within each exposure of the policeman. The final section is written as an allegory, allowing the characters to participate in ritual which eludes understanding but points to one external authority. The author's confidence, or perhaps trust, in his new mode helps him for once to create an integrated work. The message of his story and the function of his style are very close to each other. Syme and the writer go through the same process of expression with the progress of events, and the events themselves illuminate the meaning of the expression.

The action of the novel begins with the establishing of roles for the poet of order and the poet of anarchy. Paradoxically we find that the anarchist has to be far more organised to survive as such than the poet of order; and he is introduced while speaking in 'his high didactic voice, laying down the law'. Syme, on the other hand, is engaged by the police force as a free agent with no questions asked. Despite his passionate defence of respectability he is a 'meek' and 'humble' man. But the novelist provides a more important comment on the two men in his opening style. Both men are shown as definite; both use similar emblematic examples, merely interpreted from their own point of view. Their claim to full understanding makes both poets over-explain in these first three chapters. The author allows it and the action of the chapters is arrested by the very limitations that are being exposed in the characters. Neither man has a satisfactory outlook; neither the control nor the spontaneity they represent can succeed in isolation.

Within this first section a second point of stylistic importance originates. The novelist establishes certain random, rather fanciful images concerning red hair which is associated negatively with Gregory and positively with his sister. There is also a musical motif in the barrel-organ which inspires Syme. The associative and ambiguous nature of these images is appropriate to the artistic limitations of author and characters which appear in this section of the novel. As these limitations are broken down and explored, the images will come to form an integral part of the personal symbolic expression that results from a less isolated view of communication.

Syme's intended role within the police force emerges from a conversation with another policeman at the start of the central section. There is apparently a 'purely intellectual conspiracy' threatening the existence of civilisation. The police are expected to 'trace the origin of these dreadful thoughts that drive men on at last to intellectual fanaticism and intellectual crime'. These are the thoughts that 'stop thought'; Gregory himself says that the anarchists want 'To abolish God', to make themselves the sole source of meaning for the world. This of course is Chesterton's solipsistic vision. Yet here he says that total despotic control to counteract it is just as bad. Syme must find another solution to come to terms with the 'dreadful thoughts'.

The growth into anarchy by the characters in the central section of the novel, is paralleled by a growth of more and more impressionism in expression. The process begins when Syme accepts the role of Thursday and steps into the steamship that will take him to his meeting with the Council. The transition from order to anarchy is stylistically one from explanation to impressionism, and the novelist carefully combines the two aspects at the end of the first section. But both the impression and explanation are transcended by the actual objects Syme carries with him: his food, brandy and pistol. They take on a 'concrete and material poetry' which conveys his true inspiration. Syme can reach beyond impression to inspiration, and it is the growth of his ability to do so that we watch as he experiences and comes terms with anarchy.

Significantly the first anarchist council member that Syme meets is the Secretary, or Monday, the pure intellectual at the root of the conspiracy. The other men on the council each represent different uses of intellect for the perversion of logic. Syme thinks on seeing them that:

> Each figure seemed to be, somehow, on the borderland of things, just as their theory was on the borderline of thought. He knew that each one of these men stood at the extreme end, so to speak, of some wild road of reasoning. (64)

The members of the Council are all aspects of man; and Syme as the poet or definer has to discover the meaning that lies beyond their appearance. The only clue comes from Sunday when he exposes Tuesday. Tuesday stands out as the obvious choice, the madman, the fanatic; but the whole man is a pose. The Russian peasant is a harmless Cockney business man with a little blue card that identifies him as a policeman.

But it is the inspirational artist in Syme that initially proves most valuable in discovering the anarchists' identities. The initial mask of each man is established during the first meeting, and Syme describes them as 'demonic details' that he tries to shake off, but 'The sense of an unnatural symbolism always settled back on him again'. The feeling marks a process of apprehension that does not right itself until each figure is exposed. Syme counteracts the fear caused by separation of essence and form, when he hears the jangle of a barrel-organ. It suddenly recalls to him his source of true inspiration: the Church, the 'common and kindly people in the street', his humanity. As he listens, the image of the barrel-organ that the reader was briefly introduced to in section one is enriched. It becomes a metaphor, rooted in the actual and conveying the real. Through it Syme controls the fear of the vague impressions around him and pierces to their inspiration.

The first exposure in which he is directly involved is that of Professor Worms. Here Syme only instigates the exposure because the Professor reveals himself by producing his little blue card, and only then does Syme produce his. The Professor's facade was as a propounder of German nihilism. On dropping his mask he reveals a realist. Realism stands at the beginning of a self dependence that leads in the end to a denial of all authority. This is why his anarchic form is nihilism. When Syme is in the process of discovering the true inspiration his own impressions are distorted in a nihilistic manner. After a few attempts to escape the Professor who follows him after the

meeting, he feels that the 'philosophical entities called time and space have
no vestige even of practical existence'. Against this vague indefiniteness, the
distortion of nihilistic perception, Syme suddenly notices, picked 'out in
perfect silver, the great orb and cross'. He counteracts the effects of the
totally arbitrary images with the 'symbol of human faith and valour' and
gains the courage to turn and face his pursuer. When the Professor is
exposed, Syme:

> had for a flash the sensation that the cosmos had turned exactly
> upside down; ... Then came slowly the opposite conviction. For
> the last twenty-four hours the cosmos had really been upside
> down, but now the capsized universe had come right side up
> again. (85)

The peculiar effect of the professor's perverted realism was conquered by the
use of symbol which never claims total personal control; and which expresses
the essence of the order for which Syme is fighting.

In a similar manner Syme goes on to expose Bull's rationalism and
efficiency as an ordinary practicality by means of inspiration from his
personal symbol of a woman's red hair. The same symbol, along with the
barrel-organ, instigates. his exposure of the fourth member, Wednesday or
Radcliffe. His aestheticism and cynicism is the result of the reduction of
common sense by the intellectual perversion of anarchy. The common sense
of Radcliffe lets him naturally take charge of the band of policemen as they
retreat from the army which is led by Monday. In the flight from the
perverted logic of pure intellect Syme is overcome by the most dangerous
impressionism of all, the doubt of his own existence. The shadows of the
wood into which they retreat cause confusion, and the disorientation
increases until Syme wonders:

> was he wearing a mask? Was anyone wearing a mask? Was
> anyone anything ... Was there anything apart from what it
> seemed? ... He had found ... that final scepticism which can find
> no floor to the universe. (133)

The poet pulls himself out of this doubt by sheer conversation; and it is
dispelled by the appearance of a peasant cutting wood, who was 'common-
sense in an almost awful actuality'. Yet the confusion of identity experienced
recurs as one by one the men the police think they can rely on, turn about
face and help the anarchists.

From Syme's perspective Monday is the last remaining anarchist. He is the intellect that provides the basis of anarchy. Yet from Monday's own perspective, he is the last remaining policeman for he is philosophy that stops anarchy. The progress of Syme has increasingly isolated him from the rest of the world as he has defined the personal basis of the members' lives. Near the end of the chase Syme warns the Professor that he's becoming an anarchist, and Radcliffe adds 'Everyone is'. Syme has become an anarchist even though he thinks he is still a policeman. The paradox arises from the realisation that the personal meaning he has uncovered has no absolute basis. Once the personal inspiration for the men's behaviour is clarified by Syme's poetic creation, it does not seem to help to define their lives. To avoid anarchy Syme must define with reference to an external authority which means interpretation as well as creation, and this he has increasingly ceased to do.

With every normal expectation reversed, on the edge of giving in to the insanity of the solipsist, Syme's personal symbols of the red hair and the barrel-organ are now useless as a means to inspire him. He turns to a different mode of expression to counteract the impressionism of the intellect. At the last minute he picks up the old ecclesiastic lamp a helper had given him, and challenges Monday. By the allegorical meaning of 'the cross carved on it, and the flame inside', he tears away the intellectual scepticism of Monday to expose him as a policeman; in the process he also exposes himself. Allegory is externally inspired rather than personally created alone. It cannot, therefore, degenerate into impressionism or rationalism, and includes its own interpretation. This final exposure casts off human intellect to reveal external authority for action; it casts off human expression to acknowledge that it is too limited to define man. The simultaneous exposure of Monday and Syme as both policeman and anarchist is the recognition of control and spontaneity as two essential elements in man. Further it is the recognition that they cannot simultaneously exist without the acknowledgement of an external authority and inspiration; and that this authority cannot be expressed through human symbol, but only through ritual in allegory.

The creative nature of Syme's exposure in the central section of the book was necessary for him to understand his human limitations. In the final section his role as poet or definer is mainly interpretive in the light of these limitations. The last section shows the men trying to define Sunday because they realise that their personal meaning is not complete without him. Yet it is not until they become involved in the ritual he has created for them that they succeed, and Syme leads the May in the attempt. It is he who starts the totally absurd chase into the countryside.

The limits of man's understanding are underlined as each man tries to define Sunday while on the chase. Each definition is an aspect of man that is not understood. For example, Monday thinks of him as like 'protoplasm ... the final form of matter', which reminds him of all that human intellect originated in, and over which it has virtually no power. Syme begins to notice and interpret the pattern that defines Sunday only by negatives. Relating the pattern of negative definitions to his own experience, he reaches the 'secret of the whole world', that man always looks only at the back of things, never at the front. Syme realises that he has been exposing the back of people, the human nature. His great revelation is that he must search for the face, the god-like, the divine.

The revelation ends the chase, yet would not have been possible if the men had not been involved in it. The chase can be seen as performing different functions for every expressive level. As an action involving the council it is a ritual they must perform in order to understand Sunday. For Sunday it is an allegorical expression of the ritual. For Chesterton both allegory and ritual are themselves an allegorical expression of life. Rather than an absurdity without logic, it is an enigma with an unknown logic; and enigma is the central feature of Chesterton's allegory. Apart from the chase itself one of the enigmatic aspects is the dropping of notes for each man. The notes indicate on a smaller scale the function of allegory. They contain some application to the recipient, but every reader will get something different from them. For example, Syme's note reads:

> No one would regret anything in the nature of an interference by the Archdeacon more than I. I trust it will not. come to that. But, for the last time, where are your galoshes? The thing is too bad, especially after what uncle said. (164)

One response is to see the contrast between Syme's occasionally ludicrous sense of form and ceremony and his neglect of practicalities. A simpler example is found in the note to Tuesday. As the supposed anarchist Russian peasant, or 'red', his note reads, 'The word, I fancy, should be "pink"'. What is important is that the notes have some relevance for each person, but one can never understand them fully. A more important enigmatic and allegorical aspect is the use of clothes. The chase ends when a messenger arrives from Sunday to take the men to his house. Here the members are all given clothes which define them. This time their definition is not personal but absolute for Sunday's allegory does 'not disguise, but reveal'.

At the final ceremony all the animals and objects that have been encountered in the book are dancing at what seems a pointless masquerade until Sunday appears and then the dancing becomes 'as absurd as Alice in Wonderland, yet as grave and kind as a love story'. The confluence of nonsense and romance in the ritual dance indicates Chesterton's understanding of allegory as without comprehensible logic yet with an absolute goal and authority. However, the appearance of Sunday leads the men to question why the Anarchic Council was set up; why they should have suffered. Again each question is appropriate to the aspect of human nature each member represents.

As they finish questioning, Gregory, the true anarchist poet, reappears. It is after his accusation that the policemen are mere acceptors of law, never having truly suffered, that Syme makes his last definition, his final interpretation of the action of the book. The men had to become anarchists, to suffer, to define themselves, before their function within and understanding of an external system of order could become valuable. But when he questions Sunday, because it is important for his own value to know that Sunday too should have suffered, he is answered with the words 'Can ye drink of the cup that I drink of?' and Syme blacks out before the impossible knowing of God. Simultaneous with Gregory's appearance is the reintroduction of Syme's personal symbols of the 'red hair'. One again has the duality of Gregory's red hair which 'shall burn up the world' and the opposite force of his having 'red hair like your sister'. Yet just as the ambiguity and danger of authority and anarchy in man is explained, so the ambiguity and danger of the personal symbol is here resolved in face of an external authority. When Syme comes to it, it is as if his participation in ritual has strengthened his personal expression. Having defined himself in terms of an external he can use symbol with new clarity, and the novel ends with the 'gold-red hair' of Gregory's sister.

The novel as a whole does contain an overriding control by Chesterton. However, the control is constructed as ritual so that a lot depends upon the connections the reader makes with a meaning beyond the story itself. As with the previous novels, *The Man Who Was Thursday* takes place at twilight, the time of change. It is also enclosed, this time by a dream framework which is significant when one remembers that Chesterton believed dreams to present essence despite seemingly inappropriate exteriors. The movement is circular in beginning with Syme and Gregory at the start, returning to them in the last chapter. Yet here the movement does not lead to some projected human perfection of expression. It returns to the limited symbolic mode of man, showing it stabilised by participation in ritual. The parallels between the events and the style show that personal definition through understanding is linked with the human process of impression and inspiration. The ethical foundation of this understanding is not adequate to prevent the danger of anarchy or despotism. Instead definition must be approached through the knowledge of an external authority that is experienced in, and interpreted from the allegorical verbalisation of ritual. The basis of existence will then be absolute and moral.

It is important that within the novel the ritual is given by the Christian God. Therefore the characters of the book can find it perfectly revealing. Because it is written by Chesterton the ritual cannot be perfect in the reader's terms. It is humanly limited and intended to be so. The formal and obvious structuring of the book into three sections, the allegorical rather than symbolic function of the characters, and the absurdity of temporal and spatial relations, make this clear. Yet Chesterton has chosen a sufficiently strong allegory to present the meaning, in using the days of the week and their biblical interpretations. The weight of such figures transcends the limitations of the human expression, just as the ecclesiastical lamp transcended the ultimate danger of limited human understanding. Chesterton's confidence lies in this knowledge of having incorporated an external authority. Yet the novel also contains a symbolic strength that is new to Chesterton's novels and makes it possible for the reader not just to observe but to involve himself in the work. In his own terms he has both perceived essence in an acknowledgedly limited way, yet expressed it creatively and with moral responsibility as an artist.

JOHN COATS

The Return to Hugo:
A Discussion of the Intellectual Context
of Chesterton's View of the Grotesque

B orges' important short piece on Chesterton singles out, probably rightly, the two critical studies with which Chesterton made his literary *début* as in some way typical of his essential nature:

> His personality leaned towards the nightmarish, something secret, blind and central. Not in vain did he dedicate his first works to the justification of two great Gothic craftsmen, Browning and Dickens.[1]

Most readers interested in Chesterton, while grateful for this contribution to the recent increase of serious attention he has been getting, are likely to feel that Borges' reading of Chesterton's innermost spirit is wrong. Yet, they might accept that while the conclusion is false, the area of emphasis is correct. Much of vital significance about Chesterton is displayed in those combative, deliberately controversial rehabilitations, a concern, above all, with the grotesque, in experience and in art. I wish to explore Chesterton's view of the grotesque in its intellectual context, especially his return to the first formulations and spirit of Victor Hugo, which had been either forgotten or misinterpreted by his contemporaries and immediate predecessors.

From *English Literature in Transition*. © 1982 by *English Literature in Transition*.

In his two early critical forays, on Browning and Dickens, Chesterton engaged in a number of tasks. Both books were obviously and successfully rescues: of Dickens, from critics or defenders who attacked or condoned his superficiality; of Browning, from those reverent admirers who insisted on his "profundity." Characteristically good tempered, they are outstanding examples of literary polemic, the overwhelmingly convincing demolition of a false and time-wasting view of a subject. Chesterton rendered it impossible to view Dickens or Browning as George Gissing or Professor Forman viewed them. Fruitful and important as this work of demolition was, it is, perhaps, less significant than Chesterton's deeper controversial intention. Beyond the removal of misconceptions about individual authors, the underlying direction of the two books is towards a wholesale examination and defense of the "larger than) life" element in art. The studies of Browning and Dickens are seminal statements of Chesterton's aesthetic views.

Conveniently they break the "larger than life" quality into two separate strands: the nature of fable, the basis of consideration in the work on Dickens, and the "grotesque," the primary subject of study in *Robert Browning*. Chesterton sees the grotesque as the proof of Nature's energy, or rather the energy of God in nature, "energy that takes its own forms and goes its own way."[2] The grotesque is the refusal of the living force of nature to conform I to narrow aesthetic views, the conventionally "beautiful" harmony of proportion and form, the diluted heritage of Greek classicism. It is, too, evidence of an artistic energy which escapes jejune or limited notions of what is beautiful, those which concentrate on the supposed needs of civilized man, or defer to the received opinions of art critics.

Readers will at once recall instances of Chesterton's excursions into this field in his very early works *A Defence of Skeletons*, or *A Defence of Ugly Things* (both 1900), first trace a tendency which was to undergo some alteration before it culminated in *The Man Who Was Thursday* (1908) as a fictional concern, and in *On the Book of Job* (1929) in essay form. In *A Defence of Ugly Things* Chesterton, leaning (as we shall see) on Hugo's *Preface to Cromwell*, makes his most trenchant and direct attack on the Greek classical ideal of harmony and proportion. This short manifesto on behalf of the grotesque, among the very first of his articles published in *The Speaker*, is interesting because it stands at the start of his literary career, antedating even the book on Browning. He roundly attacks the classical ideal as "a worship of one aesthetic type alone."[3] The Greeks "carried their police regulations into elfland"[4] out of a timid avoidance of the wild ideas, the violent combinations of the imagination that mankind naturally loves. Consequently their fantasy is anaemic compared to fairy-tale or "Scandinavian story." "Who ever feels that the giants in Greek art and poetry were really big—big as some folk-lore giants have been?" Chesterton asks.[5] What applies in the realm of imagination affects also our way of seeing the world. Greek restraint, "this disgraceful *via media*, this pitiful sense of dignity" makes us, against our instinct, view powerful and endearing faces as ugly, silly and repulsive faces as beautiful. Left to itself, mankind spontaneously prefers "size, vitality, variety, energy, ugliness,"[6] which ultimately are qualities of Nature. "Ugliness" in aesthetics is a recognition of the primal quality of Nature or life. It is not at this stage, as it became, significantly, later in Chesterton's view, and in the view of Poe who influenced Chesterton on the matter of the grotesque, a question of humor. Rather Nature is considered as an artist breaking fresh ground by "her bold experiments, her definite departures, her fearlessness and her savage pride in her children."[7]

What interest these early statements possess is derived mainly from such light as they throw on Chesterton's mature use of the grotesque and as little seeds or faint anticipations of *The Man Who Was Thursday*. It would, however, be a mistake to view them only as anticipating Chesterton's later career. To understand their true significance it is necessary to look backwards, to see them within their intellectual context. Chesterton's liking for the grotesque and his writing on it have been discussed very much within a framework of his personality and psychology, where of necessity much must be guesswork and assumption. The history of these ideas, vitally important in a career built so consciously on intellectual controversy, has not been given sufficient attention. While Chesterton's view of the grotesque certainly grew out of his own mental landscape and his own preoccupations, it is possible to dwell too much on conjectural subconscious motives and too little on his response to what others said or failed to say.

Chesterton wrote against the current of a view of the grotesque originating in various sources, including, most likely, Walter Pater's misinterpretation of Hugo. However, a full understanding of the debate requires a still wider context. It is useful to see the direction of Hugo's original view of the grotesque and how Pater changed its tone and emphasis. Because of the tendency among other critics writing in English on the grotesque to underrate it and fail either to explore it or to do it justice, Pater's powerful and subtle views held the field at the time when Chesterton began to formulate his own theories, theories largely in opposition to Pater's, which were, in essence, a return to Hugo's first pronouncements.

Victor Hugo's name is central to the background of the debate in which Chesterton was involved, since the *Preface to Cromwell* (1827) may be taken as the seminal document on the grotesque, at least in England. Two writers,

Hugo and Hegel, mark a decisive departure from earlier views of the grotesque, and a readiness to grant the concept a new significance. Hugo's *Preface*, rather than Hegel's *Essay on the Grotesque*, was the likely point of departure for English readers because it is written in an accessible style, where Hegel is peculiarly dense and technical and likely to appeal only to a minority among professional philosophers, even in a period when Hegelianism was highly influential. It is, of course, true, as Clayborough has pointed out,[8] that the *Preface to Cromwell* uses a basically Hegelian framework—one which stresses the antithetical elements of man working towards resolution, and a tripartite division of human history into primitive or the age of the ode, classical or the age of the epic, and romantic or the age of the drama, in the last of which a synthesis of the material and spiritual is reached. The *Preface*, however, is a bright succession of striking generalizations rather than a laborious treatise. It is a lively sketch of human history offered with a polemical purpose in the context of Hugo's war against "Classical" canons in the French theater leading up to the scandal and triumph of *Hernani*, and in the current of liberalism moving towards the 1830 Revolution. Its appeal is instantaneous.

Perhaps the most significant point about Hugo's view of the grotesque is his definition of it as an aspect of necessary and desirable moral and social development, an extension of human sympathy connected explicitly with growing political freedom. First, in his sketch, comes the innocence of primitive times, "when man is just awakened," when the earth imposes no fetters on the individual man and "he is still so near God that all his meditations are ecstatic; all his dreams are visions."[9] It is a time when his "Lyre has but three strings: God; the soul; creation; but this three-fold mystery entraps everything; this three-fold thought includes everything."[10] In this first age the poetic temperament is one of prayer and finds expression in the ode. For polemical purposes, Hugo portrays the classical age which follows as a falling off from this first freedom and innocence. Dogma lays its hold on worship. Theocracy succeeds patriarchal community. An impressive gravity prevails in public and private morals and an epic spirit dominates, even in the plays. The Greek drama, Hugo states, was essentially a vast civic and religious ritual: "Its characters are still heroes, demigods, gods; its motives, dreams, oracles, fatality; its tableau, funeral rites and combats."[11] Everything was remorselessly sacrificed to one ideal standard of beauty, a perfection of physical form and a concentration on the socially exalted. Hugo sees the advent of Christianity as an attack upon a civilization which had hardened and degenerated. The new religion preached a division of flesh and spirit in man, foreign to a purely materialistic paganism. With the new more complex human model appeared a hitherto unknown sense of contradiction which Hugo calls "melancholy," the disparity between man's immortal and temporal concerns. The simplicity and harmony of pagan classicism were no longer possible.

This moral change was connected with a social change: "Up to that time catastrophes which befell empires rarely reached to the heart of the people. Kings fell, majestic personages vanished, but that was all."[12] But now, the violence which brought the Roman Empire to an end affected the great mass of the population. Influenced both by violence and Christianity, a religion of "equality, liberty and charity," a much greater sense of social equality emerged: "Man, taking thought to himself in the presence of the vicissitudes among the great began to take pity on his kind and to reflect on the bitter ironies of life."[13] The logical and fullest development of this spirit, Hugo states, is just emerging in the romantic art, especially drama, of his own time. The new spirit of this art "will feel that everything in creation is not beautiful from the standpoint of mankind, that the ugly exists besides the beautiful, the misshapen besides the graceful, the grotesque beside the sublime."[14] It will decline to "set God right" by rejecting so much of his creation, to obtain an ideal beauty by mutilation, to cut man in two.

Hugo, as might be expected from the future author of *Notre Dame de Paris*, sees the Middle Ages as the first great flood of the grotesque in heraldry, in "that wonderful architecture," in manners, in laws and eventually in church and religion. He describes it, with exhilaration and delight, as a spirit of vigor and creative power.

In considering the treatment of the grotesque by English writers in the fifty years before Chesterton, it is hard to dispute Kayser's generalization that the discussion fell back from "the high place of the definitions between 1770 and 1830."[15] Apart from the special and very important exception of Pater, a straightforward "loss of status" for the concept of the grotesque may be traced during the period 1830–1900. Much the most significant feature of this process, however, was the refusal of writer after writer to accept the notion of the grotesque as part of a social development, the historical consciousness which was the essence of Hugo's analysis of the term and its moral meaning.

At first, in Ruskin's well-known account in *The Stones of Venice* (1851–1853), the grotesque still occupied a relatively high rank. It is of course inferior, even in Dante, to the sublimity of the highest art since it results from a sportive instinct outside a perfect natures "It is evident that the idea of any kind of play can only be associated with the idea of an imperfect, childish fatigable spirit."[16] The grotesque impulse, for Ruskin, chiefly

occupies a middle rank in the human temper between the perfect and those
either too morose, dull or exhausted to invent a jest. He divides grotesque art
into the noble or terrible and the ignoble. Ruskin takes the existence of the
noble grotesque in art as a kind of index of the quality of a civilization. He
sees the phenomenon as a whole, much as Hugo had done, as a result of
Christianity's contradiction between flesh and spirit: "The fallen human soul,
at its best, must be as a diminishing glass, and that a broken one, to the
mighty truths of the universe around it."[17] Ruskin's thoughtful analysis lays
weight on the description of spiritual states, which seem to be given,
permanent facts of human nature, not on the description of any historical
process. The temperaments which produce different kinds of art, it would
seem, recur in age after age. Along with the lose of historical consciousness
and a sense of development found in Hugo is a tendency to blunt the edge of
the grotesque, to soften any bizarre or uncouth quality it might have. The
"noble grotesque," a hardly conceivable hybrid, sounds humorless as well. By
importing the notion of "nobility" Ruskin accommodates the grotesque to
contemporary tastes by limiting its capacity to shock.

Later critics showed a disposition to retreat from Ruskin's carefully
qualified but nonetheless important place for the grotesque. Clayborough
remarks that

> in the later nineteenth century when the romantic view of
> grotesque art as possessing a 'numinous' transcendental quality
> loses ground, a ... view of the grotesque becomes current
> according to which the grotesque is neither a rejection of reality
> nor an actual part of it; the view that it is a fantasy with a practical
> aspect; parody, burlesque, mockery, caricature.[18]

There seems also to lie behind their various dilutions or disintegrations of
the concept of the grotesque a persistent sense that art should be dignified
and that the grotesque must derogate from it. Art's nobility and beauty are
the supreme truth and to admit other elements would overturn the proper
and natural hierarchy of aesthetic value.

Walter Bagehot, although well aware of the grotesque on a personal
level,[19] was unwilling in his essay "Wordsworth, Tennyson and Browning; or
Pure, Ornate and Grotesque Art in English Poetry" (1864) to grant the
grotesque any significant stature except in theory: Despite a technical
admission that "grotesque art" (a term which he uses to mean ugly or
monstrous rather than fantastic) within it limits might be as valid as pure art,
he makes it clear that since grotesque subjects require highly specialized

treatment the artist had much better leave them alone. In practice, the grotesque poetry of Browning is far inferior to the pure poetry of Wordsworth or even the ornate poetry of Tennyson.[20]

In Thomas Wright, J. A. Symonds and George Santayana, there is a perceptible movement further and further away from Hugo's view of the grotesque. The constituents of Hugo's view—namely the connections between the grotesque and the religious sense; the "melancholy" awareness of human contradiction; the link between the emergence of the grotesque and the growth of a wider social and human sympathy; the essential part Hugo assigned to it in a fuller view of man and the world, freed from the mutilation caused by a limited aesthetic ideal; the notion of the grotesque as, above all, a token of creative energy—in short all the rich and suggestive ideas broached in the *Preface to Cromwell* have been abandoned. Wright's simple *History of Caricature and the Grotesque in Literature and Art* (1865) states that "the monstrous is closely allied to the grotesque and both come within the province of caricature, when we take this term in its widest sense."[21] This is, as Clayborough remarks, so loose a definition as to be almost valueless. Nevertheless the intention is plainly to rob the grotesque of deeper psychological or spiritual meaning or significance. For Symonds, in his essay *Caricature, the Fantastic, the Grotesque* (1890),

> the grotesque is a branch of the fantastic. Its specific difference lies in the fact that an element of caricature, whether deliberately intended or imported by the craftsman's spontaneity of humour, forms an ingredient in the thing produced.[22]

It is, he feels, particularly found in the Teutonic races but is lacking in Greeks and Orientals. It is scarcely necessary to observe that the notion of "caricature" like that of "nobility" in the grotesque represents a demotion of the whole category. In Symonds' view it can have no originality and must be parasitic on the "real" world. Santayana in *The Sense of Beauty* (1896) considers the grotesque simply as a name given to artistic novelty and aesthetic effect—for a while striking and new in its "divergence from the natural." When, however, the effect is more fully understood "the incongruity with the conventional type disappears and what was impossible and ridiculous at first, takes its place among the recognised ideals."[23] Santayana, as Clayborough says, seems to regard the disappearance of what is startling as highly desirable. (It is interesting to note that he, like Bagehot, depreciated the grotesque art of Browning that Chesterton was to rehabilitate.) Perhaps the ultimate point in this gradual denial of meaning and significance to the grotesque is T. Tyndall Wildridge's suggestion in *The Grotesque in Church Art* (1899) that it resulted from the copying of earlier work, "without a knowledge of its serious meaning,"[24] that it was, in fact, a form of incompetence or ignorance.

The movement from Ruskin to Santayana was nothing less than a drying up of interest in a whole category of art and experience. There are some curious paradoxes about this dwindling away of a potentiality. One is the great and continuing popularity with educated Englishmen of Victor Hugo as a playwright, poet and dramatist, his role acknowledged by critics, such as Pater, in the general development of Romanticism, for which, of course, the *Preface to Cromwell* is a prime source. Yet there persisted a strange unwillingness to take up the ideas on the grotesque contained in the *Preface*. Another anomaly in this failure of intellectual response is suggested by the recollection that it coincided, in England, with the full flood of the Gothic Revival. Surely, one might feel, there ought to have been some connection between the grotesque and the Gothic.

The paradox that this element played little part in the interpretations of Pugin, Ruskin or William Morris is readily explained. They were serious moralists, in their various ways convinced that Gothic art was connected with the simple moral goodness, religious purity or superior social organization of the medieval world which produced it. It was this which absorbed them rather than the bizarre or fantastic vision as such.

In short, the full range of insights offered by Hugo were too disturbing and wide ranging, raising too many questions both moral and aesthetic. It was preferable to see the grotesque as "caricature" or as an artist's desire for an original effect because this blunted any challenge it might have to accepted taste or moral standards. Perhaps the whole process of attenuating the sphere and meaning of the grotesque is best viewed as a rear-guard action of intellectual conservatism.

One striking exception to the process just sketched is Pater's exploration of the connection of the grotesque with the romantic spirit and its animating and vivifying role in art. This sophisticated treatment of the subject, with its obvious influence on the aesthetes of the 1880's and 1890's, is to be found in the "Postscript" to *Appreciations* (1889), an essay which first appeared as "Romanticism" in 1876. As has been suggested, because other critics abdicated from serious discussion of the grotesque, Pater's view was the most weighty and considered one available, the one Chesterton felt called upon to challenge.

Pater, recalling Hugo, describes classical restraint and romantic love of the grotesque as two "tendencies really at work at all times in art, moulding it with the balance sometimes a little on one side, sometimes a little on the other.[25] Significantly, however, Hugo's scheme of a moral and social *development* is dropped, since the two tendencies have always been present. Pater's notion of a delicate and necessary balance between two conflicting ideals as the precondition of the highest art has some affinity with the "synthesis" of romantic art in the *Preface to Cromwell* but seems much more a deliberate and calculating design on the artist's part than a cultural and social phenomenon.

The romantic spirit, according to Pater, though it loves beauty, refuses to have it "unless the condition of strangeness be first fulfilled."[26] It must be a beauty born out of the conjunction of unlikely elements, experiment and bold alchemy to produce "a charm which wrings it even out of terrible things."[27] Recognizing the piquancy of the grotesque, Pater sees it as a difficult but essential flavor in a work of art, a subtle ingredient in the whole effect. The "eager, excited" romantic spirit "will have strength, the grotesque first of all." If enough sweetness and beauty is incorporated the result will be a "genuine classic," "and a trace of distortion, of the genuine grotesque, may perhaps linger, as an additional element of expression, about its ultimate grace."[28] This is like, yet crucially unlike, Hugo's balancing of the sublime and the grotesque. Hugo suggests a broader human sympathy, Pater a more sophisticated artistic effect. Having subtly altered Hugo's views, Pater illustrates the effect he means by drawing several examples from Hugo's own novels. The "Postscript" is altogether a very deft performance which clearly influenced the Aesthetes' view of the grotesque factor in art.

Chesterton's relationship to the Aesthetic movement of the 1880's and 1890's was more complex than is often allowed. By selective and familiar quotation it might be made to seem as if he simply combatted their pessimism with cheerfulness, their morbidity with healthy-mindedness, their ideals of art with a jolly popularism. This matter of the grotesque shows the relationship in a different light. He evidently shared Pater's taste for unlikely combinations, deliberate discords, or at least was unwilling to surrender the possibilities of vitality and freshness in art which the grotesque might supply.

The persuasiveness of the views Chesterton encountered, emanating from Pater's "Postscript," must be admitted, especially set against the obvious deficiency of the Arnoldian ideal. Even in his controversy on translation with F.W. Newman there is, for most readers, a sense that Arnold is limited, that he is ignoring the value as artistic resources of the rough, the bizarre, the uncouth or the grotesque. Too much has been sacrificed to dignity and restraint. He is vulnerable to Pater's quiet but deeply subversive response. Yet, restrained as Pater characteristically is, his position is open to abuse by coarser minds, such as that of Oscar Wilde.

The "Postscript" throughout emphasizes the highly self-conscious artist exploiting the grotesque. The artist seizes on it with delight, drawn to it for the energy it brings his work. But then the artist elaborates upon it, combining it with "sweetness," achieving an "alchemy" as Hugo does, Pater suggests, in the figures of Marius and Cosette. Pater's analysis gives the process an unspontaneous, recondite flavor. Significantly, he describes those periods when this "temperament" has dominated, when

> curiosity may be noticed to take the lead, when men come to art and poetry with a deep thirst for intellectual excitement, after a long ennui in reaction against the strain of outward practical things.[29]

"Curiosity," "ennui," "thirst for intellectual excitement," a movement above all away from outward practical things—every characteristic Pater associates with the grotesque reverses Hugo's view with its stress on wider social sympathy and involvement. In more vulgar or less restrained minds than Pater's, his teachings lend themselves to mere titillation, a cold exploitation of horrible or distasteful elements for effect. In this sense Pater's views are behind that 1890's dabbling with the bizarre against which Chesterton reacted.

Chesterton's response is subtle. He senses the inadequacy of balance alone, of a purely negative kind of restraint. (His description of Arnold's ideal figure Goethe is a striking example of damning with faint praise.)[30] He is as alert as Pater to the value of the grotesque and its connection with energy in art. Without surrendering these undoubted advantages, the benefits established by Hugo of disowning a stereotype such as that of Greek or Renaissance classicism, Chesterton effects a fundamental shift in the basis of Pater's analysis of the grotesque. This may be seen partly in his account of Victor Hugo, Pater's chief exemplar.

Chesterton's essay on *Victor Hugo* (1902) belongs to the same period as *A Defence of Ugly Things* and *Robert Browning*. Its full effect, as with the book on Browning and other of Chesterton's examinations of the grotesque, is best understood if his approach is contrasted with Pater's. With Hugo, as with Browning (and, incidentally, when he examines the related concept of the fabulous in Dickens), Chesterton's first and most important effort goes to establishing a context in the recent past in which the figure and his "grotesque art" may be understood. In *Victor Hugo* the techniques employed a year later in *Robert Browning* may be seen in miniature.

Chesterton emphasizes the point that with Hugo, as with Browning, "we are divided from the generations that immediately precede us by a gulf far more unfathomable than that which divides us from the darkest ages and the most distant lands."[31] This represents a familiar preoccupation of Chesterton. Repeatedly he developed the thesis that the period from 1789 to 1871, from the French Revolution to the defeat of France by Prussia, was one cultural unit, that of the high-tide of reformist liberalism. After this hopeful and expansive period which produced the writers he rehabilitated (Dickens, Browning, and in a sense, Hugo), the age just before his own, 1871 to 1900, represented a failure of nerve, a decline into pessimism and fatalism in philosophy and literature, into loss of hope and capacity for action in politics.[32]

The twin revolutions of Romanticism and Democracy which produced Hugo, Browning and Dickens are incomprehensible because they "have conquered and become commonplace."[33] Chesterton's position is destructive of the historical detachment of the Paterian cultural arbiter moving with scholarly ease from age to age. The "languid and aesthetic collector" lavishes praise on Byzantine painting, Persian carpets and Fijian idols; but he has no real sympathy or understanding for, no involvement in his own age—the movements and ideas which, even though he chooses to ignore them, provide the background of his own mind. Without such sympathy he cannot understand the irruption of the grotesque into the work of the great nineteenth-century writers.

This is very far from being, as Pater describes it, a love of the strange stemming from an ennui of practical things, but a rescue of the seemingly mundane from insignificance, a rescue intimately connected with a new sense of human value, produced by the rise of democracy. For Hugo

> there is neither a large thing nor a small one; he has abolished the meanest and most absurd of all human words, the word "insignificant;" he knows that it is impossible for anything to signify nothing.[34]

The essence of Chesterton's view of the grotesque lies in his giving it a context in the recent past.

In his essay *On Gargoyles* (1910) Chesterton returns to the division of human history of the *Preface to Cromwell* with one significant difference. For Hugo there had been an age of primitive innocence then classicism, then romanticism. Chesterton sketches first the childlike innocence: "They worshipped the sun, not idolatrously, but as the golden crown of the god whom all such infants see almost as plainly as the sun."[35] The priest then orders the people to build a temple in a style suggestive of Hugo's age of classicism: "He would have nothing grotesque or obscure.... He would have all the arches as light as laughter and as candid as logic."[36] As in the *Preface to Cromwell*, barbarian invasion, "years of horror and humiliation," break up this simplicity and serenity. There comes the realization that "the temple is of the noon; it is made of white marble cloud and sapphire sky. But the sun is not always of the noon. The sun dies daily; every night he is crucified in blood and fire.... The sun, symbol of our father, gives life to all those earthly things that are full of ugliness and energy.... The ugly animals praise God as much as the beautiful."[37] Under this "new inspiration," they plan a Gothic cathedral, "all the possible ugly things making one common beauty"[38] But the plan was never completed. Although (almost in Hugo's very words) "this was romantic, this was Christian art; this was the whole advance of Shakespeare on Sophocles,"[39] it was never carried through. The "rich" obstructed it. The design which unified the ugly details into a scheme of grotesque beauty was lost and the result was that chaos of meaningless absurdity, Realism: "Realism is simply Romanticism that has lost its reason."[40] The political liberalism and movement towards democracy of 1789 to 1871, which might again be renewed, was presumably an attempt to redress this, restoring, incidentally, the grotesque in literature, in restoring the social and moral condition on which it must depend. Chesterton is, in effect, returning to Hugo's position of 1830, after the retreat of 1871 to 1900.

Chesterton's critique of the assumptions of aestheticism seems more often concerned with its provinciality than with its unhealthiness. Notions of what are strange or exaggerated situations or reactions are often the result of a timid and sheltered English gentility, cut off despite claims to range countries and centuries, from European culture and common humanity. The last words of Danton, for example, were very much in the spirit of Hugo and "the extravagant appropriateness of Hugo's conversations are thoroughly in harmony with the extravagant appropriateness of the actual incidents of French History."[41]

Chesterton's attitude to the word grotesque involves, among much else, an attempt to recapture from the aesthetes and decedents their most defensible insight into the nature of art, the real value of unexpected combinations and their connection with energy.

Perhaps a close comparison will show the manner in which Chesterton changed the emphasis and the tone of speaking of the grotesque adopted by the aesthetes. The change is a delicate and subtle one—far from a rude breeze of heartiness dispelling preciosity. Pater describes the pity for odd neglected characters and situations inseparable from Romanticism in these terms:

> Penetrating so finely into all situations which appeal to pity, into all special or exceptional phases of such feeling, the romantic humor is not afraid of the quaintness or singularity of its circumstances or expression, pity indeed being the essence of humor, so that Victor Hugo does but turn his romanticism into practice, in his hunger and thirst after practical *Justice!*—a justice which shall no longer wrong children, or animals, for instance by ignoring in a stupid mere breadth of view, minute facts about them. Yet the romantics are antinomian too, because of the love of energy and beauty, of distinction in passion, tended naturally to become a little bizarre, plunging into the Middle Ages, into the secrets of Italian story....[42]

Peter admits the impulse and mentions certain of its leading features. Yet the effect is odd because of the curious placing of emphasis in the passage. The instinct of pity is made to seem a recondite elaboration of feeling, highly sophisticated, tending to operate most effectively in contexts chosen for their strangeness, their "special or exceptional phases." There is something distant about this "pity," and the way Pater italicises *Justice* gives it an air of a bold, uncouth concept. "Whatever next!" he seems to be saying. The mention of sympathy for children in the context of quaint and singular emotions speaks for itself. The ideal of the detached scholar-artist could hardly be carried further. It is almost with a sigh of relief that Pater then returns to the thought that the impulse was really antinomian. The romantics were more concerned with the *bizarre* than with moral qualities of any kind. The whole passage is an act of delicate subversion, having the effect of taking Hugo's most important insight about the grotesque and draining it of value. It is all the more effective because Pater admits the impulse to wider human sympathy while he is, at the same time, gently robbing it of significance.

Contrast this with Chesterton's account of the odd prosaic details in Browning's love poems, part, as he says, of the material for that "general accusation against Browning in connection with his use of the grotesque."[43] Chesterton tackles head on and completely breaks up the false detachment of the aesthete or scholar-artist. Browning's oddities touch a common human feeling rooted in one's sense of things, not some *outré* or far-fetched artistic instinct, reacting against boredom or conventionality:

> So great a power have these dead things of taking hold on the living spirit, that I question whether any one could read through the catalogue of a miscellaneous auction sale, without coming upon things which, if realised for a moment would be near to the elemental tears. And if any of us or all of us are truly optimists and believe as Browning did, that existence has a value wholly inexpressible, we are most truly compelled to that sentiment not by any argument or triumphant justification of the cosmos, but by a few of these momentary sights and sounds, gesture, an old song, a portrait, a piano, an old door.[44]

The grotesque element here is connected with the concrete and the particular, the "little" details which affect a man "who has really lived." The "suburban street, garden rakes, medicine bottles, pianos, window-blinds, burnt cork, fashionable fur hats" of Browning's love poetry are connected with "insatiable realism" of sentiment and emotion. Thought and intellect, Chesterton remarks, can accept abstractions but sentiment must have concrete particularities, and he characteristically appeals to common experiences Browning's love poetry "awakens in every man the memories of that immortal instant when common and dead things had a meaning beyond the power of any dictionary to utter."[45] The grotesque is, in other words, the "melancholy" of Hugo, the sense of disparity and yet connection between material objects or mundane sights and spiritual or emotional realities. The most telling difference between the early views of Chesterton and those of Pater on the grotesque lies in Chesterton's assumption of a humanity shared by intellectual and non-intellectual, an involvement in the business of living common to himself and his readers, of experiences more fundamental than cultivation or the lack of it, and in his assertion that the grotesque is *natural*, a basic part of the condition of our lives, not a rare element one goes in search of.

Whether he considers the grotesque in scenery, in domestic details, or in startling emotional juxtapositions, Chesterton is concerned to point out that it forms the texture of existence. We cannot avoid it and it cuts through the pretence of intellectual detachment or indeed any of the moods and postures with which we deceive ourselves. As he points out in *A Defence of Skeletons*: "However much my face clouds with sombre vanity, or vulgar vengeance, or contemptible contempt, the bones of my skull are laughing forever."[46] His manner of treating the grotesque is more human, relaxed and less entrenched in the fallacious certainties of high culture than that of the aesthetes. Being aware that one cannot escape the grotesque makes for humility, based eventually and most importantly on a sense of mystery. As Chesterton points out, all that was profound or even tolerable in the aesthetes of the 1880's or the decadents of the 1890's was anticipated by Browning's grand conception that every point of view was interesting, however jaundiced or bloodshot. The vital difference between Browning and the decadents was his confidence that the grotesque quality of experience was a mystery too great for human comprehension, a meaning too large for human reason to fathom. Speaking of differing interpretations of the ancient fable of the blind men and the elephant, Chesterton declares:

> There is a vital distinction between the mystical view of Browning that the blind men were misled because there is so much for them to learn and the purely impressionistic and agnostic view of the modern poet, that the blind men were misled because there is nothing for them to learn.[47]

Chesterton's early efforts to expound his view of the grotesque move out of a closed circle of assumptions. We are made to feel, in a salutary way, how little we know. There are matters larger than intellect or, hard as this may be to accept, than good taste.

The first appearance of a concern with the grotesque in Chesterton's writing, itself contemporary with his first essays, is polemical. Its drift is better understood by contrast with the aesthetes' view of the subject than in relation to Chesterton's notional secret fears. To connect it as Chesterton does with democratic and liberal movements and universal human experience returns to first principles in Hugo and removes the grotesque element from the private, exclusive concern of a self-conscious artistic and cultural elite. Chesterton undertakes a campaign of demystification, a dispelling of the secretive and portentous element which, even in Pater, and much more in his cruder imitators, tended to hang about the grotesque. (He aims to let in the light as he had earlier in *A Defence of Publicity* and, of course, *The Man Who Was Thursday*.) In terms of the history of ideas, he effectively is the link with Hugo's first formulations, the restorer and begetter of the fuller meaning of the concept "grotesque" in English.

Chesterton's view of what Borges calls the "nightmarish" related more to public literary debate than to private phobias, and evidence for this fact lies in the marked change of tone between his earlier and later views of the subject. Passages suggesting that the universe and the creatures in it are wild and fantastic may be found in all periods of his writing and to a cursory view they may seem to contain much the same meaning. If, however, the earliest and some of the latest pronouncements are placed together then it appears that some important alteration has taken place. In *A Defence of Skeletons* (1901) we find this passage:

> This is the deepest, the oldest, the most wholesome and religious sense of the value of nature—the value which comes from her immense babyishness. She is as top-heavy, as grotesque as solemn, and as happy as a child. The mood does come when we see all her shapes like shapes that a baby scrawls on a slate— simple, rudimentary, a million years older and stronger than the whole disease that is called art.[48]

The emphasis here is on the innocence and goodness of the primal energy, its innate happiness. It has no enigmas. Our relation to this force in such moods is one of "lucidity" and "levity" as "simple as a dancing lunatic." Taken from its contemporary context of a debate on the nature of the grotesque this might lend itself to the charge of emotional special pleading; Chesterton is talking too loudly, he is trying to argue down some inner terror or uncertainty. And the tone of this passage, it might be remarked, may be found several times elsewhere in his early work.

However, if this extract is compared with a quotation from the essay on *The Book of Job* (1929), a shift may be detected in the inner meaning Chesterton attaches to the grotesque. The playful element found in *In Defence of Skeletons*, as in Chesterton's early references to *Job*, is much less marked. The comic and ludicrous quality of strangeness is insisted on much less than its "positive and palpable unreason":

> God will make man see things if only it is against the black background of nonentity. God will make men see a startling universe if He can only do it by making Job see an idiotic universe.[49]

What seems to have happened in Chesterton's continuing consideration of the grotesque has been a movement from the celebration of the "intrinsically miraculous character of the object itself," the wonder and delight of "the sense of the uproarious force in things," towards a feeling of the mysterious and enigmatic. Of course, this later element had been innate or implied in the earlier work, but it had been submerged in the sense of joy, of energy, of the naturalness and freedom from aesthetic or cultural constraints contained in the sense of the grotesque. The characteristic images of the essay on Job; of joy breaking "through agnosticism like fiery gold round the edge of a black cloud,"[50] or of "light seen for an instant through the cracks of a closed door,"[51] involve a somewhat different attitude to the grotesque element in nature. The strangeness of the physical world is rather an arresting oddity, destructive of facile explanations and mechanical optimism, making us suspect some great secret. In *A Defence of Ugly Things*, the gaining of a sense of joy, of a feeling of being at home in the world appears easy: "The moment we have snapped the spell of conventional beauty, there are a million beautiful faces waiting for us everywhere, just as there are a million beautiful spirits."[52] More notably, as here, the problem is seen in aesthetic terms, the need to reject a false or constricted way or apprehending the world.

In the explorations of the grotesque in the late phase, there is a moral rather than an aesthetic emphasis, and an accent on "impenetrable enigma" in the grotesque vision. There is an explicit denial of any simple solution or liberation into enjoyment, but "the refusal of God to explain His design is itself a burning hint of His design. The riddles of God are more satisfying than the solutions of men."[53] (Comments involving similar attitudes may be seen elsewhere in Chesterton's later writings.)

What the change involves is, perhaps, impossible to answer with a dogmatic certainty. One might suggest, however, that in the early work in particular, polemical necessity may have led him to dwell especially on the naturalness and universality of the grotesque and its connection with a creative energy. An attempt to explain the change in psychological terms involves multiplying hypotheses. Such an explanation requires not merely assumed emotional state or a neurosis for Chesterton, but a whole theory of that state's development into something else quite different, an elaboration of guesswork for which there is no hard evidence. If, however, one sets Chesterton's early views against contemporary and previous accounts of the grotesque, especially Pater's, then the need for just the particular accent he gave his views becomes clear. He wanted the grotesque, but he wanted it without misconceptions. By the later writings this polemical need had disappeared and much wider and more fruitful conceptions of the term "grotesque" had formed.

In *The Man Who Was Thursday* a crucial instance of the movement from joyful celebration of the grotesque towards an exploration of its deeper ambiguities can be detected. The dark inscrutable Sunday represents the manifestation of God's energies in nature, rather than God himself. Sunday's strange notes fill Syme With a joy connected with a recognition of Nature's incongruities:

> He remembered a hornbill which was simply a huge yellow beak with a small bird tied on behind it. The whole gave him a sensation, the vividness of which he could not explain, that Nature was always making quite mysterious jokes.[54]

What is important, as it is also very moving in the novel, is the acknowledgement, stated with great tenderness and pity, that there are those who do not see the jokes. Minds like the Secretary's or Gregory's, sensitive, scrupulous and literal-minded, who, despite Syme's plea, refuse to joy in the abundant energy of a grotesque creation. This point in Chesterton's development (1908) might well be taken as dividing the earlier and later phases of his understanding of the grotesque.

NOTES

1. Jorge Luis Borges, *Other Inquisitions, 1937–1952*, trans. by Ruth L.C. Simms (NY: Washington Square P, 1966), p. 88.

2. Gilbert Keith Chesterton, *Robert Browning* (1903; rpt. Lond: Macmillan, 1920), p. 149.

3. Gilbert Keith Chesterton, *The Defendant* (1901; rpt. Lond: J.M. Dent, 1922), p. 114.

4. *Ibid.*, p. 114.

5. Chesterton, *The Defendant*, p. 115.

6. *Ibid.*, p. 115.

7. Chesterton, *The Defendant*, p. 118.

8. Arthur Clayborough, *The Grotesque in English Literature* (Oxford: Clarendon P, 1965), p. 45.

9. Victor Hugo, *The Dramas of Victor Hugo*, trans. by Mm. Bido, Leloir, Pille, Maignan, Lalauze, Rochegrosse (Lond: H. S. Nichols, 1896), VIII, p. 9.

10. *Ibid.*, VIII, p. 9.

11. *The Dramas of Victor Hugo*, VIII, p. 10.

12. *The Dramas of Victor Hugo*, VIII, p. 12.

13. *Ibid.*, VIII, p. 12.

14. *The Dramas of Victor Hugo*, VIII, p. 13.

15. Wolfgang Kayser, *Das Groteske; seine Gestaltung in Malerei und Dichtung;* cited in Clayborough, p. 61.

16. John Ruskin, *The Stones of Venice* (1851–1853; rpt. Lond: Routledge, 1907), III, p. 141.

17. John Ruskin, *The Stones of Venice*, III, p. 169.

18. Clayborough, p. 49.

19. Walter Bagehot, *Literary Studies* (Lond: J.M. Dent, 1911), I, p. 31.

20. Walter Bagehot, *Literary Studies*, II, pp. 342–44.

21. Thomas Wright, *A History of Caricature and the Grotesque in Literature and Art* (Lond: Virtue Brothers, 1865), pp. 8–9; cited in Clayborough, p. 51.

22. John Addington Symonds, *Essays Speculative and Suggestive* (Lond: Chapman and Hall, 1890), p. 245.

23. George Santayana, *The Sense of Beauty* (1896; rpt. NY: Collier Books, 1961), p. 175.

24. T. Tyndall Wildridge, *The Grotesque in Church Art* (Lond: Andrews, 1899); cited in Clayborough, p. 61.

25. Harold Bloom, *The Selected Writings of Walter Pater* (NY: New American Library, 1974, p. 212.

26. *Ibid.*, p. 212.

27. *Ibid.*, p. 212.

28. *Ibid.*, p. 212.

29. *The Selected Writings of Walter Pater*, pp. 213–14.

30. Gilbert Keith Chesterton, *The Victorian Age in Literature* (1913; rpt. Lond: Oxford UP, 1916), pp. 19–20.

31. Gilbert Keith Chesterton, *A Handful of Authors* (Lond: Sheed and Ward, 1953). p. 36.

32. Chesterton, *The Victorian Age in Literature*, p. 96.

33. Chesterton, *A Handful of Authors*, p. 37.

34. Chesterton, *A Handful of Authors*, p. 40.

35. Gilbert Keith Chesterton, *Alarms and Discursions* (1910; rpt. Lond: Methuen, 1927), p. 2.

36. *Ibid.*, p. 2.

37. Chesterton, *Alarms and Discursions*, p. 4.

38. *Ibid.*, p. 4.

39. Chesterton, *Alarms and Discursions*, p. 5.

40. Chesterton, *Alarms and Discursions*, p. 6.

41. Chesterton, *A Handful of Authors*, p. 43.

42. *Selected Writings of Walter Pater*, p. 216.

43. Chesterton, *Robert Browning*, p. 49.

44. Chesterton, *Robert Browning*, pp. 50–51.

45. Chesterton, *Robert Browning*, p. 49.

46. Chesterton, *The Defendant*, p. 49.

47. Chesterton, *Robert Browning*, p. 175.

48. Chesterton, *The Defendant*, p. 48.

49. W.H. Auden, *G.K. Chesterton: a selection from his non-fictional prose* (Lond: Faber and Faber, 1970), p. 154.

50. *G.K. Chesterton: a selection from his non-fictional prose*, p. 155.

51. *G.K. Chesterton: a selection from his non-fictional prose*, p. 17.

52. G.K. Chesterton, *The Defendant*, p. 118.

53. *G.K. Chesterton: a selection from his non-fictional prose*, p. 153.

54 G.K. Chesterton, *The Man Who Was Thursday* (1908; rpt. Aylesbury, Bucks: Penguin Books, 1967), p. 160.

JOHN PFORDRESHER

Chesterton on Browning's Grotesque

Reassessing the significance of Victorian literature was a project which engaged G.K. Chesterton throughout his career as a writer. The task, as he fulfilled it, was to define those aspects of major Victorian writers which would remain important for readers of the early twentieth century. Consequently Chesterton's criticism continually compares the Victorians to his own contemporaries, Maeterlinck, Whistler, Shaw, and Yeats. Modern writers suffer in these comparisons.

At first, it might seem that Chesterton's revalidation of literary heroes from the preceding generation sprang from conservative impulses. But the matter is not so simple as that. Chesterton rediscovers the ancestors, but sees them in his own light, as representing solutions to what he takes to be certain modern problems. Transformation rather than preservation is his goal.

The first book-length contribution to this project is *Robert Browning*, published in 1903.[1] Late in life, Chesterton discounted it as "a book on love, liberty, poetry, my own views on God and religion ... a book in which the name of Browning was introduced from time to time, I might almost say with considerable art, or at any rate with some decent appearance of regularity."[2] Written rapidly, and based frequently on his memory of books rather than on systematic reference to them as he worked, Chesterton's *Browning* appears at

From *English Language Notes*. © 1987 by Regents of the University of Colorado.

first to be a continuous development of his own ideas, frequently justified simply by an appeal to the reader's common sense.[3]

But Chesterton was well aware of those who had previously written on an issue, and his argument is frequently a response to unnamed opponents combined with the unacknowledged use of ideas taken from earlier writers. If Chesterton's criticism is to be seen accurately as a part of an ongoing debate, as a significant component in the evolution of certain crucial ideas, then his enemies and his friends, and his indebtedness to each, must be clearly identified. Nowhere is this more significant and revealing than in Chesterton's celebrated discussion of Browning's grotesque, in which he tacitly replies to a damaging attack by Walter Bagehot using critical theories taken from the writings of John Ruskin.

Bagehot's 1864 essay, "Wordsworth, Tennyson, and Browning; or, Pure, Ornate, and Grotesque Art in English Poetry"[4] ensured that the term grotesque would be, as Isobel Armstrong puts it, "an indispensable word in the discussion of Browning's style...."[5] Bagehot is acutely sensitive to its history. "Grotesque" first referred to "a kind of decorative painting ... consisting of representations of portions of human and animal forms, fantastically combined and interwoven with foliage and flowers,"[6] and Bagehot's discussion assumes that it refers to the unnatural and bizarre. As he puts it, "grotesque art ... takes the type, so to say, in *difficulties* ... with abnormal specimens ... not with what nature is striving to be, but with what by some lapse she has happened to become. [The grotesque] ... works by contrast ... it makes you see ... the perfect type by painting the opposite deviation" (p. 353).[7] Bagehot assumes that in nature and life there are normal and ideal states, as well as deviation. Convinced, like Matthew Arnold, that the typical reader of his day was "*half* educated" (p. 365), Bagehot found himself looking for a neoclassical "pure art" (p. 365) to save English culture, and so suggested that Browning abandon "these out-of-the-way and detestable subjects" (p. 360), the consequence of an "*insane*" taste" (p. 359), which, though it may have been developed through a close scrutiny of "grotesque objects [which do] exist in real life ..." leads ultimately to "ugly poems and ... detestable stanzas" (p. 360). Bagehot's insistence that, in physical terms, the grotesque is "abnormal" and that, in conceptual terms, a taste for it is "insane," forces the conclusion that Browning's art, insofar as it employs the grotesque, works against what Bagehot considers the fundamental principles of poetry—to please and refresh the reader (see pp. 360 and 366).

Bagehot's attack reappeared in his collected *Literary Studies* (1878)[8] and the term grotesque soon became a regular feature of Victorian Browning criticism. So *Fraser's Magazine* says of Browning in 1879, "we fear we shall have still a losing battle to fight for him so long as he will mistake the grotesque for the great ..."[9] and Justin McCarthy in his *History of Our Times* (1880) speaks of Browning's "almost-morbid taste for the grotesque...."[10] By 1900 Santayana, in his famous attack on Browning, "The Poetry of Barbarism," could casually allude to the poet's "superficial grotesqueness" and assume the ordinary reader would grasp the nature of the fault.[11] While Chesterton never refers to Bagehot in his book on Browning, or, evidently, in any of his other writings, it is still fair to conclude that Bagehot, and those who subsequently echoed his famous attack, constitute the presumed but unacknowledged background against which Chesterton developed his own discussion of the grotesque.[12]

Chesterton's response to Bagehot's challenge is, in effect, to accept his description of Browning's art but to reverse its conclusions. To achieve this end Chesterton adopts an unusual argumentative strategy. He concedes that in Browning we find a grotesque element in such traditionally unpoetic things as "toad-stools" and "monstrous tropical birds" (p. 145)—the latter, especially, sound much like Bagehot's "abnormal specimens" (p. 353)—but Chesterton conjoins to these examples some very different ones: "stormy and fantastic clouds," "a gnarled and sprawling oak," and a "mountain" (p. 144) and calls all of them, oak and toad-stool both, "rugged." In each of these instances Chesterton seems to highlight just what Bagehot thought was their peculiarly grotesque characteristic—that they depart from the normal and the ideal—the oak, because it is twisted, the toad-stool, because it seems inappropriate for the medium of poetry. This unusual strategy permits Chesterton to subtly transfer qualities traditionally associated with the Sublime—ruggedness, fearfulness, twisted energy—to Browning's poetry, even when it is describing toad-stools. Chesterton can then go on to argue that this ruggedness is "an essential quality in the universe" and that people respond to it just as they do "to the striking of any other chord of the eternal harmonies" (p. 145). He thereby asserts, contrary to Bagehot's notions, the appropriateness of the grotesque/rugged as a subject for art, because it is present in both nature and the human spirit. In fact, Chesterton notes, it is also a stylistic property of accepted works of literature, as in the "beautifully grave and haunting" meter of "the old ballads ..." (p. 145). Finally, he argues that "the grotesque in nature, means, in the main, energy, the energy which takes its own forms and goes its own way." Thus Chesterton, accepting Bagehot's pejorative term, reverses its connotations and denies Bagehot's neoclassical aesthetic values. He asserts that the unusual is not abnormal, and by associating the unusual with the sublime concludes that it embodies in a special way the energy inherent in all created things. "The verse sprawls," he says, "like the trees, dances like the dust; it is ragged like the thundercloud, it is top-heavy like the toadstool [sic]. Energy which disregards the standard of classical art is in nature as it is in Browning" (pp. 149–150).

This deft and elegant defense may have sprung fresh to Chesterton's mind. But it is far more likely that as he thought and wrote about his subject he recalled earlier discussions of the grotesque. The most proximate, and the most significant, was undoubtedly that of John Ruskin. Just when Chesterton read Ruskin, and how much he read, is not at all clear from available sources.[13] In his writings Chesterton speaks as if he enjoyed a comprehensive grasp of Ruskin's oeuvre, and given his delight in reading we might assume he had a fairly strong recollection of Ruskin's major works, on which he could draw, consciously or unconsciously.

But, typically, his use of Ruskin's ideas is highly personal, constituting in itself a rethinking and hence transformation of Ruskin's notions into a Chestertonian mode. As he was to admit a few years after he published the book on Browning: "such combative figures [as Ruskin] produce a reaction which is almost simultaneous with their energy ... any man who speaks truth and, speaks anything less than the full and divine truth draws attention to all the doctrines that he himself omits ... his incompleteness exasperates ... We disagree with Ruskin as we disagree with a friend gone wrong ... the irritation against a friend is a thing that grows and bears fruit like a living orchard."[14] While specifically referring to other issues here, Chesterton may be expressing how he felt when he began to write about Browning's grotesque, and recalled the celebrated passages from Ruskin's *Stones of Venice* III (1853) and *Modern Painters* III (1856) which develop a complex, penetrating, and comprehensive theory of the grotesque in art and literature.

At the start of his discussion in *Stones of Venice* Ruskin divides the grotesque into "two elements, one ludicrous, the other fearful ..." and thus he can separate grotesque art into "sportive grotesque and terrible grotesque...."[15] Ruskin's second division derives from the tradition of the Sublime. It is God's purpose in creation, he argues, to stir a sense of "fear which arises out of contemplation of great powers in destructive operations ..." (XI, p. 163), whose energy has been roused by sin and whose threatening consequence is death. But if a human mind cannot enter into "the complete depth ..." of these realities, it will instead dwell on them in some "irregular manner," which becomes then the terrible grotesque (XI, p. 166).

Chesterton took this aspect of the Sublime and transformed it for his own purposes. He too perceives a divine power in nature which finds expression in the grotesque. But Chesterton gives it the far more positive name "energy," and while, like Ruskin, he sees this energy in the "thunder-cloud" and the "toad-stool" (p. 149), it becomes in his argument a source not of terror but of pleasurable delight, producing a sense of "uproarious force" in all things (p. 150). Consequently Chesterton's discussion of the "rugged" conspicuously omits mention of the "fear" Ruskin finds evoked in the "imagination" by "scenic magnificence" (XI, p. 163).

Bagehot had argued that a taste for the grotesque was "*insane*" (p. 359), delighting in the abnormal rather than the natural. Reversing the polarity of the argument, Chesterton concedes that in his oddest moments the poet does indulge in "a kind of demented ingenuity ..." (p. 153), but that this tends to "touch the nerve of surprise" in the reader, and concludes that just because it is unexpected the grotesque can "draw attention to the intrinsically miraculous character of the object itself" (p. 151). Bagehot prepared the way for Chesterton's argument in saying that the art of the grotesque "works by contrast" (p. 353). But what for him seemed dangerously odd becomes for Chesterton vitally illuminating: turn St. Paul's cathedral upside down and people will suddenly see it again as it actually is, "intrinsically miraculous."

This shared sense that there is an aspect of the irrational, or even the "insane" in grotesque art, echoes one of the most significant passages in Ruskin's discussion of the terrible grotesque. Any time, according to Ruskin, that the mind fails to perceive the truth precisely, either from "fear operating upon strong powers of imagination" or from "the failure of the human faculties ... to grasp the highest truths" (XI, p. 178), the resulting imperfection of understanding is grotesque. Thus dreams are grotesque, and because "the noblest forms of imaginative power are also in some form ungovernable ..." they share in "the character of dreams ..." (XI, p. 178) and their "strange distortions and discrepancies ..." (XI, p. 179) are also grotesque. Products of the imagination struggle to present the sublime through symbol, but the discrepancy between sign and reality troubles the mind with a "thrill of mingled doubt, fear, and curiosity ..." because the thing represented is "other and greater than it seems ..." (XI, p. 182). Such a discrepancy is grotesque,[16] and so this quality can ultimately be seen as inherent in "all things amidst which we live.... there is a deeper meaning within them than eye hath seen, or ear hath heard; and ... the whole visible creation is a mere perishable symbol of things eternal and true" (XI, p. 183).

At this point it becomes clear that Chesterton's suggestion that the grotesque has the ability to "touch the nerve of surprise and thus to draw attention to the intrinsically miraculous character of the object itself" (p. 151)—is a repetition of Ruskin's typically nineteenth-century conclusion that the entire world is an inadequate sign of the Divine. The gap, the discrepancy between sign and substance, produces that sense of disparity we call the grotesque, a sense which, in Ruskin's words, evokes in us that "thrill of mingled doubt, fear, and curiosity...."

But there is a difference of tone in the final impression made by the two arguments. Ruskin's is the more somber. His God evokes fear through intimations of sin and death in the terrible grotesque, whereas Chesterton's sense of the miraculous perceives an "uproarious force" in things, and he ends his discussion of that "sense of wonder provoked by the grotesque ..." with a flippant reference to a question posed in the *Book of Job*: can one keep a "hippopotamus as a household pet ...", a question Chesterton sees as "curiously in the spirit of the humour of Browning" (pp. 151–152).

Having thus transformed what had seemed to Bagehot a glaring fault into a triumph of art and vision, Chesterton goes on to acknowledge that there are moments in Browning's poetry in which a lesser grotesque appears, a "perfectly childish ... indulgence in ingenuities" (p. 152), a "rhyming frenzy" which is "the horse-play of literature" (p. 153), a "buffoonery" or "frivolity" in using language. "His mind," Chesterton concedes, "was like a piece of strong wood with a knot in it" (p. 154). And in this we see another echo of Bagehot's "*insane* taste."

Ruskin saw this "ludicrous," or "sportive" grotesque (XI, p. 151), as a mode which arises from the human need for play. Life for most, he says, is "irksome and troublesome, demanding an expenditure of energy which exhausts the system...." But when toil is over "those noble instincts, fancy, imagination, and curiosity ..." reappear and "exert themselves" by some form of "fantastic exercise," a sort of "leaping and dancing of the heart and intellect ..." (XI, p. 154). The typical product of this spirit is the grotesque ornament one finds in Gothic architecture, a result, according to Ruskin, "of a rejoicing energy in uncultivated minds" (XI, p. 159). But a similar release of energy in the work of a person of superior intelligence and ability produces "a false grotesque ... the result of the *full exertion* ..." of mind for a "*frivolous*" intention, such as the Renaissance grotesques in the Vatican, which Ruskin derides as "the fruit of great minds degraded to base objects" (XI, p. 170).

When Chesterton, partly echoing Bagehot, finds fault with Browning for his "childish ... indulgence in ingenuities" (p. 152), his "rhyming frenzy" that is the "horse-play of literature" (p. 153) and when he notes an element of "buffoonery" in Browning's love for "learning as an enjoyment and almost a frivolity" (p. 154), he appears to be adopting the imagery and even the language describing Ruskin's playful grotesque; and in fact to be arriving at a similar, if rather less severe, judgment on its merits. Both Ruskin and

Chesterton see this sort of creating as an outburst of energy and link it to a childlike liberation of high spirits, ingenious but purposeless invention, and joking. The term "frivolity" (Ruskin XI, p, 170; Chesterton, p. 154) summarizes the nature of their fault-finding. Minds like Raphael's and Browning's have higher ends to serve. But while Ruskin severely chastises such work as "base," degrading to its creator, Chesterton is more inclined to pardon the trait in Browning as little more than a "childish ... indulgence."

While Chesterton uses' Ruskin's theory of the grotesque to overturn Bagehot's attack as well as to respond to the aesthetic pessimism and pervasive materialism of the 1890's, his Ruskin has undergone a typically Chestertonian transformation, and sees a brighter world. The terrors of the sublime have given way to delight in a divinely uproarious force, while the buffoonery of the mind at play is condoned as a momentary overflow of ungovernable energy.

In the same year that *Robert Browning* was published, Chesterton's transformation of Ruskin reappeared in an essay which portrays Ruskin as "a great humorist," arguing that "half the explosions [in his writings] which are solemnly scolded as 'one-sided' were simply meant to be one-sided, were laughing experiments in language ... he saw the humour of his own prejudices ... [and] deliberately exaggerated them by rhetoric. One tenth of his paradoxes would have made the fortune of a modern young man with gloves of an art yellow."[17] While we cannot be sure about the color of Chesterton's gloves, his debt to Ruskin's ideas does seem pretty clear.

NOTES

1. Quotations from this book, cited below in the text, refer to G.K. Chesterton, *Robert Browning* (London, 1936).

2. G.K. Chesterton, *The Autobiography of G.K. Chesterton* (New York, 1936), p. 95. Yet P.J. Keating, in a recent survey of Browning scholarship, concludes that it "remains unsurpassed as a general introduction" to Browning's art. P. J. Keating, "Robert Browning: A Reader's Guide" in *Robert Browning: Writers and their Background*, ed. Isobel Armstrong (Athens, Ohio, 1975), p. 315.

3. "His memory for literary passages was prodigious ... I think it safe to say no one had read the works of Dickens or Browning or Ruskin or Stevenson as thoroughly as he." Gary Wills, *Chesterton: Man and Mask*. (New York, 1961), p. 62.

4. First published in *The National Review* (November, 1864) xix, pp. 27–67, and frequently reprinted in his *Literary Studies*. Alastair Buchan, *The Spare Chancellor* (London, 1959) notes this was "the last of his major essays on literary figures ... [and] his most ambitious attempt at the definition of poetry" (p. 88). Perhaps, as Norman St John-Stevas argues in his *Walter Bagehot* (Bloomington, 1959), Bagehot's literary criticism suffered from "his lack of scientific scholarship, and a narrowess of reading ..." (p. 37) but

nevertheless this essay constituted a part of the upsurge in serious critical attention given Browning in the 1860's. See Charlotte Crawford Watkins, "Browning's 'Fame within these four years.'" *Modern Language Review* LIII, 4 (October, 1958), pp. 492–500.

5. Isobel Armstrong, "Browning and the 'Grotesque' Style" in *The Major Victorian Poets: Reconsiderations*, ed. Isobel Armstrong (Lincoln, 1969), p. 93. The absence of any thorough history of Browning's critical reception prevents any more certain assertion.

6. Definition from the N.E.D. reprinted in Arthur Clayborough, *The Grotesque in English Literature* (Oxford, 1965), p. 253. Clayborough gives a thorough analysis of the term's semantic development (pp. 1–20) and then traces its use by writers of the last three centuries.

7. Norman St John-Stevas (ed.), *The Collected Works of Walter Bagehot* (London, 1965) II, p. 353. Subsequent quotations cited in the text come from this edition.

8. Ed. R.H. Hutton. See Norman St John-Stevas, *Walter Bagehot*, I, p. 25.

9. "Three Small Books: By Great Writers" from *Fraser's Magazine* July 1879. Reprinted in Boyd Litzinger and Donald Smalley, *Browning: The Critical Heritage* (New York, 1970), p. 464.

10. Justin McCarthy, *A History of Our Own Times* (London, 1879), II, p. 379. In the same sentence, McCarthy compares Browning's grotesque to the etchings of Callot. Chesterton draws the same parallel in *Robert Browning* (p. 149) and this may indicate Chesterton had recently consulted McCarthy; though, as Clayborough notes in *The Grotesque* (*op. cit.*) such comparisons were frequent (p. 9).

11. George Santayana, "The Poetry of Barbarism" in *Robert Browning*, ed. Philip Drew, (London, 1966), p. 18.

12. Other writers on Chesterton have already suggested Bagehot as Chesterton's unnamed adversary. See, for example, Lawrence J. Clipper, *G.K. Chesterton* (New York, 1974), p. 20. Sprug, in his remarkable index to Chesterton's works, has no entry for Bagehot. Joseph W. Sprug, *An Index to G.K. Chesterton* (Washington, D.C., 1966).

13. The major biographies of Chesterton do not systematically record his early reading and there is no published edition of his letters or of the evidently significant early notebooks. Michael W. Higgins' "Ruskin and Chesterton: A Common Spirit" *The Chestertonian* V, 1 (Fall/Winter 1978–1979), pp. 62–78, unfortunately provides no information on this critical issue.

14. G.K. Chesterton, "John Ruskin" from *The Book Fair* (1908). Reprinted in his *A Handful of Authors* (New York, 1953), pp. 148–149.

15. John Ruskin, *The Works of John Ruskin*, Ed. E.T. Cook and Alexander Wedderburn (London, 1904) XI, p. 151. Subsequent quotations, all derived from this edition, will be cited in the text.

16. "A fine grotesque is the expression, in a moment, by a series of symbols thrown together in bold and tearless connection, of truths which it would have taken a long time to express in any verbal way, and of which the connection is left to the beholder to work out for himself; the gaps, left or overleaped by the haste of the imagination, forming the grotesque character." *Modern Painters* III. Ruskin. *Works*. V. D. 132.

17. G.K. Chesterton, "Ruskin." First published in September 1903. Reprinted in *Varied Types* (New York, 1908), pp. 217–218.

ELMAR SCHENKEL

Visions from the Verge: Terror and Play in G.K. Chesterton's Imagination

It was probably on 4 March 1881 when Dr Watson's attention was caught by a peculiar piece of writing entitled 'The Book of Life'. After perusing it, he pronounced it to be 'ineffable twaddle'. The article turned out to be written by Sherlock Holmes himself and gave an outline of his methods in a strange mixture of rationalist argument and philosophical camouflage. 'From a drop of water', said the writer, 'a logician could infer the possibility of an Atlantic or a Niagara without having seen or heard of one or the other. So all life is a great chain, the nature of which is unknown whenever, we are shown a single link of it' (Doyle 29). The Platonic overtones—particularly in view of the initiation to be undergone by the candidate in the Science of Deduction and Analysis—not only give the lie to Holmes's alleged philosophical and literary deficits listed by Watson in *A Study in Scarlet* (1887) but are also elements in the ideological forces that shaped the genre of the detective story.

Time and again critics have pointed out the structural resemblances between detective stories and earlier religious literature such as the sermon or the Puritan quest. Hence these stories in their secular moulds make use of very traditional elements of Western myths and spiritual attitudes. Whatever the form may betray it is also true that the fathers of the first detective stories, Poe and Doyle, created protagonists who were not able or, willing to

From *Twentieth-Century Fantasist: Essays on Culture, Society, and Belief in Twentieth-Century Mythopoeic Literature*. © 1992 by The Macmillan Press.

bridge the gap that had become apparent since the days of Enlightenment—
the abyss between religious consciousness and rational analysis, emotion and
thought, body and soul, spirit and nature. Instead, Dupin and Holmes in
their armchairs cultivate an intellectually-oriented approach which can be
seen as a culmination of the age of rationality, while at times they fall into a
dreamlike stupor and resort to drugs or black-letter volumes to dispel their
acedia or *ennui*. Like Dr Jekyll and Mr Hyde they represent the fictitious
modern self, 'founded as it were on its own physical encapsulation, [...] a false
self, *without* reality' (Barfield 52).

It is part of G.K. Chesterton's achievement to have created completely
obverse kinds of detectives: Basil Grant in *The Club of Queer Trades*, Gabriel
Gale in *The Poet and the Lunatics*, and Father Brown, who serve to express
Chesterton's spiritual unease with the modern self. Since detectives are
agents addressing disorder in both a social and psychological sense, they are
also part of larger value-systems. Taking Father Brown as a starting point, I
shall look at the kind of monsters and monstrosities that cause disorder, guilt
and fantasy in Chesterton's fictional world, in order to discuss the strategies
he deploys in controlling and channelling the ambiguous forces of the
imagination.

Set against the dual or schizoid character of the two major nineteenth-
century detectives, Father Brown's outlook and method encompass the moral
and human essence of both the criminal and the sleuth, or, to put it in a more
old-fashioned way, he acknowledges the essential reality of the *soul*. Since
crime for the meek priest is, in most cases, of a moral and psychological
order, very often derived from one of the vices of Christian theology, such as
pride, greed or lust, his methods of detection belong also to a moral order.
Intuition and imagination and a good deal of down-to-earth realism restore
the earlier 'dissociation of sensibility'; indeed at times Brown needs to get rid
of reason in order to solve a problem: 'His head was always most valuable
when he had lost it.' ('The Queer Feet', *The Complete Father Brown* (*CFB*),
44). Yet he demonstrates a deep knowledge of human nature when he
denounces the unreasonable. When Flambeau, in his criminal days disguised
as a priest, expresses romantic feelings about the universe and the infinite, he
is faulted: '"You attacked reason"', said Father Brown. '"It's bad theology."'
('The Blue Cross', *CFB*, 23). It is this sense of the richness of human nature,
its evasiveness, its fantasising and enacting faculties, its mimicry and its
creative and criminal imagination that constitutes the appeal of the Father
Brown stories. Instead of being a romantic outsider with scientific
aspirations, an aesthete and an expert, a logical machine and an addict, the
detective is now a mirror of the criminal and is highly conscious of his own

shortcomings and guilt. In theological terms, it is original sin which connects both and is the cause for real or imagined monstrosities. Wilfred Bohun, the village priest who tends to drop hammers on people from the spire of his church, cries out on being discovered: "'How do you know all this? ... Are you a devil?" "I am a man", replied Father Brown gravely; "and therefore have all devils in my heart".' ('The Hammer of God', *CFB*, 130). While Holmes drowns any sense of evil he might harbour in his 'exasperating solos' in violin-playing or cocaine, Father Brown makes it the centre of his investigation. Hence the stories, especially those in which the pot-boiler formula is less visible and which thus achieve a greater unity of plot and symbolism, deal with more than simple problem and solution sequences. Evil cannot be eradicated from a fallen world—in 'The Hammer of God' the criminal priest is submitted to the judgement of God—and no solution of an individual case can replace universal redemption. The beginnings of the stories evoke the fallen world of sin and mystery and illustrate the ambiguity of the imagination itself.

Bessière was the first to point out the antinomical structure of modern fantasy, seeing it as revolving around a centre of the impossible that is formed by a fundamental polysemy or 'opening' (Bessière 62). The very titles of fantasies indicate this since they convey 'notions of (1) invisibility, (2) impossibility, (3) transformation, (4) defiant illusion' (Jackson 23), and a brief look at Chesterton's titles will also attest to it. The riddles with which the reader is confronted in the plots reinforce the sense of an antinomical world. In story after story, nightmare and mystery are evoked in such depth and detail that one can easily subscribe to Borges's influential statement on Chesterton:

> He asks if a man might not have three eyes, or a bird three wings; he speaks, to refute the pantheists, of a dead man discovering in Paradise that all the angelic hosts have his own face over and over; he speaks of a jail of mirrors; he speaks of a labyrinth with no centre; he speaks of a man devoured by metal automatons; he speaks of a tree that gobbles up birds and puts forth feathers instead of leaves ... He defines close-at-hand objects with remote, exotic images, even atrocious ones; [...] if he speaks of night, he perfects an ancient horror (*Apocalypse*, 4:6) and calls it a *monster made of eyes*. (Borges, 120f., trans. Lindstrom 274)

It has been pointed out that in most of the stories the central event is located in 'twilight, a recurrent Chesterton symbol for the limitation of human perception and for a somnambulistic life ever subject to metamorphosis or awakening' (Scheick 109).

Chesterton's strong sense of colour, manifested in all his narratives from *The Man Who Was Thursday* to *The Flying Inn*, is in itself an indication that the reader is asked to enter a world of unresolved and non-conceptualised experience. Colour not only informs the atmospheric qualities of settings but can become the expression of the chaotic forces of the imagination. There is no formula which can translate and resolve these phenomena. For Chesterton, as for some of his characters, colour presents a temptation to which there is no theological or philosophical counterpart. Take Leonard Quinton in 'The Wrong Shape', the celebrated writer of wild Oriental poems and romances, who

> drank and bathed in colours, who indulged his lust for colour somewhat to the neglect of form ... This it was that had turned his genius so wholly to eastern art and imagery, to those bewildering carpets or blinding embroideries in which all the colours seem fallen into a fortunate chaos, having nothing to typify or to teach. He had attempted ... to compose epics and love stories reflecting the riot of violent and even cruel colour; tales of tropical heavens of burning gold or blood-red copper; of eastern heroes who rode with twelve-turbaned mitres, upon, elephants painted purple or peacock green [...] (*CFB* 90)

But so had Chesterton. Much as this is directed satirically against the decadence of the 1890s, Quinton's affinity with parts of Chesterton is obvious, in particular if one considers that one of his decadent tales was entitled 'The Curse of the Saint', which is close to Chesterton's own 'The Curse of the Golden Cross'. The solution of the murder in 'The Wrong Shape' is found in a typographical detail (quotation marks), and can be seen as an attempt to frame the whole event in a fictional parenthesis as in a dream. Yet the parenthesis cannot account for the abysses gaping at the reader from the inside of the indented text. What Chesterton takes to be the Orient, with its emphasis on a lush appearance hiding horrible truths, is a world his imagination feeds on in order to overcome it in one story and to immediately take it up again in the next: a process demonstrating that both author and reader connive in a shared obsession or *Wiederholungszwang* (compulsive repetition). Ernst Block has pointed out that this destruction of appearances and the reconstruction of something untold is essential to the apparatus of detective stories, which reveal an affinity to gnostic world models (Bloch 247ff.).

The 'East' confronting the detective is a form of chaos which can only be translated into order by the act of narration. Father Brown himself is not immune to this inner chaos since one of his reactions is to resort, as did his creator at times, to xenophobic projections: 'Don't you ever feel that about Eastern art', he asks his friend Flambeau in the same story. 'The colours are intoxicatingly lovely; but the shapes are mean and bad—deliberately mean and bad. I have seen wicked things in a Turkey carpet' (*CFB* 92).

That appearances in a postlapsarian age are not consistent with reality and that truth suffers from separation and fragmentation is clearly seen in the many references to architecture. Buildings proclaim the false pretensions and ambitions of the sinful builders and inhabitants in much the same way as atmosphere and setting. There is a sense of postmodern eclecticism and preposterousness: houses built like a T, houses with no exits, houses within houses, Eastern imitations, Babylonian halls in a big hotel or a classical colonnade concealing an Arctic jungle ('The Dagger With Wings').

One of the strangest examples of fantastic architecture is found on an American-type skyscraper with the 'oiled elaboration of its machinery of telephones and lifts': 'It was an enormous gilt effigy of the human eye, surrounded with rays of gold, and taking up as much room as two or three office windows.' ('The Eye of Apollo', *CFB* 131f.) While the use of the eye as a focus of power reminds one of Stevenson's 'The Dynamiter', the grotesqueness of this appearance reflects the abysmal absurdities of neo-pagan sunworship, one of the modern fads that, for Chesterton, have superseded the common sense of traditional religion. The anthropomorphic quality of this building stimulates, as in Poe's 'The Fall of the House of Usher', fantasies of persecution and paranoia. Any divine symbol can be diverted from its original sense and assume; evil connotations if the context is sufficiently inflected by sins such as greed or lust for power. The use of anthropomorphic qualities is in keeping with Chesterton's attitude towards the imagination which blends horror with the holy. As he points out in *Heretics*, anthropomorphism is not a means of explaining the world, as common sense (in the wake of nineteenth-century positivism) still maintains, but rather a means of increasing awe vis-à-vis a mysterious creation:

> The final cure for all this kind of philosophy is to walk down a lane at night. And one who does this will discover very quickly that men pictured something semi-human at the back of all things, not because such a thought was natural, but because it was supernatural; not because it made things more comprehensible, but because it made them a hundred times more

incomprehensible and mysterious. For a man walking down a
lane at night can see the conspicuous fact that as long as nature
keeps to her own course, she has no power with us at all.... so long
as a tree is a tree, it does not frighten us, at all. It begins to be
something alien, to be something strange, only when it looks like
ourselves. When a tree really looks like a man our knees knock
under us. And when the whole universe looks like a man we fall
on our faces. (*Heretics* 152).

For Chesterton it is Gothic architecture which epitomises the ambivalence
of our imagination. For here anthropomorphism, allegory and
personification combine, and the chaotic forces of nature colonise human
orders of the real. When Father Brown speaks to Wilfred Bohun in 'The
Hammer of God' they stand on the Gothic spire of the church of Bohun
Beacon. It is significant that Bohun with his morbid thirst for beauty loves
Gothic architecture more than he loves God. But even Father Brown
experiences the scene as a temptation, the temptation of a world without
limits, boundaries, rules; of what in his system of thought could be called the
'Eastern', that is, the pagan and mythical element of the imagination:

Immediately beneath and about them the lines of the Gothic
building plunged outwards into the void with sickening swiftness
akin to suicide.... it poured like a cataract into a voiceless pit. For
these two men on the tower were left alone with the most terrible
aspect of the Gothic: the monstrous foreshortening and
disproportion, the dizzy perspectives, the glimpses of great things
small and small things great; a topsy-turvydom of stone in the
midair ... A carved bird or beast at a corner seemed like some vast
walking or flying dragon wasting the pastures and villages below.
The whole atmosphere was dizzy and dangerous, as if men were
upheld in air amid the gyrating wings of colossal genii ... (*CFB*
129)

Not only is this image of the Middle Ages a far cry from conventional
conceptions of a static Dark Age but the type of Gothic depicted here can be
seen as a spatial representation of essential qualities in fantasy and
imagination which cannot thrive without a sense of the void, the threat of
nihilism and absence; both psychology and cultural history provide us with
numerous examples of this function of the imagination. Chesterton
expounded this ambivalence in the essay 'On Gargoyles' which introduces

his collection of essays Alarms and Discursions. Gargoyles are seen here as the emblems of his own imaginative essays in which he refutes, as part of his battle against modernity, a phoney and superficial realism that is unable to control the million monsters of ugliness. Chesterton's general view of his essays may well serve as a succinct formula for the position of his art in the modern context:

> This row of shapeless and ungainly monsters which I now set before the reader does not consist of separate idols cut out capriciously in lonely valleys or various islands. These monsters are meant for the gargoyles of a definite cathedral. I have to carve the gargoyles, because I can carve nothing else ... (*Alarms and Discursions* 7)

The implied message here is that as long as you maintain a larger perspective and are able to focus chaos may be kept under control: 'For there is nothing so delightful as a nightmare—when you know it is a nightmare.' (Ibid. 17). A gargoyle seen from too close, without the cathedral as its controlling parenthesis, turns into pure horror. The onlooker then may succumb to the dissolving qualities of the imagination as the decadents and Chesterton did in the 1890s (if we are able to believe his many statements in his *Autobiography*) (1936, 80ff.).

But the aesthetic parable only works because it is informed by a moral idea. Again it is the meek little priest who points out to the hammer-throwing priest—in a sense his criminal alter ego—that 'heights were made to be looked at, not to be looked from' (*CFB* 129). The temptation really is one of pride, a vice closely connected to all Nietzschean superman fantasies. Bohun is tempted because 'he had in his hand one of the most awful engines of nature; I mean gravitation ...' (*CFB* 130). Ultimately it is humility which helps a human being focus things and people properly and helps prevent individual and collective hallucinations and insanity.

Many criminals in the Father Brown stories suffer eventually as their egos feed too much on a sense of superiority. It makes them prone to use the powers of mimicry, camouflage, art and enchantment, which they indeed possess, to the detriment of other people and to the exaltation of their own personalities. The characteristic sin of the false mages appearing in the stories ('The Song of the Flying Fish', 'The Eye of Apollo', 'The Red Moon of Meru') is spiritual pride (Robson 619, 623ff.).

Critics have pointed out the staginess of many Chestertonian settings (Scheick 107; Ribstein 142) and this enactment of fantasies not only goes back to Chesterton's favourite hobby of 'toy theatres' but is fairly central to his imagination. The stage is the place of hallucination and artifice, yet it is confined by a framework of walls and curtains, a time schedule and the audience, all of which provide a parenthetical structure to the emergent fantasies. Criminals are actors and artists using disguise and deception in order to pursue their vicious aims. 'A crime', says Father Brown in 'The Queer Feet', 'is like any other work of art ... crimes are by no means the only works of art, that come from an infernal workshop.' The centre of a work of art, as of crime, he continues, is a simple fact 'that is not itself mysterious. The mystification comes in covering it up ...' (*CFB* 51f.). Or, as he contends, when confronted with a criminal novelist in 'The Dagger with Wings', mystification comes in when the power of story-telling is perverted and the true story is told the wrong way round (*CFB* 421f.). Detective and critic, then, have faculties and aims in common, but so have the writer of mystery stories and the mystic. For the author of mysteries, as Chesterton put it, 'is enjoyed not because he creates mystery, but because he destroys mystery' (*All Things Considered* 87ff.), while the 'mystic is not the man who makes mysteries but the man who destroys them' (*William Blake* 131).

Piercing the veil of deception and delusion is certainly a value derived from Enlightenment and Christianity. But whereas humility may, be the end of a story it is certainly not its beginning. The reader can only be engaged when common things are seen in a strange light and grass is not yet or no longer green. Gabriel Gale, the poet, painter and detective, likes to stand on his head in order to see the world differently, like St Peter, maintaining 'that the main object of a man's life was to see a thing as if he had never seen it before' (*The Poet and the Lunatics* 52ff.). Here Chesterton's aesthetics is in keeping with contemporaneous art movements such as Russian Formalism with its emphasis on 'making strange'. Psychologically speaking, the beginning is always presented as a threat and the ensuing story is meant to contain and possibly undo this threat. *The Club of Queer Trades* (1905), in which Father Brown's predecessor Basil Grant appears as the genial solver of mysteries, opens with a death threat. Major Brown discovers behind a wall a large bed of pansies arranged in gigantic capital letters that form the sentence 'Death to Major Brown'. Of course it turns out to be a misunderstanding, but the fact remains that there are people in the modern world who feed on threats—those engaging 'The Adventure and Romance Agency' in order to have a thrill as a relief from modern *ennui* and boredom: 'The Adventure and Romance Agency has been started to meet a great modern desire ... the desire for a larger theatre of events—for something to waylay us and lead us splendidly astray.' (*The Club of Queer Trades* 31). The thrill-providing agency and thrill-seeking individual thus become literal renderings of writer and reader, for like Major Brown we are always hurled into other people's stories when we read fiction. And just like the Agency, many writers since the Romantics have attempted to recreate an experience of childhood, 'that godlike time when we can act stories, be our own heroes, and at the same time dance and dream' (Ibid. 32). In this sense the Agency becomes a mediator between adult ego and child ego as it opens up the possibilities of games in an adult world. Fantasy and game, however, are for Chesterton in close proximity since both change habitual perceptions of the world and afford a new primeval freshness to a weary modern humanity: according to him, mysterious murder stories are 'professedly a toy, a thing that children "pretend" with' (quoted by Gardner 2). His imagination conjures up a topsy-turvydom, a world turned upside down which corresponds closely to what Bakhtin discovered as the experience of carnival in literature: 'Scandals and eccentricities destroy the epical and tragical integrity of the world, they form a breach in the stable, normal course of human affairs and events and free human behaviour from predetermining norms and motivations' (Bakhtin 96).

Threat can also appear in the form of scandalous madness as it does in 'The Noticeable Conduct of Professor Chadd' in the same collection. Professor Chadd, having been appointed the keeper of the Asiatic manuscripts, suddenly breaks off verbal communication and is seen standing on one leg. The problem is solved by Basil Grant—in a mode anticipating R.D. Laing's therapies—when he discovers that the Professor is trying to communicate non-verbally. Grant then begins to mimic him and to exchange messages until the two men dance jigs and hornpipes. Like Father Brown, Grant practises a kind of negative capability, accepting a limited transformation in order to understand. The threat of insanity is thereby overcome and turned to good use—to ethnological research in this case.

The writing of *The Man Who Was Thursday* can be seen as such a carnivalesque communication or dance as Chesterton's imagination itself. The centre of this vision, as he repeatedly pointed out (in the poem dedicated to E.C. Bentley prefixed to the novel or in his *Autobiography* (102)), is a nightmare and from nightmare, which Chesterton links to the morbid fantasies of his youth, all kinds of gargoyles and grotesque scenes are generated. The novel reads like a big psychological machine transforming anarchists into policemen and appearances into realities while keeping up the atmosphere of permanent threat. There is the imminence of cannibalism, the possibility of reality's losing its very consistence: 'Was there anything that was apart from what it seemed?' (*The Man Who Was Thursday* 127). The protagonist, Gabriel Syme, again and again has a close shave of 'that final scepticism which can find no floor to the Universe' (*Thursday* 127). Bodies fall apart only to reassemble and to assume a new disguise, as in the case of Professor de Worms who confesses that he cannot trust his own bodily machinery (ibid. 148). When he is recognised as a policeman we know that he was an impostor mimicking a real German Nietzschean professor, a representative of that nihilistic modernism Chesterton so eagerly attacked in all, his writings.

As for Sunday, this wild shifter of shapes is not only the grotesque image of pantheism as it was perceived in the 1890s, but represents also uncontrollable imagination itself. For Chesterton this bizarre tale of riddles and revelations was another attempt at exorcising the temptation inherent in cultural and psychological chaos by implementing narrative parentheses. It is difficult to explain why the red-haired woman appears only at the beginning and the end of the novel. But it seems that woman is part of those parenthetical forces containing nightmare—more than once Chesterton was, as it were, saved from the verge by a virgin. This also implies that women are rarely participants in the fictional horror and fun to be found in Chesterton's fantasies, since women represent maturity and sanity.

Stephen Medcalf has described the essence of Chesterton's imagination as a fourfold motion: '... from fantasy (imagined transcendency) through a fact whose primitive essence is realized by being set in fantasy, and then after a new attitude of the mind has been set up, to a transcendence found in the fact ...' (Medcalf 100). The process leading to the discovery of transcendence found in facts presupposes illusion, deception and distortion which are characteristic of grotesque vision. Annihilation and multiplication of the ego are as much part of this process as are hallucination and hilarious terror.

In this at least, Chesterton is close to such modernist explorers of the psychic abysses as Marcel Proust or Virginia Woolf—with the important difference that he derived a lot of laughter from the modern predicament. This has long been a major obstacle to his being taken seriously by the academic establishment. But nightmare as well as silliness are significant elements in the process of what one might call, following James Hillman, 'soul-making'. Dream, horror, anthropomorphism, allegory and any type of image-oriented language which transcends the real by being non-literal, contribute to this soul-making which takes place on the verge of order: 'Because our psychic stuff is imagery, image-making is a *via regia*, a royal road to soul-making' (Hillman 23). Stories then have the function of giving them sense.

The actual source of Chesterton's fantasies is a deep insecurity about reality, a sense of the unreal in the midst of what is conventionally seen as 'reality' or even as 'the laws of nature'. For Chesterton, the supreme parenthesis was Christianity, as he so vigorously demonstrated in *Orthodoxy* (1908) or *The Thing* (1929). In terms of chaos and order one could concur with the view that 'the only satisfactory reading is one that recognises the dynamic relation between the opposing forces of dishevelment and unity, with the eventual triumph of the religious man's outlook' (Lindstrom 275). Dreams like stories in their process of fragmentation and reconstruction reveal the 'elemental truth that it is the spiritual essence behind a thing that is important, not its material form' ('The Meaning of Dreams' 32). Chesterton's stories, then, are ways of experiencing the unconscious without giving in to its ultimate demands. Detective story, fantastic fiction and fairy tale merge as methods of containing horror, nightmare and death. All of his fantasies, imaginary games, and carnivals, however, implicitly reflect the role of the arts in modern society. Since art has two faces—with skill and craft belonging to consciousness, and the evocation of dreams, images and illusions stemming from the unconscious—its ambivalence is the main problem for Chesterton. The criminal (the anarchist, the eccentric, the writer, the painter) mostly performs artistic miracles which the other artist (the detective, professor, priest or policeman) must unravel using both reason and intuition. The concept of 'contradictory integration' emerges as one that encompasses the width of Chesterton's striving: integration first of all as a psychological technique for maintaining an equilibrium between fantasy and reality; secondly as a theological strategy, since Chesterton thought the multiplicity of his ideas and contradictions could best be contained in the fantastic medievalism of Catholicism; and thirdly, integration can be seen in his ideas about distribution as an effort to readjust society, individuals and resources—a political strategy which was intimately bound up with his 'cult of limits' (d'Haussy 145–9), and foreshadows more recent attempts to find a third way beyond capitalism and communism.

Another term for this 'contradictory integration' is paradox. We do not have to go out of our way, then, to look for the reason Chesterton was so fond of (and reviled for) this rhetorical device. It is in paradox that the power of parenthesis resides since in this concentrated contradiction both worlds, frame and picture, are seen as belonging to one world. Reason and madness, maturity and childishness, order and chaos together reflect the transcendental nature of the world much more truthfully than any one quality by itself. The mental structure of paradox provides space for the essential ambiguity of Chesterton's thought and imagination. Where this space is not provided, dogmatism flourishes and a spirit of exclusion takes over—to the detriment of reality, if one considers some of Chesterton's political interventions. In contrast, his use of fantasy underlines the fact that one never gets closer to reality than when giving it up. As one critic (Kenner 22) has pointed out—and here both the detective story writer and the mystic coalesce—'the stuff of reality, which reason has somehow to discover, is paradoxical stuff'.

WORKS CITED

Bakhtin, Mikhail. *Problems of Dostoevsky's Poetics* (Ann Arbor, MI: Ardis, 1973).

Barfield, Owen. *History, Guilt, and Habit* (Middletown, Ct.: Wesleyan University Press, 1979).

Bessière, Irène. *Le récit fantastique: la poétique de l'incertain* (Paris: Larousse, 1974).

Bloch, Ernst. 'Philosophische Ansicht des Detektivromans', in *Gesamtausgabe* 9 (Frankfurt/M.: Suhrkamp, 1977), 242–63.

Borges, Jorge Luis. 'Sobre Chesterton', in *Otras Inquisiciones* (Buenos Aires: Emecé, 1960), 119–23.

Chesterton, Gilbert Keith. *William Blake* (London: Duckworth, 1910).

———. *Heretics* (London: John Lane The Bodley Head, 1919).

———. *Alarms and Discursions* (London: The Library Press, 1926).

———. *All Things Considered* (London: The Library Press, 1926).

———. *The Poet and the Lunatics* (London: Cassell, 1929).

———. *Autobiography* (London: Hutchinson, 1936).

———. *The Man Who Was Thursday* (Harmondsworth: Penguin, 1937).

———. *The Club of Queer Trades* (Harmondsworth: Penguin, 1946).

———. 'The Meaning of Dreams', in *Lunacy and Letters* (London: Sheed & Ward, 1958), 33–8.

———. *The Complete Father Brown* (Harmondsworth: Penguin Books, 1981).

Conlon, D.J. (ed.) *G.K. Chesterton: A Half Century of Views* (Oxford: Oxford University Press, 1987).

Doyle, Sir Arthur Conan. *A Study in Scarlet* (London: John Murray and Jonathan Cape, 1974).

Gardner, Martin. 'Introduction' to Chesterton, *The Annotated Father Brown* (Oxford: Oxford University Press, 1987), 1–12.

D'Haussy, Christiane. *La vision du monde chez G.K. Chesterton* (Paris: Didier, 1981).

Hillman, James. *Re-Visioning Psychology* (New York: Harper & Row, 1975).

Hugh, Kenner. *Paradox in Chesterton* (London: Sheed & Ward, 1948).

Jackson, Rosemary. *Fantasy: The Literature of Subversion* (London: Methuen, 1981).

Lindstrom, Naomi. 'The Argentine Reading of G.K. Chesterton', *Chesterton Review* 6 (1979/1980), 272–9.

Medcalf, Stephen. 'The Achievement of G.K. Chesterton', in John Sullivan (ed.), *G.K. Chesterton: A Centenary Appraisal* (London: Elek, 1974), 326–35.

Ribstein, Max. *G.K. Chesterton: Création romanesque et imagination* (Paris: Klincksieck, 1981).

Robson, W. W. 'G.K. Chesterton's "Father Brown" Stories', *The Southern Review* 5 (1969), 611–29.

Scheick, William J. 'The Twilight Harlequinade of Chesterton's Father Brown Stories', *Chesterton Review* 4:i (1977/1978), 104–14.

ED BLOCK JR.

G.K. *Chesterton's* Orthodoxy *as Intellectual Autobiography*

It goes without saying that G.K. Chesterton's *Orthodoxy* is not the "slovenly autobiography" he called it. It is, rather, the complex record of a remarkable intellectual odyssey. Brought up in the late Victorian Age, when agnosticism and a host of other dangerous "isms" were afoot, it is little wonder that in *Orthodoxy* Chesterton reveals, if only implicitly, traces of the deep emotional and psychological turmoil that he had undergone in the 1890s. It is also little wonder that *Orthodoxy* everywhere manifests Chesterton's indebtedness to that same Victorian Age, even as the book represents a dynamic appropriation of that tradition.

Orthodoxy is a response to that tradition which, according to the book's own best images, treats the re-discovery of Christianity as a fairy tale adventure and an excursion into unfamiliar territory which turns out, in the end, to be a return to the familiar and the secure. In light of Chesterton's thus characterizing his intellectual autobiography as a vintage nineteenth-century romantic adventure, it may prove a bit surprising when I assert that the book also refutes some of the most pernicious claims of late twentieth-century postmodernism. The point of this interpretive argument will be that Chesterton's *Orthodoxy* remains an important and durable personal testimony to the shaping power which Chesterton gave to his own life, within his own historical period. Put another way, *Orthodoxy* remains as good an antidote for

From *Renascence* 49, no.1 (Fall 1996). © 1997 *Renascence*.

1990s nihilism as it was for Chesterton an antidote for 1890s nihilism. If one goal of an autobiography is to show the individual's personal creative response to difficult psychological, and intellectual conditions, then *Orthodoxy* deserves to be called a classic of the genre.

I do not claim any new insights about the relation of Chesterton's life to the sense of self which emerges in *Orthodoxy*. From reading Chesterton's 1936 *Autobiography*, however, as well as biographies by Maisie Ward, Michael Ffinch, and Alzina Stone Dale, it seems obvious even to an outsider that *Orthodoxy* might be seen as an expression of intense relief after what was demonstrably a period of emotional and psychological unrest. It is plausible to argue that aspects of *Orthodoxy* reflect by inversion Chesterton's turbulent adolescence, his plunge into *fin de siècle* agnosticism, and his flirtation with diabolism.

In the 1890s Chesterton had experienced a late and painful adolescence, depressions, and periods of mental anguish. Plunging deeper into doubt (including a doubt of the external world), he found himself in the situation of many a fin de siecle thinker. In the *Autobiography* he says: "It was as if I had myself projected the universe from within, with all its trees and stars, and that is so near to the notion of being God that it is manifestly even nearer to going mad. Yet I was not mad, in any medical or physical sense; I was simply carrying the skepticism of my time as far as it would go" (*A* 88).

Chesterton also records that his moral state was in similar disarray. "And as with mental, so with moral extremes. There is something truly menacing in the thought of how quickly I could imagine the maddest, when I had never committed the mildest crime.... As Bunyan, in his morbid period, described himself as prompted to utter blasphemies, I had an overpowering impulse to record or draw horrible ideas and images; plunging deeper and deeper as in a blind spiritual suicide" (*A* 89). As Michael Ffinch notes: "His fits of depression became more and more frequent, he filled his notebooks with grotesque and often sadistic figures, and there appeared for the first time a woman in what might be called an 'inviting position'. Seeing some of his wild drawings at this time, two of his closest friends thought Gilbert might be going mad" (Ffinch 39).

Chesterton further describes his situation in terms that sound like depression: "What I may call my period of madness coincided with a period of drifting and doing nothing; in which I could not settle down to any regular work" (*A* 76–77). This period of "madness" was compounded by Chesterton's feelings of guilt at having toyed with the planchette or ouija board. "I am not proud of knowing the Devil. I made his acquaintance by my own fault; and followed it up along lines which, had they been followed further, might have led me to devil-worship or the devil knows what" (*A* 76).

Orthodoxy reflects these struggles in the often alarming issues and images it employs: dueling, disorientation, revolutionary destruction; and even in chapter-titles that intimate larger themes, like "The Maniac," and "The Suicide of Thought." A less sympathetic critic might say that *Orthodoxy* depicts the recollections of a childhood whose deepest fears and certainties about himself are disclosed, obliquely and artfully altered to show their best face. To set the argument of *Orthodoxy* upon a suitably scientific fact, Chesterton, in chapter two, rejects a religious perspective, saying, in effect: since we can't agree on the existence of evil, let's at least agree that there is such a thing as insanity. I remember feeling a thrill of recognition when I first read that famous line: "Men deny hell, but not, as yet, Hanwell" (*O* 25). Read in light of Chesterton's adolescent experiences, this sentence carries an added weight of somber experience—if not suffering—which lends it even greater credibility as genuine autobiographical insight. To anticipate a bit my points about *Orthodoxy* and postmodernism, I might add that my earlier "thrill of recognition" has become an almost uncannily chilling feeling as I realize that some today do seek to deny Hanwell, or that there may need to be Hanwells. Even if British playwright Peter Shaffer (in his play, *Equus*) does not himself seriously question psychological "Normality," his depiction of a psychiatrist who does wonder whether there is such a thing as normality, and whether it is a good, anticipates some recent claims of postmodernism.

To show that *Orthodoxy* does more than merely reflect inversely some of Chesterton's adolescent mental suffering, I would quote an additional passage which seems weighted with personal experience. Having shown with more than a bit of whimsical comparison that it is the lunatic who cannot accept causeless actions, Chesterton assumes a more serious tone as he states: "Every one who has had the misfortune to talk with people in the heart or on the edge of mental disorder, knows that their most sinister quality is a horrible clarity of detail; a connecting of one thing with another in a map more elaborate than a maze" (*O* 31–32). Chesterton here reveals an empathy and vivid perception that shows his familiarity with the experience. From this it is easy to conclude: Chesterton knows whereof he speaks. His insight implies some familiarity with the very disconcerting reality of Hanwell.

From this vivid evocation of the reality of madness, Chesterton fashions an argument leveled at the madness of nineteenth-century deterministic thinking. Observing that "the madman's explanation of a thing is always complete, and often in a purely rational sense satisfactory" (*O* 32),

Chesterton goes on to point out the "narrow universality" of such explanations. He observes that "a small circle is quite as infinite as a large circle, but, though it is quite infinite, it is not so large." Modulating the observation into an image that might attract the attention of a—perhaps mad—postmodern literary critic, Chesterton anticipates the theme of suicide in chapter five, observing that "a bullet is quite as round as the world, but it is not the world" (*O* 33). As an antidote to the claustrophobia of the determinist's closed circle of argument, Chesterton then offers the intimation of a larger whole. But to explain the source and significance of that larger whole, I shall first have to introduce my second theme: Chesterton's re-appropriation of his Victorian background.

Previous critics have praised or noted Chesterton's Edwardian qualities. One thinks, for instance, of his chauvinistic, Eurocentric stance, or allusions to dated political and scientific terms and concepts. Among the terms that come to mind, I frankly find it at worst whimsical and perhaps even somewhat satiric when, for instance, Chesterton proposes to use scientific terms for the Resurrection and Ascension, suggesting that they be called "Levitation" and "Regalvanisation." As a Victorianist, however, I am moved by the degree to which Chesterton dynamically responds to and actively appropriates the tradition of thought and artistic expression which preceded the Edwardian Era, and with which Chesterton was intimately and demonstrably familiar. One need only remember that Chesterton would become well-known for studies of Robert Browning, Charles Dickens, and Percy Shelley to suspect the importance of nineteenth-century thought in *Orthodoxy*. Besides the texture of more comprehensive and cosmopolitan literary allusion which includes Marcus Aurelius, Leo Tolstoy, Henrik Ibsen, and Friedrich Nietzsche, there are numerous specific references to the late eighteenth and nineteenth-century English tradition: to William Cowper, Matthew Arnold, Alfred Lord Tennyson, H.G. Wells, and Bernard Shaw, just to name some of the most prominent. A first way to demonstrate Chesterton's dynamic appropriation of this tradition, then, is to discuss three other prominent Victorians who figure more centrally in *Orthodoxy*. They are Thomas Carlyle, T. H. Huxley, and (now Venerable) John Henry Cardinal Newman. Chesterton's use of these authors' ideas highlights a common tradition of English philosophical and literary thought of which he is a beneficiary, and to which he is a contributor.

As a first step to making the madman of chapter two aware of a larger whole, a larger and less insane world in which to live, Chesterton says, "How much happier you would be if you only knew that these people cared nothing about you! How much larger your life would be if your self could become smaller in it" (*O* 34–35). Sounding most proximately like a phrase from Thomas Hardy's *Tess of the d'Urbervilles* (Hardy 77), the last phrase and a later definition of madness (*O* 40) clearly appropriate ideas central to the thought of Thomas Carlyle. Carlyle's philosophy in *Sartor Resartus* is based upon Goethean *Entsagung*, or renunciation of self. Carlyle's complex fictional narrator says: "Make thy claim of wages of zero, then; thou hast the world under thy feet. Well did the Wisest of our time write: 'It is only with Renunciation (*Entsagen*) that Life, properly speaking, can be said to begin'" (Carlyle 153). Like Chesterton, Carlyle had wrestled with thoughts of nihilism and feelings of depression. It is little wonder that Chesterton finds Carlyle's thought congenial. Like Carlyle, too, Chesterton is objecting to the insane, deterministic cast of modern scientific thinking.

If Chesterton is objecting to deterministic scientific thought, how then, especially in the face of his obvious and frequent criticism of T.H. Huxley, do I presume to claim that Chesterton appropriates Huxley? Chesterton, it turns out, is objecting not so much to Huxley's thought as to the image of Huxley as presented by his sometime student, H.G. Wells. To understand the next stage of Chesterton's argument for a larger, more comprehensive view of reality, and Chesterton's use of Huxleyan thought, it is necessary to sketch briefly a few of Chesterton's first principles.

In chapter four of *Orthodoxy*, "The Ethics of Elfland," Chesterton makes this observation: "We have always in our fairy tales kept this sharp distinction between the science of mental relations, in which there really are laws, and the science of physical facts, in which there are no laws, but only weird repetitions" (*O* 91). This statement could as easily have been uttered by the Huxley who wrote "Methods and Results" or *Man's Place in Nature*. Relying upon a tradition of empirical logic that stretches back through David Hume to Francis Bacon, Huxley sought to argue that we know nothing certainly except mental relations. In an equally famous essay, "On the Physical Basis of Life," he had sought to explain gravitation using the example of stones falling to the ground.

> I suppose if there be an "iron" law, it is that of gravitation; and if there be a physical necessity, it is that a stone, unsupported, must fall to the ground ... It is very convenient to indicate that all the conditions of belief have been fulfilled in this case, by calling the statement that unsupported stones will fall to the ground, "a law of Nature." But when, as commonly happens, we change will into must, we introduce an idea of necessity which most assuredly

does not lie in the observed facts, and has no warranty that I can discover elsewhere. (Huxley 161).

It is, to me, somewhat whimsical when Chesterton later alludes to just such laws of Nature, and with one exception, in just such terms as Huxley might have used.

> When we are asked why eggs turn to birds or fruits fall in autumn, we must answer exactly as the fairy godmother would answer if Cinderella asked her why mice turned to horses or her clothes fell from her at twelve o'clock. We must answer that it is <u>magic</u>. It is not a "law", for we do not understand its general formula. It is not a necessity, for though we can count on it happening practically, we have no right to say that it must always happen. It is no argument for unalterable law (as Huxley fancied) that we count on the ordinary course of things. (*O* 93)

Though Chesterton mistakes Wells's popularization of Huxley's ideas, he actually states a position—minus the word "<u>magic</u>," with which not only Huxley but John Henry Newman would have agreed.[1] Something very like the same point is implied by John Henry Newman in his *Tamworth Reading Room* letters, his *University Sermons*, and the *Essay in Aid of a Grammar of Assent*. In the *Apologia Pro Vita Sua*, too, he states: "'What do I know of substance or matter? just as much as the greatest philosophers, and that is nothing at all.';—so much is this the case, that there is a rising school of philosophy now, which considers phenomena to constitute the whole of our knowledge of physics" (*Apologia* 185). No wonder Huxley himself had quipped that there was a whole primer of skepticism in Newman's writing. Showing what there is of Newman in Chesterton that is not in Huxley will, after a further delay, make possible a return to Chesterton's argument about madness in chapter two of *Orthodoxy*.

I turn, therefore, to the third major appropriation, John Henry Newman. Perhaps because Chesterton acknowledges Newman's importance in his preface, critics have felt little challenge to trace more exactly Chesterton's appropriation of Newman's ideas in *Orthodoxy*. Yet I see Newman's thought as so thoroughly imbuing Chesterton's text that I was tempted to subtitle this paper "A Poor Man's Apologia," or—in a fit of postmodern imaginativeness—claim that, at the very least, *Orthodoxy* is an anxious re-inscription of the *Apologia*. What Chesterton derived from Newman was this greater, more expansive sense of the whole which constitutes reality. The ideas of Newman and Chesterton also resemble each other partly because both accept a living tradition of Christian Aristotelian metaphysics and logic.

One similarity which initially strikes the reader are the similar circumstances which brought Newman to write the *Apologia* and Chesterton to write *Orthodoxy*. Both had experienced various kinds of "conversion" earlier in life. Newman had experienced several. Chesterton had demonstrably changed from a depressed youth to an exuberantly optimistic young man. At a later stage in life, both were challenged by other writers to explain themselves. Like Newman responding to Charles Kingsley, Chesterton, in response to a challenge from G.S. Street, decided to explain how and why he had traversed those dangerous times called adolescence and the twenties, arriving where he had on the threshold of full maturity.

If I had to list three or four of the most striking similarities between Newman and Chesterton, I might start by noting that Chesterton's urging that a man must stop thinking if he is to go on living (*O* 37) is a gloss on Newman's powerful injunction in *The Tamworth Reading Room* letters: "Life is for action. If we insist on proofs for everything we shall never come to action" ("Tamworth Reading Room" 204). I would also note Chesterton's acknowledgment of the agnostic's honest disbelief (*O* 262), and his assertion that it was "an enormous accumulation of small but unanimous facts" (*O* 265) which led to his personal belief. These assertions, along with reference to "miscellaneous and scrappy evidence" or "loose but living experience" are Chesterton's more self-effacing equivalent of Newman's acknowledgment of the fact of non-belief, and for the "antecedent probabilities" for belief about which he speaks so vigorously in the *University Sermons* and the *Grammar of Assent*.

This similarity, of course, is founded on their both accepting the philosophical necessity of belief before reason.[2] "To accept everything is an exercise," Chesterton says, "to understand everything is a strain" (*O* 29). This is Chesterton's colloquial paraphrase of the following statement which Newman makes in the *Grammar*:

> Of the two, I would rather have to maintain that we ought to begin with believing everything that is offered to our acceptance, than that it is our duty to doubt everything. The former, indeed, seems the true way of learning. In that case, we soon discover and discard what is contradictory to itself. (*Grammar* 294)

Along with statements like, "The man who begins to think without the proper first principles goes mad" (*O* 48), and references to the arrogance and infinite appetite of man (*O* 54) or the skeptical tendency of reason (*O* 59), these statements recall not only Wells's essay, "Doubts of the Instrument" and Newman's *University Sermons*, or the *Grammar of Assent* but the famous fifth chapter of the *Apologia*.

Besides the striking similarities between Newman and Chesterton, however, there are a number of less obvious ones, like the reference to the balancing act that Christianity manages (*O* 180 ff.) and to point of view (*O* 38) as the fundamental disposition for distinguishing reality. These, along with reliance on ordinary peoples' views (*O* 86) and what is learned at a mother's or a nurse's knee are all echoes of a fundamental position in Newman's thinking. These lesser similarities culminate in Chesterton's affirmation of the Church as "a truth-telling thing" (*O* 291). This is a specific example of what Newman describes when, using the analogy of a child believing its mother's assertions, he says: "Her veracity and authority is to him no abstract truth or item of general knowledge, but is bound up with that image and love of her person which is part of himself, and makes a direct claim on him for his summary assent to her general teachings" (*Grammar* 35).

The reader who sees the Victorian period as deeply homogenous, despite apparent heterogeneity is probably most taken by Chesterton's similarity to Newman when Newman, Chesterton, and Huxley are most alike. As intimated earlier, the science of mental relations vs. physical fact, and of logical necessity implying no physical necessity (*O* 93), as well as reference to "inner syntheses which we do not possess" (*O* 94), are manifestations of all three thinkers' scrupulous employment of reason within limits. The way in which postmodernists feel that they have surpassed such critical reasoning has been in the doubt they cast on the linguistic instrument itself. But here, too, Chesterton and Newman have preceded the postmodernists in ways with which Huxley too would have approved. The focal point of Chesterton's language skepticism comes when he observes that "All descriptions of the creating or sustaining principle in things must be metaphorical, because they must be verbal ... All terms, religious and irreligious, are open to this charge" (*O* 141–42). On the face of it, such a statement sounds skeptical, but taken with reference to "stars bent on being understood" (*O* 107), we can see that such a statement sensitively argues a connatural view of knowledge. It points to an apprehension of reality that only metaphor can approach. Chesterton, it turns out, employs the philosophical rigor of Hume, Huxley, and Newman against what the late

Walker Percy would have called the dilution of pure science by scientism.[3] All three, Newman, Huxley, and Chesterton, better understand the limits of science than those postmodern proponents of gnosticism who would seek to "fix" (in both senses of the term) by increasingly complex congeries of technological, legal, but ultimately mechanical means the fundamentally broken nature of human beings and their thinking—not to mention natural things. Chesterton's complaint about "the modern world [being] solid for modern Calvinism" (*O* 106) is as true today as it was ninety years ago.

An additional observation related to this "scientific fatalism" reveals an even more fascinating side of Chesterton's belief system. When he rejects such fatalism, denying that "the leaf on the tree is green because it could have been anything else" (*O* 105), he affirms a scientific as well as a poetic principle. His claim that "the leaf is green precisely because it might have been scarlet" (*O* 105)—like the even more enigmatic claim that "every colour has in it a bold quality as of choice" (*O* 106)—affirms a providential, poetic view related to that with which he began the chapter: "The vision is always solid and reliable. The vision is always a fact. It is the reality that is often a fraud" (*O* 82). Though we might unpack this statement in a variety of ways,[4] it expresses a fundamentally "connatural" view of human knowing. It is an insight aptly and beautifully expressed in an early poem of Adrienne Rich called "Design in Living Colors," a poem probably indebted to T.S. Eliot. It describes a medieval tapestry-like scene and ends with the following lines:

> We are the denizens of a living wood
> Where insight blooms anew on every bough
> And every flower emerges understood
> Out of a pattern unperceived til now. (Rich 67)

After seeing the hard-headed skepticism of Chesterton's position, even with respect to language, we might gloss this poetic insight by reference to a Chestertonian contrast which has all the sharp suspicion of language, thought, and rationality wrapped up into one statement. "All that we call common sense and rationality and practicality and positivism," he says, "only means that for certain dead levels of our life we forget that we have forgotten. All that we call spirit and art and ecstasy only means that for one awful instant we remember that we forget" (*O* 97). Here, as Carlyle, Newman, and Huxley would agree, the labels that we give to certain kinds of experience tend to obscure their actual meaning, while still disclosing their significance in our lives.

By this circuitous route we are able to see why Chesterton, back in chapter two of *Orthodoxy*, takes Ernst Haeckel so much to task as representative of deterministic thought's insanity, claiming that "(according to Haeckel) the whole of life is something much more grey, narrow, and trivial than many separate aspects of it. The parts seem greater than the whole" (*O* 40–41). Haeckel, and with him modern deterministic science, fails to envision the greater whole to which Newman's thinking had led Chesterton. Rejecting false verbal traps and hewing close to the mystery behind life-giving metaphors, Chesterton shows us how he was able to begin the return to sanity. The early chapters of *Orthodoxy* thus manifest a vigorous mind rejecting the cant, solipsism, and paralysis of much late nineteenth-century thought in favor of something that he will, in later chapters, re-discover to be the perennially new troths of Christianity.

Another way to discuss Chesterton's appropriation of his Victorian predecessors is to show how *Orthodoxy* reflects the re-emergence of favorite—I want to say archetypal—themes and images of his childhood experience. These are the experiences to which W.H. Auden refers when he quotes Chesterton himself: "There is at the back of every artist's mind something like a pattern or type of architecture. The original quality in any man of imagination is imagery. It is a thing like the landscape of his dreams, the sort of world he would wish to make or in which he would wish to wander; the strange flora and fauna of his own secret planet; the sort of thing he likes to think about" (Auden 268). Auden's observation is particularly valuable inasmuch as it is the expression of like finding like. Auden thought enough of Chesterton's insight to make it a central motif of an important literary critical essay, "Reading."

As Auden points out, "In 'The Ethics of Elfland' Chesterton tells us how his own 'pattern' was derived from fairy-stories" (Auden 268). What Auden does not bother to point out is that the larger context within which this pattern receives its elaboration and development is the late nineteenth-century fascination with romance and the many forms in which it became available not only to children but adults as well. Chesterton names "Grimms' Fairy Tales or the fine collections of Mr. Andrew Lang" (*O* 98), thereby acknowledging two of the most popular (and prominent) sources. He also refers somewhat critically to the fairy tale qualities of W. B. Yeats (*O* 99). The tradition, however, does not end there. A related aspect of that tradition is continuously suggested by references to "tawdry romances," "penny dreadfuls," "a boy's book" (*O* 253), and "a serial story in a magazine" (*O* 253), not to mention ghost stories (ch. 9, esp. 276). It is also hinted at in the use made of Daniel Defoe's *Robinson Crusoe*. That tradition is one identified with another favorite Victorian of Chesterton's, Robert Louis Stevenson. Like the shadow of Newman, the shadow of Stevenson is one which falls most charmingly over *Orthodoxy*, lending it pleasing tones and suggestive highlights. From the numerous references to sailing, navigating, and outdoor adventure generally; and to even more specific images and situations suggesting courageous and intrepid explorations, the spirit of Stevensonian romance is clear.

A final appropriation of a Victorian predecessor is that of Robert Browning. Chesterton's indebtedness to Browning is fourfold. But it is also both more diffuse and more intimately related to Chesterton's central ideas than some of his other indebtednesses. Chesterton's "loyalty" to the world, for instance, along with his claim for its "meaningfulness," take part of their coloring from the energetic optimism that Browning manifested and that Chesterton shared. Near the end of chapter four Chesterton combines the Newmanian and the Browningesque as he concludes, "There was something personal in the world, as in a work of art; whatever it meant it meant violently" (*O* 117). From Newman, Chesterton derives the insight of a personal force at work in the world; from Browning's poem, "Fra Lippo Lippi," he derives the idea and even the phraseology denoting intense meaningfulness. From loyalty to this meaningful world there also derives Chesterton's Browningesque willingness to venture out, take a risk, and make a commitment. This may also explain Chesterton's love of Stevenson, for within the adventurer—which Stevenson certainly was—is often a hidden venturer.[5] A fourth feature of Chesterton's indebtedness to Browning I shall discuss in my concluding remarks.

From the evidence of *Orthodoxy*, then, Chesterton was a man who, initially attracted by the nihilism of the 1890s, felt drawn to find a reason for why things were, rather than dwelling on why they were not. From this felt need arose a real assent to the truth of what he had experienced in childhood, in family, in fairy tales. And having made this assent, he was able to find his way back to that reason for going on with life; for acting rather than remaining passive. Seen in this way, Chesterton's vigorous affirmation of life is yet another mirror reflection of his earlier depression and inanition. In his *Autobiography* Chesterton succinctly summarizes his indebtedness to the nineteenth century when he says: "This way of looking at things with a sort of mystical minimum of gratitude, was of course, to some extent assisted by those few of the fashionable writers who were not pessimists; especially by Walt Whitman, by Browning and by Stevenson" (*A* 90).

In this concluding section I shall turn from Chesterton's relation to the past and deal, instead, with the way in which the "style" of *Orthodoxy* anticipates and preempts a number of supposed discoveries of post-modernism. Of course Chesterton may have learned an aspect of this style from another Victorian predecessor, Oscar Wilde. Auden observes that Chesterton couldn't escape the influence of the decadents. "Oddly enough, since he so detested them, Chesterton inherited from the aesthetes of the 1880s and 1890s the conviction that a writer should be continuously 'bright' and epigrammatic" (*A* 264). This very penchant for the 'bright' and clever epigram or paradox also relates Chesterton to much postmodern critical writing. But as Chesterton's own piece on Wilde indicates (*Illustrated London News*, March 11, 1911), he knew the excesses as well as the virtues of paradox. And though Auden may be right when he says that Chesterton can become a parody of his own "brightness," his oppositions and paradoxes invariably result in visionary disclosure of some aspect of a larger, more significant whole with which we have become too familiar, too comfortable, too self-assured.

It is largely through repetitions, variations on the binary opposition between familiarity and unfamiliarity, that Chesterton manages his famous paradoxes. To speak theoretically for a moment: what is a paradox but a sudden revelation of sameness in difference; of truth in apparent fallacy or contradiction. Already in this way of putting it one might see paradox as the very intimation of a larger whole, a way of seeing something which turns apparent fallacy into luminous truth. *Orthodoxy* is built upon a series of such polarities and oppositions which are, nevertheless, related to each other. The most familiar and striking is the analogy of the yachtsman. With this analogy Chesterton points to a fundamental epistemological fact; the fact that we know by comparison, by the recognition of sameness and difference. Our self first comes to know itself at least partly through recognition of otherness. *Orthodoxy* calls attention to a series of such important oppositions.

Among the paradoxes with which Chesterton anticipates and in fact preempts postmodernism, I find three most persuasive. Returning for a moment to the climax of chapter four, we find an anticipation of postmodernism even as it recapitulates features of nineteenth-century thought. In employing the image of the materialist as madman, Chesterton reverses Spencer and Wells, claiming that their expansive (that is, imperialist) thoughts have "turned mankind into a small nationality" (*O* 111). Chesterton then transforms the idea of Hanwell into Reading Gaol, anticipating not one but two of the late Michel Foucault's most famous insights. In a Chestertonian (or postmodern) frame of mind, I am inclined to believe Foucault was the plagiarist, and that his ideas about prisons and asylums are mere pedantic elaborations of Chesterton's almost uncannily creative analogy. Chesterton's most uncanny repetition may be his conjecture that, in time, he could have invented the marriage vow (226). Such a claim for re-discovery challenges in boldness that made in Jorge Luis Borges' story, "Pierre Menard, Author of the Quixote" (Borges 36–45).

Two related passages are even more somber and uncanny. In chapter five, his chapter on loyalty, Chesterton stops us abruptly at one point as he reasons that we must look upon our world as both an "ogre's castle and our own cottage" (*O* 130). Here the senses of unfamiliarity and familiarity are raised to an intensity that readers might find more than a bit uncomfortable. Finally, in chapter nine Chesterton seeks to show the importance of Catholic doctrine and discipline by using the image of protective walls. He asks us, in true Stevensonian fashion, to imagine a fairy tale island.

> We might fancy some children playing on the flat grassy top of some tall island in the sea. So long as there was a wall round the cliff's edge they could fling themselves into every frantic game and make the place the noisiest of nurseries. But the walls were knocked down, leaving the naked precipice. They did not fall over; but when their friends returned to them they were all huddled in terror in the centre of the island; and their song had ceased. (*O* 269)

This brief parable has much in common with postmodern tendencies. Chesterton does not interpret. He lets the metaphor speak. Of course it is easily interpretable in the best deconstructionist fashion. The image of protective barriers lost might be meant to inspire fear, timidity, and ultimately acquiescence. But in the striking contrast there are also numerous prescient features that suggest the fundamentally sound reasons for walls.

As a final example of Chesterton refuting postmodernism I should like to turn to a more positive instance of the familiar and the unfamiliar, the self and the other. It is also one which returns us to the final connection with Browning. In chapter eight, "The Romance of Orthodoxy," Chesterton locates Christianity's liberating quality in its being founded on an opposition, a separation. "No other philosophy makes God actually rejoice in the separation of the universe into living souls. But according to orthodox Christianity this separation between God and man is sacred, because this is eternal. That a man may love God it is necessary that there should be not only a God to be loved, but a man to love him" (*O* 246). In postmodern terms, we might say that even the world of religious experience is inconceivable without the recognition of self through a transcendent other.[6] A sundering postmodern *différance*—a recognition of self and other, familiar and unfamiliar—which makes possible all other knowledge, all other distinctions.

But as if this revelatory opposition were not enough, Chesterton carries it even further. A few pages later he proposes to consider the revolutionary idea that "Christianity is the only religion on earth that has felt that omnipotence made God incomplete. Christianity alone has felt that God, to be wholly God, must have been a rebel as well as a king" (*O* 256). This paradoxical statement recalls what Chesterton says of Browning as a poet of the two-fold hope. This strikingly paradoxical statement is also a way to deal with the Incarnation in a fashion that, as Ezra Pound would have said, "makes it new." Chesterton does indeed make it new. A few lines later he says: "It is written, 'Thou shalt not tempt the Lord thy God.' No; but the Lord thy God may tempt Himself; and it seems as if this was what happened in Gethsemane. In a garden Satan tempted man: and in a garden God tempted God" (*O* 256–257). This is yet another strikingly paradoxical way of trying to suggest an idea, a whole, which is beyond human understanding. Chesterton does it in this case—consciously and perhaps even somewhat unconsciously—in order to return to the pervasive theme which we have seen has relevance to his own transformation. Of Christ's agony in the garden Chesterton says; in that garden "He [Christ] passed in some superhuman manner through our human horror of pessimism. When the world shook and the sun was wiped out of heaven, it was not at the crucifixion, but at the cry from the cross: the cry which confessed that God was forsaken of God" (*O* 257). In this striking insight Chesterton has even anticipated modern orthodox theologians like Hans Urs von Balthasar, who uses this profound paradox to elaborate a Christology based on Jesus' experience of "Godforsakenness."[7] Without descending to jargon, Chesterton is here imagining God as transcendentally other, yet personal; a thou for our selves; a complete whole whose very completeness makes not one but two other persons necessary, God the Son and God the Holy Spirit. God is a Trinity who, together, nevertheless call for, in some strange manner "need," our loving response.

Largely through his paradoxes, then, Chesterton awakens us to the truth of revelation; to the revelatory nature of seeing the world as a Christian sees it. In this way *Orthodoxy* becomes for us, as I suspect it was for Chesterton himself, an antidote to pessimism and skepticism, the very embodiment or celebration of a grateful acceptance of Being and existence.

In what might be termed its "graceful returns upon acceptances," *Orthodoxy* recalls a poem ("The Fountain") by the poet, Donald Davie. In it Davie, alluding to an image employed by the skeptical British philosopher Berkeley, compares thought to a fountain, which

mounts

> From bland assumptions to inquiring skies,
> There glints with wit, fumes into fancies, plays
> With its negations, and at last descends,
> As by a law of nature, to its bowl
> Of thus enlightened but still common sense. (Davie 60)

In an age that is rightly cautious of the "tyranny of common sense," Chesterton subtlely incorporates trenchant logic with the most experientially based observations and intuitions. Expressing his view of life in paradoxes which—like Heidegger, but so much more effortlessly—disclose the truth suddenly, he embodies an acceptance of revelation and mystery making of *Orthodoxy* an intellectual autobiography and a classic example of "enlightened but still common sense."

NOTES

1. It is also the ground for Newman's arguing in his *Essay on Miracles* that miracles are not exceptions to natural law, but part of a larger conception of that law or plan.

2. The same assertion of belief before reason occurs in another famous Catholic's thinking: Hans Urs von Balthasar in his "A resume of my thought," pp. 470–72.

3. Chesterton even anticipates the "amnesiac" thought experiment which Percy was so fond of using. See Percy, p. 17.

4. It is even explicable in terms of the thought of such providential scientific seers as Loren Eiseley. See Eiseley, "The Secret of Life," pp. 195–210.

5. A true venture is founded on desire for the reward as well as a calculation of the cost—hence the reason that buying a two-dollar lottery ticket is not really a venture or, if so, one which cheapens the original meaning of the term. I won't risk a jump across an abyss if it is merely to show off. I might, however, make such a venture if my life is endangered. I shall risk a dangerous swim to save a drowning child, but not merely to demonstrate my breast stroke.

6. Balthasar, *Heart of the World*, pp. 35; 39–40.

7. Balthasar, *Truth is Symphonic*, p. 167 inter alia.

WORKS CITED

Auden, W.H. "Chesterton's Non-Fictional Prose." *Gilbert Keith Chesterton: A Half Century of Views*. Ed. D.J. Conlon. New York: Oxford UP, 1986. 262–268.

Balthasar, Hans Urs von. *Heart of the World*. San Francisco: Ignatius Press, 1979.

———. "A résumé of my thought." *Communio* 15 (Winter, 1988): 468–473.

———. *Truth Is Symphonic*. San Francisco: Ignatius, 1987.

Borges, Jorge Luis. *Labyrinths*. New York: New Directions, 1964.

Carlyle, Thomas. *Sartor Resartus*. *Collected Works I*. London: Chapman and Hall, 1896.

Chesterton, Gilbert Keith. *Autobiography*. New York: Sheed and Ward, 1936. Cited in the text as (*A* page).

———. *Orthodoxy*. New York: Dodd and Mead, 1959. Cited in the text as (*O* page).

———. *Illustrated London News, The Collected Works of Gilbert Keith Chesterton XXIX*. San Francisco: Ignatius, 1987. 51–54.

Dale, Alzina Stone. *The Outline of Sanity: A Biography of Gilbert Keith Chesterton*. Grand Rapids: W.B. Eerdman's, 1982.

Davie, Donald. *Collected Poems 1950–1970*. New York: Oxford UP, 1972.

Eiseley, Loren. *The Immense Journey*. New York: Random House, 1957.

Ffinch, Michael. *Gilbert Keith Chesterton*. San Francisco: Harper and Row, 1986.

Hardy, Thomas. *Tess of the d'Urbervilles: A Critical Edition*. 2nd ed. New York: Norton, 1979.

Huxley, T.H. *Collected Essays I*. Rpt. 1917. New York: Greenwood Press, 1968.

Newman, John Henry. *Apologia Pro Vita Sua*. Ed. David J. DeLaura. New York: W.W. Norton, 1968.

———. *Essay in Aid of a Grammar of Assent*. Notre Dame: Notre Dame UP, 1979.

———. "The Tamworth Reading Room." *Essays and Sketches II*. Ed. Charles Fredrick Harrold. New York: Longmans, Green, and Company, 1949.

Percy, Walker. *Lost in the Cosmos: The Last Self-Help Book*. New York: Farrar, Strauss, and Giroux, 1983.

Rich, Adrienne. *A Change of World*. New Haven: Yale UP, 1951.

Ward, Maisie. *Gilbert Keith Chesterton*. New York: Sheed and Ward, 1943.

JOHN McCABE

On Reading Chesterton's Chaucer

G.K. Chesterton opens his book on Chaucer with a cautionary admonition to the reader to beware "possible mistakes" and "inevitable pitfalls" (*Chaucer* 9). Then he begins his colossal stride across the span of some six hundred years, cape flying, walking stick in hand, sure of foot at every step. We hang on for dear life.

I hear that caveat, and I apply it to myself. To consider together these two titans of the world of English letters is a daunting task. The six centuries that separate Chaucer and Chesterton are marked by profound linguistic shifts and cultural fissures. To bring these two figures into a single focus requires that we enlarge our perspective and adjust our sense of proportion. Both of these writers are, as a matter of fact, masters of proportion. Chesterton, for example, records his surprise at the moment that he realized that the world could be thought of as something small because it is something complete (*Orthodoxy* 63). This is a perspective (and emotion) that he shares with Chaucer's Troilus, when, having been released in death from the double sorrow of his life:

> His lighte goost ful blisfully is went
> Up to the holughnesse of the eighthe spere ...
> And down from thennes faste he gan avyse

From *Renascence* 49, no.1 (Fall 1996). © 1997 *Renascence*.

This litel spot of erthe, that with the se
Embraced is ...
And in hymself he lough right at the wo
Of hem that wepten for his deth.
    (*Troilus and Criseyde* V 1808–1809; 1814–16; 1821–22)

Matters of proportion become matters of perspective. I will want to argue that the great accomplishment of Chesterton's study of Chaucer is that he makes the world of Chaucer habitable again, even for a reader of the twentieth century. He brings it down to size, so to speak, without ever diminishing what he identifies as a distinguishing mark of the poetry of Chaucer: its spaciousness (*Chaucer* 241). Anyone who has known a happy home, however small, however humble, knows what it means to speak of the spaciousness of home. Chesterton makes us feel very much at home in the spaciousness of Chaucer. He set out as a twentieth-century pilgrim to join these fourteenth-century pilgrims on the road to Canterbury and found that his journey took him home.

Chesterton observed in the opening of *The Everlasting Man* that "there are two ways of getting home, and one of them is to stay there" (9). He might have added: to stay there reading. Chaucer would have understood that; he, like Chesterton after him, confesses to be a bookish man: "On bokes for to rede I me delyte" (*Legend of Good Women* 3). In his dream visions, he gives us several amusing portraits of himself—alone, at night, after a day of important "busynesse" (for Chaucer was something of a man of state), poring over his books by candlelight, dozing off into improbable dreams, dreams that became the stuff of his poems, peopled by the books he read, from Virgil and Ovid to Boethius and Dante and Petrarch, and he made them all his own, in his own inimitable way, with a deep reverence and a lightness of touch. Chesterton remarked of Chaucer: "His own touch was as light as a feather; but the feather came truly from an angel's wing" (*Chaucer* 59).

It was fashionable in some critical circles throughout the nineteenth century, and well into the twentieth, to view Chaucer as a medieval eccentric: literally, as someone who removed himself from the center of his culture, who turned his back upon his religious heritage and set England and English poetry on a new track.[1] There is a half-truth here: Chaucer did set poetry on a new track, but he didn't do it by turning his back upon tradition. Chesterton considers the matter of Chaucer's orthodoxy by comparing Chaucer's religious attitudes with those of a more overt religious poet of the same period, William Langland, the author of the fiercely prophetic poem *Piers Plowman*. Chesterton concludes that Chaucer shares with Langland "exactly the same fundamental ideas about the nature of repentance and the authority of Christ... [and] exactly the same fundamental belief in the sacramental and ecclesiastical system of the Middle Ages" (*Chaucer* 249). Chesterton recognized that the poetry of Chaucer is rooted in orthodoxy, and he announced to a skeptical audience that the joy and hilarity that emanate from the poetry of Chaucer is the same joy that irradiates the writings of Aquinas. Chesterton was at home in the world of Chaucer, and found it "sane and cheerful and normal" (12), because Chaucer was at home in the spacious world of classical Christendom.

It is characteristic of Chesterton and appropriate to a study of Chaucer for Chesterton to find the configuration of fourteenth-century orthodoxy in the constellation of three books:

> Suppose at some time some medieval man had only three medieval books. And suppose those three were, first, some version of the works "of Aristotle and his philosophy"; second, the Divine Comedy of Dante; and third, the *Summa* of St. Thomas Aquinas. This is not to possess books but to possess worlds ... A man might own a whole Circulating Library of modern novels and minor poets, without having anything like such a comic conspectus, or complete consideration of all sides of the real world. But the vital point to seize, in connection with the particular case of Chaucer, is that the philosophy ... was one which aimed at a certain equilibrium, achieved by giving so much weight to one thing and so much less or more to another ... That thing was a poised and proportioned thing. (282–83)

The genius of the criticism of Chesterton lay less in the practice of *explication de texte* and more in the discovery that Chaucer sustained an easy conversation with Aristotle, Aquinas, and Dante. Chesterton puts the question directly: "What, it may be asked, has Chaucer to do with Dante? What did he actually inherit from Dante? I answer, the spaciousness" (241). Chesterton recognized that, though Chaucer may have come upon the wisdom of this inherited culture in fragmentary fashion, he received "enough of its culture to be filled with its fulness" (283). Chesterton could have been echoing Matthew Arnold when he observed that the comedic world of Chaucer has "largeness and liberty," but he was entirely original when he wrote:

> The mind of Chaucer was capacious; there was room for ideas to play about in it. He could see the connexion, and still more the

disconnexion, of different parts of his own scheme, or of any scheme. (26)

Two words from this passage, "capacious" and "play," are key for a reading of Chesterton on Chaucer.

The term "capacious" is very like the one I earlier drew from Chesterton to describe the poetry of Chaucer: namely, that it is "spacious." "Spacious," I would suggest, is a visual image: it is, obviously, a spatial thing, some wide and deep and unencumbered place. "Capacious," too, may refer to something wide and deep and unencumbered, but it is less a place and more a potentiality, less static and more active, a *capax*, an ability to see and to take in and to hold in delight. Chesterton at one point speaks of "an unruffled and radiant receptivity" in Chaucer (273). This is a clear-eyed seeing of the manifold but real order of things, and a spontaneous delight in their deep-down freshness. Thus capaciousness is linked to playfulness. Chesterton finds around Chaucer what he calls a "penumbra of playfulness ... a halo of humor" (26–27). Sanity and cheerfulness come together in that both flow from his theology (278). This is like the dance of Peace and Justice, Truth and Love, celebrated in Psalm 85.

The "spacious/capacious" qualities that Chesterton uncovers in the poetry of Chaucer are qualities that accompany, or are the consequence of, the "cosmic philosophy" that links Chaucer with Dante and Aquinas. This philosophy may appear in Chaucer in "a leisurely and allusive fashion, but it was there all right." Chesterton describes the "feeling" aroused by this philosophy as "a sort of reasonable repose" (242). In one of his most eloquent passages Chesterton expands on this idea:

> There is at the back of all our lives an abyss of light, more blinding and unfathomable than any abyss of darkness; and it is the abyss of actuality, of existence, of the fact that things truly are, and that we ourselves are incredibly and sometimes almost incredulously real. It is the fundamental fact of being, as against non-being; it is unthinkable, yet we cannot unthink it, though we may sometimes be unthinking about it; unthinking and especially unthanking. For he who has realized this reality knows that it does outweigh, literally to infinity, all lesser regrets or arguments for negation, and that under all our grumblings there is a subconscious substance of gratitude. (36)

This passage could as well have appeared in Chesterton's study of Thomas

Aquinas, published a year after his study of Chaucer. In all likelihood, he had for some time been working on these studies simultaneously. There are any number of passages in the book on Aquinas that resonate with this same language:

> Now nobody will begin to understand the Thomist philosophy, or indeed the Catholic philosophy, who does not realize that the primary and fundamental part of it is entirely the praise of life, the praise of Being, the praise of God as the Creator of the Word. (*Saint Thomas Aquinas* 105)

Or again:

> There is a general tone and temper of Aquinas, which is as difficult to avoid as daylight in a great house of windows. It is that positive position of his mind, which is filled and soaked as with sunshine with the warmth and the wonder of created things. (119)

For Chesterton, the "light of the positive" that he experienced in the philosophy of Aquinas becomes "the business of poets" to make resplendent. Philosophy and poetry are different but complementary modes of praise:

> That light of the positive is the business of poets, because they see all things in the light of it more than do other men. Chaucer was a child of light ... He was the immediate heir of something like what Catholics call the Primitive Revelation; that glimpse that was given of the world when God saw that it was good ... These things belong to the same world of wonder as the primary wonder of the very existence of the world ... for it is only rarely that we realize, like a vision of the heavens filled with a chorus of giants, the primeval duty of Praise. (*Chaucer* 37)

Chesterton ascribes to Aquinas the appellation "St. Thomas of the Creator" (*Saint Thomas Aquinas* 119); he ascribes to the poetry of Chaucer the quality of "gusto," of "zest," which is "a certain appetite for things as they actually are, and because they actually are" (*Chaucer* 166).

"Creation was the greatest of all Revolutions," Chesterton observed (*Chaucer* 37). Chaucer brought about an English poetic revolution of his own in his evocation of Creation as sempiternal in the opening lines of "The General Prologue of The Canterbury Tales." Here is embodied the medieval notion of *Natura Naturans*: Nature being renewed and renewing itself in an ongoing celebration of Creation. The images figure forth new life: April pierces the dryness of March, sweet showers bathe the veins of every plant with a "licour" so powerful—with such "vertu"—as to engender a blossom. The West Wind is a spirit that breathes forth ("inspired hath") the tender shoots. What is quickened in Nature is matched in Grace: the natural and the supernatural orders are inseparable in this syntax. After the temporal subordinate clauses, the main clause and consequence follow:

> Thanne longen folk to goon on pilgrimages,
> And palmeres for to seken straunge strondes ...
> The hooly blisful martir for to seke,
> That hem hath holpen when that they were seeke.
>   ("General Prologue" 12–13; 17–18)

This vision of nature and of human nature is Incarnational and sacramental and redemptive. Quietly obtrusive, the concluding descriptive clause "whan that they were seeke" strikes a discordant theme. Chaucer brings us up short with what is for the modern age the scandal of the medieval consciousness of sin, the moral blighting of nature.

I do not know why medieval sinfulness should be such a stumbling block for the modern age. We surely have sins enough of our own, but we insist on taking pride in the progress we have made in virtues of self-fulfillment, and we scorn as superstitious the medieval regressive penchant for the naming and cataloging of sins.

Chaucer thought it neither regressive nor negative to name a sin a sin, nor did he think it lacking in charity, nor invasive of privacy, nor a measure of his lunacy, to depict individuals in various states or acts of sinfulness, but his depiction of the sin or the sinner is never mean-spirited. Chesterton makes us aware of how Chaucer never loses his balanced composure, his sane sense of cheerfulness, his generosity. Chesterton finds Chaucer in *Troilus and Criseyde* to achieve "something new," a refined balance between the demands of jesting about lovers and jeering at false love, conventions long associated with the tradition of romance. Chaucer revealed a finer spirit:

> He jested without jeering and reproached without raving. The charity of Chaucer toward Cressida is one of the most beautiful things in human literature; but its particular blend belongs entirely to Christian literature. (*Chaucer* 144)

Chesterton calls this "the more merciful view." Even in satire Chesterton finds Chaucer's sensibilities to be all on the side of sympathy. He observes: "He does not want the Friar and the Wife of Bath to perish; one would sometimes suspect that he does not really want them to change" (210). There is a fine sense of tact shown here on Chesterton's part, because the nearly irresistible impulse of most modern readers of the portraits in "The General Prologue" is to move in on them with a reformer's zeal. For those who find scandal in the portrait of the monk who turns the order of the monastic world topsy-turvy, Chesterton offers this consolation: "To those troubled in spirit by the divine disturbance of humor, it will be obvious that Chaucer is simply chaffing a monk for his cheek in not being a monk at all" (*Chaucer* 254). In recounting the foibles and vices of even the scoundrels among the pilgrims to Canterbury, Chaucer "cannot contain himself for gladness at the thought of such sociable eccentricities." These characters, in all their moral shabbiness, evoke from him "an impulsive movement to applaud what he does not approve ... Their impudence gave him so much pleasure that he could not withhold a sort of affection based on gratitude" (271–72). In calling the Pardoner a "gentle Pardoner," Chaucer was not confusing his moral categories. Instead, this ability to maintain equanimity, and even good humor, in encountering evil

> reached the sort of balanced and delicate habit of mind, the habit
> of looking at all sides of the same thing; the power to realize that
> even an evil has a right to its own place in the hierarchy of evils;
> to realize, at least, that in the abysmal relativities of Hell and
> Purgatory, there are even things more unpardonable than the
> Pardoner. (274–75)

Chaucer has his Parson in his sermon give us a pithy description of the consequences of sin: "And ye shul understonde that in mannes synne is every ordre or ordinaunce turned up-so-doun" (*The Canterbury Tales* X, 260). Centuries later, Chesterton will echo these words in his comments about our being born "upside down:"

> The primary paradox of Christianity is that the ordinary
> condition of man is not his sane or sensible condition; that the
> normal itself is an abnormality.

This is the inmost philosophy of the Fall. This paradox, Chesterton concludes, has "one special application" and leads him to "the ultimate idea of joy" (*Orthodoxy* 158).

A great achievement of medieval culture was to reconcile the opposition between gravity and gaiety. Chesterton found gravity and gaiety in the medieval epoch to be interwoven and complementary—as complementary as is *The Canterbury Tales* to the *Summa Theologica*. Chesterton observes:

> The meaning of Aquinas is that medievalism was always seeking a center of gravity. The meaning of Chaucer is that, when found, it was always a center of gaiety. (*Chaucer* 288)

Here—in their encounter with sin—we encounter especially the freshness and the freedom of Chesterton and of Chaucer, because their freshness flows from their delight in freedom. The idea of freedom is absolutely fundamental to the thought of Chesterton. The whole of the poetry of Chaucer, as Chesterton rightly sees it, is a celebration of

> the spirit that made Dante acclaim freedom as the first of divine gifts ... In the very center of the Christian cosmos, everything pivoted on the idea that the human heart could be given to God or withheld from him. The highest affections of the soul could turn this way or that, to the divine or the diabolic; and the supreme charity was valued because it was not enforced. (146)

It is ironic that the narrators in the poetry of Chaucer should be charged so often with simplicity, because simplicity—in its medieval manifestation—is not a simple thing. "A light touch," Chesterton remarks, "is a mark of strength and not of weakness, in spiritual as in bodily things" (143). I have come to think that in one respect at least Chaucer outdistanced his master Dante, and that was in the gift of an exquisite sense of humor, in his spirit of playfulness. His mirth is a kind of magnanimity that springs from an impulse of gratitude. Aristotle recognized a form of this in the virtue of *eutrapelia*; Aquinas, and the Greek fathers of the Church before him, likened this virtue to the spirit of Wisdom, which is said to play before the Lord.[2] I think it fair to say that what we admire about the Divine Comedy is its solemnity, its grandeur. But grandeur is not deeper than gaiety; nor is solemnity wiser than mirth: both are manifold aspects of the same human spirit, different, if distant, reflections of the infinite Wisdom of God. If we say that Dante excelled in one and Chaucer in the other, we may be forgiven for a moment of being, with Chesterton, partisan for Chaucer in thinking that Chaucer chose a more difficult path to the stars. What I mean to say is that it must be, really, as easy to hate in Hell as it will be, we are told, to love in Heaven. The virtues and vices we find portrayed in the *Inferno* and the *Paradiso* are etched in fearsome clarity, seared in the flames of hate or love. But what is one to do in this middle spot of earth—"that with the se embraced is"—where the movements of the human heart are subtle, difficult to catch in flight, quick to change. Chesterton saw this in Troilus: "We see these shifting and conflicting crosslights shining or darkening on the figure of Troilus" (271). To put it another way: we can't imagine any character in Dante as being any other way than as graven for us; but we can't imagine the pilgrims on the road to Canterbury unless as being—always—just one step shy of conversion.

Chesterton says of Chaucer: "God had given him a remarkable talent for seeing what good there was in things" (150). Chesterton had once described how his discovery of Christianity had led him to another discovery:

> I had found this hole in the world: the fact that one must somehow find a way of loving the world without trusting it; somehow one must love the world without being worldly. (*Orthodoxy* 79)

Twenty-five years later, we find Chesterton celebrating the imagination of Chaucer for giving expression to exactly this kind of freedom. Chesterton describes the imagination of Chaucer:

> He had set up, as part of the structure of his own mind, a sort of lower and larger stage for all mankind, in which anything could happen without seriously hurting anybody, and an upper stage on which walked the angels of the justice and the mercy and the omniscience of God. (*Chaucer* 272)

So also for the Canterbury pilgrims: they are enveloped in the love of their poet/creator, who, we trust with equanimity, will call forth from them the good that is in them. Why else does Chaucer have the Parson step forth at the gates of the shrine of Thomas à Becket with his call to confession and his promise of redemptive grace. Chaucer was blessedly wise to know that contrition follows upon gratitude, and not the other way around, and that forgiveness is nourished in joy. The Parson proclaims that Christ has conquered Satan, Heaven has vanquished Hell:

> For certes oure sweete Lord Jhesu Christ hath spared us so
> debonairly in our folies, that if he ne hadde pitee on mannes
> soule, a sory song we myghten alle synge. (*The Canterbury Tales* X,
> 315)

So Chaucer sings a happy song; he could not do otherwise. In the words of
Chesterton: "Chaucer had the one thing needful ... He had Charity; that is
the heart and not merely the mind of our ancient Christendom" (275).

NOTES

This essay is an adaptation of a paper presented to the Midwest Chesterton Society
at their spring Conference on June 9, 1995.

1. For a survey of shifting scholarly and critical assessments of Chaucer's orthodoxy
during the early part of the twentieth century, see Robert W. Ackerman's essay, "Chaucer,
the Church and Religion."

2. For a discussion of *eutrapelia* in the *Summa Theologica*, cf. IIaIIae. 168, 2–4: also
IaIIae. 11, 3 on enjoyment; refer also to Hugo Rahner, S.J., *Man at Play*, 1–2, 27–30.

WORKS CITED

Ackerman, Robert W. "Chaucer, the Church and Religion." *Companion to Chaucer Studies*.
    Rev. ed. New York and Oxford: Oxford UP, 1979, 21–41.
Chaucer, Geoffrey. *The Works of Geoffrey Chaucer*. 2nd ed. Ed. F. N. Robinson. Boston:
    Houghton Mifflin, 1957.
Chesterton, G.K. *Chaucer*. London: Faber and Faber, 1932.
———. *The Everlasting Man*. Image Books Edition. New York: Doubleday, 1955.
———. *Orthodoxy*. Image Books Edition. New York: Doubleday, 1955.
———. *Saint Thomas Aquinas*. Image Books Edition. New York: Doubleday, 1956.
Rahner, Hugo. *Man at Play*. New York: Herder and Herder, 1967.

MARIAN E. CROWE

G.K. *Chesterton and the Orthodox Romance*
of Pride and Prejudice

What do erotic love, adventure stories, and orthodox faith have in common? G.K. Chesterton would answer resoundingly with one word: romance. His use of the same word for three apparently disparate entities may be careless and indiscriminate, or it may disclose a valuable insight into what Chesterton clearly sees as three of the richest human experiences: falling in love, telling stories, and believing the Christian faith. His use of the same word, romance, to describe all three suggests that he sees some commonalities among them. This essay will argue that Chesterton's claims about the nature of romance are wonderfully illustrated in what is arguably the greatest romantic novel of English literature, Jane Austen's *Pride and Prejudice*. Chesterton's comprehensive view of the romantic—including not only erotic experience but stories and faith as well—suggests that a broader understanding of romance may account for some of the power of this novel.

Why discuss Austen in light of Chesterton or vice versa? Chesterton certainly admired Austen's work. He claimed in *The Victorian Age in Literature* that she "knew much more about men" than the Brontës or George Eliot (109). In "On Jane Austen in the General Election," he describes her as a "shrewd and solid psychologist" (197). He also states in a preface he wrote for Austen's early Love and Friendship [sic] that there is "an infallible force to her irony" and a "stunning weight to her understatements"

From *Renascence* 49, no.3 (Spring 1997). © 1997 Renascence.

(xv). The most compelling reason, however, for using Chesterton's ideas as a lens through which to view the romance in *Pride and Prejudice* is simply that this novel with its four romances, its analytical intelligence, and its moral seriousness, is one of the best, most complete illustrations in fiction of the way Chesterton's ideas play out in human experience. The novel translates Chesterton's analysis into love stories that resonate deeply with readers and raises his paradoxes from the level of verbal wit to that of a fully realized truth about the way many people experience that mysterious event known as falling in love. Furthermore, Chesterton's ideas suggest why the romance in *Pride and Prejudice* goes beyond courtship or a mating ritual. The novel is romantic, not only because it is a love story, but because it has the thrill of adventure, the satisfying closure of story, and the exciting engagement with ultimate questions that characterizes faith.

Some of Chesterton's most intriguing statements about romance are found in "On Certain Modern Writers and the Institution of the Family" in his collection entitled *Heretics*. In addition, I draw on two chapters from *Orthodoxy*, "The Paradoxes of Christianity" and "The Romance of Orthodoxy." These works show that for Chesterton anything truly romantic involves a paradoxical conjoining of accident and free will. The excitement of romance stems from its power to keep together in creative tension two apparent opposites (the two parts of the paradox), but keeping their individuality fully intact. Thus, in a Chestertonian romance, separateness is valued as much as union.

Chesterton sees paradox at the heart of almost everything he values highly. Accordingly, it is not surprising that he sees paradox as essential to romance (eros), Romance, (story), and orthodoxy.[1] In *Orthodoxy* he asserts that romance is rooted in a "double spiritual need, the need for that mixture of the familiar and the unfamiliar which Christendom has rightly named romance" (10). He insists that both deliberate, conscious choice and contingency, accident, surprise are essential for Romance and strongly suggests that the same is true for romance. Similarly, the reason he finds orthodoxy "one whirling adventure" (*Orthodoxy* 101) is that "Christianity got over the difficulty of combining furious opposites, by keeping them both, and keeping them both furious" (94).

The paradoxical nature of romance—the fact that it must be both accidental *and* freely chosen—is for Chesterton a key factor in rating a relationship or a story as more or less romantic. *Pride and Prejudice* with its four couples dramatizes romances in which varying degrees of strategy and surprise are involved. In fact, Jane Austen, with her predilection for using paired absolutes as titles, might also have considered naming the novel *Reason and Mystery* or *Freedom and Compulsion* or *Strategy and Surprise*. In Chesterton's schema the extent to which each romance is both a free choice and a rational act would place it on the hierarchy of the truly romantic.

Each couple—Elizabeth–Darcy, Jane–Bingley, Charlotte–Collins, Lydia–Wickham—incorporates a different proportion of strategy and spontaneity, illustrating the way in which this paradoxical conjoining of free will and accident flavor and define and even rank the quality of the romance. Furthermore, if Chesterton's ideas are valid, Austen's predictions of marital happiness for the four pairs of lovers may reflect a substantive link between the degree of Chestertonian romance and the likelihood of future happiness.

Chesterton's primary requirement for romance is that it is fortuitous. In "On Certain Modern Writers and the Institution of the Family" he calls family life a romance precisely because it is unplanned and unchosen:

> This is, indeed, the sublime and special romance of the family. It is romantic because it is a toss-up. It is romantic because it is everything that its enemies call it. It is romantic because it is arbitrary.... It is a thing that chooses us, not a thing that we choose. (190–91)

Chesterton calls falling in love "the supreme romantic accident" and argues that "in so far as we do to some extent choose and to some extent even judge—in all this falling in love is not truly romantic, is not truly adventurous at all" ("Certain Modern Writers" 191). Thus Chesterton sees romance and adventure as closely linked, if not actually equivalent.

Romance also involves limits; in fact, it thrives on them. Chesterton calls it a mistake of the moderns to see constraints as inimical to romance and argues that they are mistaken to "imagine that romance would exist more perfectly in a complete state of what they call liberty" (195). Carrying over his theory to Romance in the sense of a story, Chesterton claims that "in order that life should be a story or [R]omance to us, it is necessary that a great part of it, at any rate, should be settled for us without our permission" (194). Romance and adventure seem to be conflated, with free choice apparently having little part in either.

If true romance, according to Chesterton, is an adventure and a surprise, then a courtship that is more strategic and purposeful would be less romantic. The first romance in the novel to be completed with a marriage is also the one that is first in the order of strategy. Charlotte's romance is conscious, deliberate, purposeful. Marriage "had always been her object; it was the only honorable provision for well-educated young women of small fortune, and however uncertain of giving happiness, must be their pleasantest preservative from want" (122–23). So when she learns that Elizabeth has refused Mr. Collins's offer of marriage, Charlotte is determined to have him. Seeing him approaching her home, she sets out "to meet him *accidentally* in the lane" (122, emphasis added). By the time they enter the house, they are engaged. Although she claims to feel "all the good luck of it" (123), Charlotte's engagement is much more a matter of strategy than luck. Whereas Chesterton insists that "in so far as we have certainly something to do with the matter ... falling in love is not truly romantic, is not truly adventurous at all" (191), Charlotte has everything to do with the matter. The strategy, the lack of spontaneity and surprise make it the most unromantic of romances by Chesterton's standards.

Chesterton, of course, is explicitly concerned *only* with the degree of romance in a relationship—not the longevity or happiness of a marriage. Yet the novel is clear enough about the probable future course of all four courtships to suggest that Chestertonian romance may be a predictor of later marital happiness. In Charlotte's case, her marriage will probably be peaceful and relatively stable. She is willing to do what is needful to satisfy Collins and play the role of clergyman's wife. What it will not be is confrontational; and, therefore, the marriage that they form will thereby miss the mark for Chesterton. It will miss the element of adventure and thus will not be a true romance. It will, however, have one of the other hallmarks of romance, for Chesterton also says that "To be in a romance is to be in uncongenial surroundings" ("Modern Writers" 195). Charlotte *is* in uncongenial surroundings. However, her strategy for survival seems to be to remove herself as much as possible from the source of tension (Mr. Collins), to be passive and compliant. When Elizabeth visits her, she notes that Charlotte chooses to spend most of her time in a small room in the back of the house rather than in the larger and more comfortable dining room. Elizabeth discerns that "her friend had an excellent reason for what she did, for Mr. Collins would undoubtedly have been much less in his own apartment had they sat in one equally lively" (168). Charlotte chooses not to act a role in this would-be drama. She acts by not acting. So the Collins marriage will be peaceful and systematic—but not dramatic. One *could* do worse.

Perhaps Lydia and Wickham *do* actually do worse. Elizabeth's flighty youngest sister, who runs off with the dashing Mr. Wickham, appears at first glance to have the kind of romance of which Chesterton would probably approve. It is an elopement—exciting, spontaneous—the very epitome of adventure. On closer inspection, however, their romance and subsequent elopement prove not to be quite so spontaneous and unplanned. Lydia's greatest goal is to be "married before three and twenty!" (221). She is not only "prepared to fall in love" ("Modern Writers" 191), an attitude which for Chesterton is antithetical to true romance, she is *determined* to do so.

Mr. Wickham, Lydia's partner in her "romantic" adventure, certainly is not captivated by the same romantic myth and mania for spouse hunting that has such a firm grip on Lydia. Yet their sudden elopement seems to suggest the romantic love that Chesterton says "does take us and transfigure and torture us" ("Modern Writers" 191). Wickham's motivation, however, has much more to do with money than with transfiguring love. His original motive for running away with Lydia is to escape some gambling debts and to have a little fling with an attractive girl while he is at it. He does not intend to marry her at all, for he is in hopes of "making his fortune by marriage, in some other country" (323). Therefore, Wickham's romantic adventure is not really romantic at all. He has struck a good bargain. While his running away with Lydia may seem impulsive and spontaneous, in fact, it is very calculated and mercenary, the immediate instigating factor not being Lydia at all, but some bad debts. It is not surprising, therefore, that the closing pages of the novel inform us that after their marriage, "his affection for her soon sunk into indifference; hers lasted a little longer" (387).

Jane and Bingley are certainly not as calculating as Charlotte Lucas, Lydia Bennet or Mr. Wickham. Though charmed with each other when they meet, they are not quite what Chesterton would call "prepared to fall in love," nor do they "jump into it" ("Modern Writers" 191). Jane seems genuinely surprised at Bingley's attention to her. "I was very much flattered by his asking me to dance a second time. I did not expect such a compliment" (14), she tells Elizabeth. In fact, Jane's lack of artifice is so effective that Darcy genuinely believes her to be indifferent toward his friend. Both these young people are in the way to fall in love, but are not actively pursuing it.

Bingley, in fact, runs away from it—or more accurately—allows himself to be pulled away from it by the arrogant—if well-meaning—Darcy, who believes a match with Jane would not be prudent. Jane is even more passive than Bingley. She spends several months visiting the Gardiners in London, and apart from making one visit to Bingley's sister, never attempts to contact Bingley or let him know that she is in town. Jane holds herself firm and steady, waits for love to come to her, and when it does not, accepts her loss as graciously as possible. When the two finally are reunited, it is more by the efforts of others than by their own direct actions. Bingley and Jane may not exactly jump into romance, but they do need a little push before they tumble gleefully into it, even if that push consists only of permission from an authority figure.

If Chesterton's formula for romance is right, if it *should* be arbitrary and unplanned, if one is acted upon rather than acting, then Jane and Bingley, who seem bemused, even amazed, by what is happening to them, should be lovers *par excellence*. But they are not. Here is where the other half of the paradox enters.

Chesterton also insists that free choice is essential to Romance in the sense of story. In *Orthodoxy* he argues that

> a story is exciting because it has in it so strong an element of will, of what theology calls free will.... Christendom has excelled in the narrative romance exactly because it has insisted on the theological free will. (136–37)

This point is also made in "On Certain Modern Writers and the Institution of the Family," where Chesterton claims that "a story has behind it, not merely intellect which is partly mechanical, but will, which is in its essence divine" (193). In fact, he goes on to say, "When Thomas Aquinas asserted the spiritual liberty of man, he created all the bad novels in the circulating libraries" (193–94). It is difficult to read Chesterton's remarks on both Romance (story) and romance (eros) and not conclude that the two are conflated in his mind. Furthermore, it is hardly a simple linguistic coincidence that Chesterton uses the same words, *romance* and *romantic*, to attempt to pinpoint what is so exciting about both stories (Romance) and falling in love (romance), for free choice *and* accident seem to be essential to both. Romance to be truly romantic must be arbitrary, surprising, unplanned. Yet romance devoid of conscious, careful human choice is beneath our dignity as human beings. If falling in love is also an adventure story, free will and rational conscious choice are critical, and lovers as well as questing knights must call on the resources of the rational. To be truly romantic, a romance must be a Romance.

In Jane and Bingley's romance there is too *little* choice, too *little* use of the rational. Most readers, however, share Elizabeth's expectations of felicity for Jane and Bingley, based on "the excellent understanding and super-excellent disposition of Jane, and a general similarity of feeling and taste between her and himself" (348).

Darcy and Elizabeth's romance is strongly characterized by accident and surprise. They take an immediate dislike to one another and are most definitely *not* "prepared to fall in love." Nor do they in any sense deliberately or consciously "jump into it" ("Modern Writers" 191). Unlike Jane and Bingley, who are nudged apart, Elizabeth and Darcy are each running as hard and as fast as they can in the opposite direction.

Robert Polhemus, in his book *Erotic Faith: Being in Love from Jane Austen to D.H. Lawrence*, suggests that Darcy and Elizabeth's romance is a blend of the accidental and the rational, but he apportions the accidental to Darcy and the rational to Elizabeth. He argues that although Elizabeth "comes to love [Darcy] by the end, it is not at all clear that she ever falls in love with him. In their romance, man falls in love with woman ..." (29). For Polhemus the difference between loving and "falling in love" is the difference between "a rational blend of affection and desire for a person, and an involuntary, often blind, power of emotion that seizes one" (53), the latter, of course, being closer to what Chesterton means by the unplanned, unwilled adventure of romance. Of course, Darcy's coming to love Elizabeth is more mysterious in the context of the novel because, as Polhemus points out, "we can only speculate about the inner process that first moves him to love and what it means to him" (48). Being reticent about the inner lives of her male characters, Austen concentrates on Elizabeth's inner experience. Nevertheless, Austen's careful, analytical probing of Elizabeth's inner life does not exclude the possibility that her feeling for Darcy is also like an "enchantment, something ineffable" (Polhemus 48). Arguing that "the origin of love [is] the instinctive attraction that Darcy [and not Elizabeth] feels, Polhemus suggests that the story "needs first Darcy's libido to push him into the fortunate erotic fall" (50) and that Elizabeth's coming to love is based on gratitude and esteem. Nevertheless, the intensity of Elizabeth's feelings about Darcy, in repeated references to his tall stature and good looks, suggests that a good deal of erotic energy, even if not consciously acknowledged, is swirling around Elizabeth too.

Chesterton insists that "the thing which keeps life romantic and full of fiery possibilities is the existence of these great plain limitations which force all of us to meet the things we do not like or do not expect" ("Modern Writers" 194–95). Therefore he would probably consider it extremely romantic when Darcy can no longer deny the reality and force of his attraction, proposes, and is shocked by Elizabeth's assertion that he is "the last man in the world whom [she] could ever be prevailed upon to marry" (193). Darcy is as astounded by Elizabeth's refusal as she is by his proposal. The shock they both experience creates a kind of psychic space in which they can enter the next phase of falling in love, a phase in which the rational will play a much greater part. In order to leave the euphoria of initial infatuation and sexual attraction and begin to really see the other, the lovers must pry away the encrusted residue of self-righteousness and moral blindness. The shock they both receive when Darcy proposes provides the energy to begin this process.

Toward the end of the novel when Darcy says, "I was in the middle before I knew that I *had* begun" (380), he points up how mysterious their relationship has been. Yet Elizabeth, looking back on the same relationships, finds it "perfectly reasonable" (380). It is the mystery that thrusts them into the place where they must begin the rational work of analyzing the self and of learning the truth about the other. If, as Chesterton asserts, "To be in a romance is to be in uncongenial surroundings," their embarrassment and humiliation place Darcy and Elizabeth in a romance. Now they must begin the hard work of becoming worthy to be true lovers. Realizing that, apart from Darcy's offensive manners, she really knows nothing substantial against his character and that she has been "blind, partial, prejudiced, absurd" (208), Elizabeth takes a step to retrieve the rational. She faces herself honestly: "I have courted prepossession and ignorance, and driven reason away, where either [Darcy or Wickham] were concerned. Till this moment I never knew myself" (208). For Darcy, too, the moment is inexpressibly painful and forces him into self-analysis. Later he admits to Elizabeth that her refusal of his marriage proposal has forced him to see himself as he really was:

> "What did you say of me that I did not deserve? For, though your accusations were ill-founded, formed on mistaken premises, my behaviour to you at the time had merited the severest reproof. It was unpardonable. I cannot think of it without abhorrence." (367)

When Elizabeth rejoices in the "wisest, most reasonable end" (347) of Jane's romance (and presumably her own), she is highlighting the rational component of romance. Is this just wishful thinking on the part of Jane Austen, child of the Enlightenment? Certainly it is true, as Tony Tanner claims, that "Elizabeth loves for the best reasons, and there are always reasons for loving in Jane Austen's world" (134). Some readers, however, see Elizabeth's studied analysis of the growth of their relationship as the self-deluded attempts at rationality of a young woman caught up in the throes of romantic passion. She is simply in love.

Perhaps another way of looking at it would be to say that the reasons play backward. Polhemus's analysis here is insightful:

> Austen sees loving as potentially a rational act, and falling in love

> as a mysterious, prerational, disruptive process for the individual. This orderly person imagines that some disruption of order is necessary to foster new love beyond familial limitations and bring about a deepened and expanded sense of self, feminine belief in personal progress, and rational marriage. (53)

As lived, romance *is*—as Chesterton so rightly saw—a surprise and an adventure. Seen in retrospect, Elizabeth's "perfectly reasonable" plan reveals itself. What Chesterton seems to demand of true lovers is to live the adventure, trust in the reasons—and through it all—to *pay attention*.

In fact, it is their capacity for attention—serious, steady, careful attention—that makes it possible for Darcy and Elizabeth to change, that makes their love dynamic rather than quiescent. Simone Weil's concept of attention suggests a way of understanding its function here. In her essay "Reflections on the Right Use of School Studies with a View to the Love of God," Weil argues that sustained attention increases one's capacity to know the truth: "every time that a human being succeeds in making an effort of attention with the sole idea of increasing his grasp of truth, he acquires a greater aptitude for grasping it" (52–53). Weil sees attention as a highly moral act, for "every time that we really concentrate our attention, we destroy the evil in ourself.... A quarter of an hour of attention is better than a great many good works" (56). This kind of attention, however, is not simply a fierce act of the will. It is as passive as it is active. "Above all," continues Well, "our thought should be empty, waiting, not seeking anything, but ready to receive in its naked truth the object which is to penetrate it" (56).

Chestertonian romance—at least as exemplified by Darcy and Elizabeth—seems to combine both active and passive elements and to include a great capacity for attention. Like the highly-patterned eighteenth-century dances that Darcy and Elizabeth perform and that are reflected in the structure of the novel,[2] true romance involves going forward, going backward, and standing still. It requires being open, present, and attentive to the conditions that life brings, being in readiness for whatever surprising marvels may appear. At the same time it requires engaging actively with whatever *does* appear, studying it with energy and zest, and using it as a lens with which to see the self. Here is where Jane and Bingley's romance falls short of Elizabeth and Darcy's.

Darcy and Elizabeth pay *attention* to their lives in ways that few of the other characters do. They study them, with a great deal of seriousness—not only to get what they want in order to make their lives more comfortable (as do Charlotte, Lydia and Wickham)—but in order to *understand* them. Thus, their use of the rational, of conscious, deliberate choice, is unlike that of Charlotte and Lydia, because it is focused on self-knowledge rather than self-advancement. It is reflective rather than manipulative.

The way that Darcy and Elizabeth's erotic experience incorporates surprise, attention, seriousness and separateness—all qualities that Chesterton associates with the romantic—foregrounds this couple against all the others of the novel and suggests why the four romances inevitably rank themselves into a hierarchy. Indeed, here it becomes more than just a rhetorical flourish that Chesterton conflates the use of the word romance to denote both an erotic male–female relationship and an adventure story. In particular, Chesterton seems to have in mind the medieval Romance, which is in a very literal sense a journey, a movement from one geographical place to another. Gawain must go to the green chapel in order to confront the green knight and face his own guilt. Darcy and Elizabeth's relationship suggests much more movement than do any of the other romances. Their romantic journey begins with surprise and a notable absence of strategy; it culminates in astonishment that issues in a rational, purposeful and serious examination of the self. This movement is what makes Darcy and Elizabeth so much more dynamic than the other three couples, who all, more or less, remain where they began, the Collinses and the Wickhams with their strategy and the Bingleys with their passivity. Is this proportion realistic? For how many people does romance serve as a catalyst for emotional, psychological, or spiritual growth? About one in four? Austen is probably not far off the mark here.

Another quality that gives Darcy and Elizabeth's relationship its excitement, its tension, and its seriousness is an example of what Chesterton sees as the distinctive characteristic of Christian love of God and of neighbor: separateness. In the chapter entitled "The Romance of Orthodoxy" in *Orthodoxy*, he points out Christianity's emphasis on the transcendence of God, in contrast to Buddhism and other religions, which stress the immanence of God and the unity of all created beings. For Chesterton, this insistence on otherness is important, not only for our understanding of the Deity, but for comprehending human love as well.

> I want to love my neighbor not because he is I, but precisely because he is not I.... If souls are separate love is possible. If souls are united love is obviously impossible.... Christianity is on the side of humanity and liberty and love. Love desires personality; therefore love desires division. (*Orthodoxy* 131)

It is the separateness of Darcy and Elizabeth that makes them so interesting. The other three couples all seem to meld into units: the improvident Wickhams, the congenial Bingleys, the clerical Collinses. Although separateness might seem to characterize the Collinses (with Charlotte hiding from her husband in the other room), in fact, their lack of meaningful interaction and Charlotte's excessive deference to her husband disallow the kind of separateness Chesterton has in mind. Elizabeth and Darcy, on the other hand, achieve a love that not only allows but encourages the definiteness and singularity of their personalities. This separateness means that they love in a way that is, at times painful, but also exciting. Their love seems to have about it a kind of aggression that the Spanish philosopher Miguel de Unamuno ascribed to the virtue of charity:

> For true charity is a kind of invasion—it consists in putting my spirit into other spirits, in giving them my suffering as the food and consolation for their sufferings, in awakening their unrest with my unrest, in sharpening their hunger for God with my hunger for God. It is not charity to rock and lull our brothers to sleep in the inertia and drowsiness of matter, but rather to awaken them to the uneasiness and torment of spirit. (282)

Darcy and Elizabeth will certainly never "lull each other to sleep in the inertia and drowsiness of matter." On the other hand, Jane and Bingley, for all their delight in each other, will most probably never awaken each other "to the uneasiness and torment of spirit." Their sameness, their easy compatibility makes their romance common wine compared to Elizabeth and Darcy's champagne. Likewise, Charlotte and Collins in their prudent strategies, and Lydia and Wickham in their willful self-indulgence, lack the sharp delineations of Elizabeth and Darcy, whose separateness creates the possibility for greater happiness. "I am happier even than Jane," says Elizabeth, "she only smiles, I laugh" (383).

Chesterton has great enthusiasm for romance in all its forms: eros, story and orthodoxy. He focuses on the experience itself but is less interested in following out the trajectory to connect the quality of romance with its ability to effect happiness. Most of Chesterton's praise for free will pertains to Romance (story) rather than romance (eros). When speaking of eros, he has much more enthusiasm for accident, surprise, and spontaneity, and has less to say about free choice. His preference raises the question of whether romance devoid of conscious deliberate choice is really good. Is Chesterton's recipe for romance also a recipe for unhappiness?

As noted, all four of the romances in *Pride and Prejudice* strongly suggest what kind of marital happiness or unhappiness each couple will achieve. Austen is clear about the fact that (at least in terms of their marriages) the Wickhams and Collinses will be unhappy, the Bingleys happy, and the Darcys supremely happy. Those whose romances are strongly characterized by strategy are doomed to unhappiness. The Bingleys, who let romance "happen" to them, are rewarded with happiness. But the best outcome (laughter as opposed to smiles) is reserved for the couple who are both swept up in a surprising, unplanned adventure, but who meet that adventure with all the resources of the rational. One might argue, of course, that the happy endings for the "good" characters are nothing more than Austen's conformity to a literary convention. Such an analysis, however, is inadequate. That the question of future happiness is more than just a literary convention to Austen is suggested by the care and attention with which she delineates all the instances of the opposite—marital disharmony: poor Charlotte, who is a good person, sympathetically portrayed, reduced to the stratagem of hiding from her husband in another room, the reference to Lydia and Wickham's growing indifference to one another, and most poignantly, the utter lack of harmony and affection in the marriage of Elizabeth's parents. Romance involves *real* risks. Chesterton emphasizes in his chapter "The Romance of Orthodoxy" that the dangers a hero faces must be serious and real:

> In a thrilling novel ... the hero is not eaten by cannibals; but it is essential to the existence of the thrill that he *might* be eaten by cannibals. The hero must (so to speak) be an eatable hero. So Christian morals have always said to the man, not that he would lose his soul, but that he must take care that he didn't. (*Orthodoxy* 136)

Austen is determined to demonstrate, through the lives of the Collinses, the Wickhams, and the Bennets, that the fate that Jane and Elizabeth escape is entirely possible for them. Since the dangers that threaten them are real, their success is exciting—and romantic.

Pride and Prejudice illustrates the Chestertonian paradox but rearranges it slightly. Whereas Chesterton seems to privilege spontaneity, accident, contingency, Austen gives a much higher place to the rational and its attendant qualities of attention, seriousness, and autonomy (separateness).

For both Chesterton and Austen, however, both parts of the paradox are essential for the best, the most romantic, love.

In "The Romance of Orthodoxy" Chesterton argues that part of Christianity's uniqueness consists in its insistence on keeping two apparently contradictory truths (such as Christ's divinity and His humanity), but keeping them both intact instead of blending them into an amalgam of the two. "It separated the two ideas and then exaggerated them both" (*Orthodoxy* 94). Using the analogy of color, Chesterton maintains that the Church "has always had a healthy hatred of pink. It hates that combination of two colours which is the feeble expedient of the philosophers. It hates that evolution of black into dirty white which is tantamount to dirty gray" (97). Darcy and Elizabeth are more romantic lovers than anyone else because they are more surprised and more rational than anyone else. Chesterton would say they are more "colourful."

The romance of Elizabeth and Darcy shares another characteristic of orthodoxy: its excitement and sense of narrowly escaped danger. Not only does Chesterton say of orthodoxy, "Nothing was ever so perilous or so exciting," but he compares it to a "heavenly chariot [that] flies thundering through the ages, the dull heresies sprawling and prostrate, the wild truth reeling but erect" (*Orthodoxy* 100–01). This image seems also to fit Elizabeth and Darcy, whose intelligence, discrimination, honesty and attention allow them to live with a kind of plenitude and integrity not possible for most of their contemporaries.

Pride and Prejudice with its four courtships provides a spectrum of erotic experience against which the reader recognizes that the most romantic love affair is that in which the lovers are most free, and at the same time, least free, are most rational and least rational. Of all the couples, Darcy and Elizabeth are the most separate, autonomous, distinctive individuals. Like the adventure of orthodox faith, their union keeps two apparent opposites yoked in a creative tension, allowing each to be fully itself. Yet they are fully engaged with each other. They are serious, they listen, they pay attention, they take risks. Real dangers threaten. Metaphorically, if not literally, they travel a great distance to meet. Like a medieval Romance, their love is a journey. Largely characterized by contingency and surprise, it gains in dignity and excitement by the careful but non-manipulative use of reason, reflection, and conscious, deliberate choice. Surely for Chesterton and for Austen's devoted readers, Elizabeth and Darcy are the most romantic of lovers.

Notes

1. For the sake of clarity I use romance with a small *r* to mean eros and Romance with a capital *R* to mean story. Chesterton's practice is to use the small *r* for both.

2. See Dorothy Van Ghent, 105.

Works Cited

Austen, Jane. *Love and Freindship [sic], and Other Early Works*. Preface by G.K. Chesterton. London: Chatto & Windus, 1922.

———. *Pride and Prejudice*. London: Oxford UP, 1932.

Chesterton, G.K. "On Certain Modern Writers and the Institution of the Family." *Heretics*. New York: John Lane Co., 1914.

———. "On Jane Austen in the General Election." Come to Think of It. New York: Dodd, Mead & Co., 1931.

———. *Orthodoxy*. Garden City: Image Books, 1959.

———. *The Victorian Age in Literature*. London: Williams & Northgate, 1925.

Polhemus, Robert. *Erotic Faith: Being in Love from Jane Austen to D.H. Lawrence*. Chicago: U of Chicago P, 1990.

Tanner, Tony. *Jane Austen*. Cambridge: Harvard UP, 1986.

Unamuno, Miguel de. *Tragic Sense of Life*. Trans. J.E. Flitch. New York: Dover, 1954.

Van Ghent, Dorothy. "On *Pride and Prejudice*." *The English Novel: Form and Function*. New York: Harper and Row, 1953.

Weil, Simone. "Reflections on the Right Use of School Studies With a View to the Love of God." In *Waiting on God*. Trans Emma Craufurd. London: Routledge and Kegan Paul, [1951].

ROBERT L. CASERIO

G.K. Chesterton and the
Terrorist God Outside Modernism

It is as true of democratic fraternity as of divine love; sham love ends in
compromise and common philosophy; but real love has always ended in
bloodshed.... In a garden Satan tempted man; and in [Gethsemane] God
tempted God. He passed ... through our human horror of pessimism....
And now let the revolutionist choose a creed and a god.... They will not
find another god who has himself been in revolt.... They will find only
one divinity who ever uttered their isolation; only one religion in which
God seemed for an instant an atheist.... The chief merit of the old
orthodoxy is that it is the natural foundation of revolution and reform.
— G.K. Chesterton, *Orthodoxy* (1908)

Perhaps the modern age secretly corresponds to the true destination of
a theology.
— Jean-Luc Nancy, 'Of Divine Places' (1986)

1

G.K. Chesterton's *The Man Who Was Thursday* (1908) purports to
differentiate modernist insiders and anti-modernist outsiders; and to
expound the difference in terms of religious belief, art and politics.
According to the book's spokesman for modernism, Lucian Gregory,

From *Outside Modernism: In Pursuit of the English Novel, 1900–30*. © 2000 by Macmillan Press
Ltd.

modernists are anarchist-terrorists, whose priority involves 'the lawlessness of art and the art of lawlessness'.[1] 'An artist is identical with an anarchist' (12); and an anarchist is identical with a terrorist (there will be more to say about this controversial identification). Here is a cento of Gregory's claims that add up to his modernist manifesto:

> 'The man who throws a bomb is an artist, because he prefers a great moment to everything. He sees how much more valuable is one burst of blazing light, ... than the mere common bodies of a few shapeless policemen. An artist disregards all governments, abolishes all conventions ... The poet is always in revolt.... We [modernists] do not only want to upset a few despotisms [including God's] and police regulations.... We dig deeper and blow you higher. We wish to deny all those arbitrary distinctions of vice and virtue, honour and treachery, upon which mere rebels base themselves.... We have abolished Right and Wrong'.
> The Man Who Was Thursday, 12, 13, 23

Opposed to these claims, which Chesterton calls the product of 'dirty modern thinkers' (42) is Chesterton's protagonist Gabriel Syme, who apparently is outside modernism. He is 'a poet of law' and order and respectability (11)—a detective, in other words!—and he becomes an undercover agent in order to hunt down 'Sunday', the secret head of a powerful international modernist-anarchist-terrorist group.

But there is more to learn from The Man Who Was Thursday than this differentiation of modernist from anti-modernist. We find that the ins and outs of modernism are not as simple, not as dependent on clear contrasts as the book's antagonists initially declare, or as Chesterton himself belatedly avows. The Man Who Was Thursday presents us with the problem of Chesterton's last comment about his narrative. Made in 1936, the last comment appears to be a palinode. Chesterton retracts any indefiniteness, especially of a scandalous kind, attaching to his portrayal of the character named Sunday, who turns out to be legible for all intents and purposes as God. God is the leader of modernist anarchist terrorists! No wonder the retraction seems absolute. Because he made Sunday be 'the mysterious master' both of 'anarchy and ... order', Chesterton says that the doubleness 'led many readers to infer that this equivocal being was meant: for a serious description of the Deity' (185). But Chesterton calls the inference a 'lunacy,' an 'error,' based on readers' refusals to attend to the novel's subtitle, 'A Nightmare'. Only in 'a nightmare' could the Deity be the equivocal being—

the 'elemental elf', as Chesterton puts it—called Sunday (185f). In reality the Deity is as unequivocal as the contrast between modernist and anti-modernist, between Gregory and Syme.

Unfortunately for his own unequivocal intentions, two matters resist Chesterton's assertion. The fact that *Thursday* is a narrative is not addressed by Chesterton's closing-off of inferences. The narrative inspires the alleged lunatic error about Sunday, because the narrative is a story and not an argument. The narrative intends to argue that terrorists and anarchists do not exist, that only the fear of the existence of anarchy and terrorism exists; even so, the narrative itself, despite its intentional argumentation, makes God still look like a terrorist. It thereby makes the anti-modernist poet of law and order also look like his opposite.

The second internal resistance to the palinodic claim arises from Chesterton's not having the sense to stop (or from Chesterton's *having* the sense not to stop) at his sentences, in his 1936 comment, about error, which condemn his readers for their response to the narrative (that is, 'lunacy led many to infer that this equivocal being [Sunday] was meant for ... the Deity.... But this error was entirely due to the fact that they ... had not read the ... subtitle' [185]). Not stopping at the sentences about error, Chesterton goes on to describe 'the world of wild doubt and despair which the pessimists were generally describing' in 1908. He remarks that he pitched his narrative to that despair, and hence, he says in the last sentence of his 1936 note, he included in the narrative 'a gleam of hope in some double meaning of the [pessimists'] doubt' (186): This admission is puzzling, because it undermines the definiteness of the assertion about the error of identifying Sunday with God. If doubt can have 'double meaning,' then there would seem to be no problem, either with doubt or with equating God and Sunday. In light of such double meaning, what is doubtful would be also hopeful; what is doubtful in meaning would also be trustworthy. By analogy, error in reading would be as good as accuracy. If doubt can have double meaning, so then can 'a nightmare', which, in the light of a logic of double meaning, can be inferred to mean a dream of bliss, as well as a nightmare.

Chesterton must have known that the last sentence in his note suggests the inference. So why does he end his palinode with a reminder of double meaning, hence of indefiniteness? One possible answer is trivial: the answer that suggests the double meanings inherent in language make it impossible for Chesterton to be dogmatic and definite no matter how much he wants to be dogmatic and definite. This answer claims that language makes heretics of us all. I find this answer trivial, because it makes heresy no less easy than easy orthodoxy; it arrives at a conclusion by retreating from difficulties. I would

like to pursue another hypothesis: namely, that Chesterton in 1908 as well as
in 1936 wants his definite reading of his own book to mean that the path of
definiteness can only be arrived at through double or multiple ambiguous
and equivocal meanings, which are the necessary detour whereby a sure
direction or aim, and a certain belief, are discovered and achieved. A
hierarchy is intended: the means to certainty is equivocal, but only
equivocation can clear a path for certainty, which then subordinates
equivocation. The idea is that the value of definiteness depends on an
indefiniteness which must accompany, and is intrinsic to the discovery of
definiteness. It is necessary to be lost in order to be found might be another
formula for this process. But, in Chesterton's version, the mode of loss is
literary equivocation, the kind of double meaning or ambiguity—indeed a
multiple meaning not just a dual one—which Syme, the anti-modernist hero
of *Thursday*, sneeringly says enables his antagonist Gregory, the modernist-
anarchist, to 'be' a terrorist just by putting on an act. In spite of what Syme
says, Chesterton, in surprising contrast to his hero, permits himself a
submission to doubleness and even to multiplicities and indeterminacies of
meaning. The narrative of *Thursday* implies that, for Chesterton, putting on
an act—especially via double meanings—makes it possible to end by not
putting on an act, by achieving single-minded significance via a dubious
means. The two processes, certainty and uncertainty, are inextricable, not
because they are mutually undecidable and indivisible, but because the
equivocation of meaning clears a space for, and helps secure, a final certainty.

I think it is useful to differentiate between two kinds of doubleness in
Chesterton's work because in the long run the differentiation might help us
think about what is inside or outside modernism, and also help us think about
our beliefs concerning modernism—and concerning belief. What the
anarchist Gregory stands for is the equivocal discourse associated by
Chesterton with error—with the kind of error that identifies God and
'elemental elf'. Double meaning never resolves, or exits from, the realm of
equivocation and multiple significances. But what Syme stands for, after all,
is both the detour of writing into double or multiple meaning and also
writing's detour-transformed emergence into a new definiteness. I propose
calling this second form of equivocation 'double-writing'. 'Double-writing',
in the sense I use it, is double because it pairs equivocal or indefinite
discourse with a purpose to resume and to consolidate definiteness, after
provocatively wandering away from the latter. The neologism, clumsy and
perversely equivocal as it is, means to keep in our minds a double process, a
dependence of resolved and unequivocal certainty upon a process or medium
of multiple and uncertain meanings, whereby what is ultimately resolved

discovers itself. Double-writing uses indefiniteness and ambiguity to produce analytic revelations or thoughts about states of affairs whose direct portrayal can not be achieved without their being twinned, for a long albeit finally limited time, by an indirect portrayal.

Modernism tends to stand for the cultivation of equivocal and multiple meanings, not for 'double-writing'. If modernism rightly stands for a cultural breakthrough of a new emphasis on indefiniteness—if, that is, modernism stands for what we can illustrate by mentally traversing texts from *The Turn of the Screw* to Katherine Mansfield's ambiguous stories to *Between the Acts*, *Finnegans Wake*, and *Molloy*—then Chesterton's double-writing is outside modernism.[2] But I have found myself wondering, thanks to Chesterton, if modernism is not also outside of itself. It would be outside of itself if it does not fully match the way we have tended to read it the way that focuses exclusively on unresolved multiple meaning and ambiguity, in the exclusive emphasis Chesterton fends off or (at least) supplements. Suppose modernism in general, no less than *The Man Who Was Thursday*, is the double-writing Chesterton uses as an ultimate exit from error, as after all a foil to equivocation. Chesterton wouldn't be an outsider at all, if the supposition were tenable. To be tenable, we should have to discover two sides or simultaneous structures in notable modernist works: a side that is multiple and ambiguous in meaning, and a side in which there is a contrasting unequivocal resolution of multiplicity and ambiguity. I think the more we look for these simultaneously present structures the more we will find them; we tend not to find I them, I suggest, because we insist that one side is modernist, and the other is outside modernism. In modern narratives about anarchist-terrorism these two sides are most prominent; indeed, this particular political thematics, I suggest, magnetizes narrative artists because it makes vivid the tense conflict and collaboration of ambiguous meaning and disambiguating resolution.

The supposition that modernism as we have known it is inside out, so that we haven't known it much; that it has the two-sided structure just proposed gains in credibility once the proposal is brought to bear on literary history. Terrorism (which Chesterton conflates, rightly or wrongly, with anarchism) is a central formal inspiration and a central thematics of Anglo-American and international fiction, throughout the century. Ignorance of the continuity has helped create another outside to modernism, our so-called postmodernism; but the continuity and the impact of anarchist terrorism on literary culture suggests that we have only various modernisms to contemplate, and not a divide between one modernism and another, of course, because Chesterton identifies, as the original terrorist, the god who blows up Job, Chesterton thinks there is more to modernism than modernity. But Chesterton's intuitive construction of modernist literary history, whereby modernism is an anarchist-terrorist plot, bears scrutiny. If we keep in mind the possibility that, in Henry James's career, the modernist (and proto-postmodernist) *The Turn of the Screw* is logically and artistically inseparable from *The Princess Casamassima*, if we keep prominently in mind the canonicity of Conrad's *The Secret Agent* (1907) and Gide's *Les Caves du Vatican* (1914) and *The Counterfeiters* (1926), we might be more receptive to the possibility that comments like the following, which are excerpted from postmodern remarks made to a novelist by a spokesman for terrorism, derive from a central tradition:

> 'The only possible heroes for our time ... live willingly with death.... Terror is the only meaningful act.... Who do we take seriously? Only the lethal believer.... Everything else is absorbed ... Only the terrorist stands outside. The culture hasn't figured out how to assimilate him. It's confusing when [terrorists] kill the innocent. But this is ... the language of being noticed, the only language the West understands.... It's the novelist who understands the secret life, the rage that underlies obscurity and neglect. You're half murderers, most of you [novelists].'[3]

These remarks from Don DeLillo's, *Mao II* (1991) hark back to Chesterton's anarchist-terrorist poet Gregory, whose personal atmosphere is 'violent secrecy. The very empyrean [over his] head seemed to be a secret' (11), and who speaks on behalf of pairing 'the lawlessness of art and the art of lawlessness'. Chesterton calls what Gregory speaks up for as 'old cant' (10), perhaps because in 1908 it was already a while since Alfred Jarry had taken to brandishing guns at literary banquets, where he put on an act as a terrorist. But is the tradition I propose from Jarry to DeLillo merely male and/or elitist? I'd suggest that the tradition more than touches on militant suffragism and women's writing: consider how Woolf's Outsiders Society in *Three Guineas* has an anarchist resonance. But, as in the cases of Doris Lessing and Muriel Spark, the relation of women's writing to terrorism intensifies after World War Two. To be most persuasive about anarchist-terrorism's place in literary history I will have to cross our 1930 boundary in this volume: a trespass I plead is necessary for keeping 1900–30 up to date. To broach this problem of tradition and current life I have scarcely space to deploy the limited constellation of four *Thursday*-related fictions I mean to use (I have mentioned only one—DeLillo's). Of course, to hang a tradition on five texts, or even on the entire ten or so I've name-dropped thus far, can't do more than initiate a speculation.

2

After this hypothesis of a tradition, and before a further pursuit of it, I take up the formal or structural characteristic, the double-writing I've mentioned, and show its link to the thematizing of terrorism that is a tradition inside modernism, and is just as much a tradition outside it, even in religious orthodoxy as Chesterton defines it.

Terrorism insists that everyday randomness shall be transformed, shall be made to express overwhelming political certainty: the personal is the political, terrorism declares with a vengeance. The insistence makes everything which is casual and random, everything which is indefinite, speak the univocal definiteness of political conviction, of religious conviction too. Like writing that uses multiple meanings to disclose a new single determination of thought or reality, terrorism's disruption of what is quotidian insists that we grasp reality in the shocking light of a novel all-unifying determination. In an age of terrorism, I might add, if there is a link between terrorism and double-writing, when the formal characteristic of sudden powerful disambiguation appears in literary texts which do *not* refer explicitly to terrorism, the lack of explicit reference suggests the indirectness by which traditions always show their impact. In an age of terrorism, that is, the appearance of double-writing, no matter where, arguably will recall terrorism whenever an artist uses ambiguous meanings in order to harness them, and to put them to the service of arriving at awesome certainty.

But is there fiction that does this work of securing certainty? And have we attended to fiction on these terms? If the answers seem negative, this is because literary criticism of modernist and post-modernist fiction tends to celebrate, as happy and liberating, as progressive, such fiction's multiple and ambiguous meanings. But the latter often are differently intoned within modernist fiction. For example, in the last chapter of *The Secret Agent* the newspaper report of Winnie Verloc's suicide—with its famous key sentence 'An impenetrable mystery seems destined to hang for ever over this act of madness or despair'—exemplifies the escape of Winnie's life and death from a single, determinate meaning.[4] The way the key sentence echoes in the anarchist Ossipon's head intensifies the escape: the sentence breaks up into non-sequential, inconsequential pieces, in a way that mimes the mystery, from first to last, of Winnie's story. Literary critics are likely to see this breaking apart of meaning, at least in the abstract, as an intellectual, moral and political virtue. And yet Ossipon is maddened by the sentence's expressive metamorphic ambiguity, because of its distance from the truth, which he is in the position to grasp definitively. There is no mystery about Winnie! Her story—its unjust waste of life and humane purpose—explodes mystery and ambiguity. Her tale is exactly 'simple,' as Conrad's subtitle for the novel points out; her meaning is simplicity itself. What is outrageous is the idea that there is any ambiguity about her, and Stevie's, and *her class's,* fate; what is outrageous is the idea that the world of international conflict and police surveillance in which she and her class are caught has multiple meaning. It has only one meaning: the destruction of Winnie and her kind. It can only mean exactly what the anarchists and terrorists in the novel think: that the world's oppression of a social class is an infamy to be eradicated. This simple side of the tale is the double-writing I have described. Of course, Conrad makes us feel an unrelieved, unresolved ambiguity in the story, and an explosive 'simplification' of the ambiguity, at once. He does the same in *Under Western Eyes* (1911). There the enforced ties of apolitical Razumov to the anarchist-terrorist Haldin show Conrad dramatizing the two structural sides of modernist writing—ambiguity and disambiguating, single-minded double-writing—at the level of character. Razumov has no interest in seeing the world with Haldin's single-minded determination; yet Razumov will emerge from a world of ambiguous meanings with a single-minded force of conviction that derives from Haldin's foreclosure of Razumov's multiple possibilities of life.

Does this structural phenomenon, and this political theme, inter-identify anarchism and terrorism, at the price of grave injustice? Anarchism and terrorism are not *prima facie* or intrinsically the same; they have had divergent histories. Indeed the history of terrorism has seemed to outlast the history of anarchism. Did the latter not have its last gasp in the student revolts of 1968, and its next-to-last gasp in the Spanish Civil War? And has terrorism not become a thing apart from anarchism, especially since its arguable motives—authoritarian ideology, a will to dominate, a cynical exploitation of media sensationalism—are far distant from anarchist libertarianism? Moreover, we have seen terrorism become an instrument of the political right, indeed of the religious right; surely this is not to be tied to the anarchist heritage.

Yet from 1870 to 1900 the history of anarchism also is, undeniably, the history of terrorism. From the emergence of Bakunin to the Parisian bombings that led to the Trial of the Thirty in 1894 to the assassination of King Umberto of Italy in 1900, anarchism and terrorism develop side by side. Indeed the development takes the form of the novelistic structure I have been describing. On the one hand, anarchism stands for a liberation of social order from single-minded determinations; for a generous break-up of the pieces of the whole into a productive decentred multiplicity of elements. Anarchist order is the promise of an ever-metamorphic non-hierarchic social form, a happy version of Ossipon's indeterminate 'sentence'. But to initiate this happiness the famous propaganda of the deed—terrorism—came to seem indispensable. And the modes and effects of this terrorism in the 1890s especially was as intense and diverse as it has been in recent decades. (In Paris alone there are 11 terrorist dynamitings between 1892 and 1894; to be sure, these killed 'only' nine persons. The nine do not include President Carnot, assassinated by an anarchist.) And when we read statements of motive by the anarchist-terrorists—'I shall not be striking an innocent if I strike the first bourgeois I meet'; another believes that his deeds will be 'The cry of a whole class which demands its right'—we can recognize the double-writing impulse enacting itself politically.[5] The multiple meanings of bourgeois life, the ambiguities which saturate the life of whole classes, are (at least in the terrorist's intention) transformed and resolved by the propaganda of the deed. The innocent bystander, blown up by history, and the innocent spectator of the explosion, thereby forcibly are persuaded of what their 'innocence' refuses to admit: that the indeterminacies, the free-floating significances, of personal or of group life are illusions. As in this century's latter end, in the last century's finale terrorism is the re-telling of the ambiguities. The re-telling disambiguates everyone's place in political and economic conflict; it insists, with brutal democracy, that we all are—for certain—equally political agents and combatants. Fused together, from 1870 on towards the Great War, the anarchist and the terrorist seem to represent a concordance of political antitheses—anarchist libertarianism, terrorist authoritarianism.

The fusion-contrast extends to ways of knowing the world, and perhaps still partly determines how we frequently experience knowledge—knowledge in general; knowledge of terrorism—as a dilemma. The libertarian thread of anarchist tradition accepts every form of knowledge or belief, in a manner that implies a generous openness to multiple meanings, and a pragmatistic mixture of doubt and credulity about epistemology, belief, or truth. But, in contrast to this libertarian thread, the terrorist insists that what he explodes into the world is an absolute certainty. The certainty would be betrayed by openness or doubtful uncertainty. It is worth noting that among present-day scholars the forms of the search for the truth about terrorism fall into curiously appropriate complementary contrasts. Half the scholarship, emphasizing the ambiguous character and the indeterminate effect of terrorism in our era, insists on the historical multiplicity of what is wrongly attributed to terrorism as its single identity. Because of this unenlightened wrongheadedness, according to the scholarship, terrorism has gained an exaggerated presence and importance. This scholarly side of the issue tends to respect, even to justify, the anarchist past, and to separate it, in spite of history, from the terrorism that is or should be, after all, an object of scholarly scepticism. Such scepticism is exemplified in Walter Laqueur's *The Age of Terrorism* (1987). In spite of naming an era of terrorism, Laqueur uses his book to reduce 'the age' to something like a figment of collective imagination. Under his scrutiny, the meaning of terrorism is decentred— even exploded. So detached is he from respect for, or from belief in, his terrorist subjects that he seems curiously anarchistic himself—that is, when he is not appearing to be as certain as any terrorist in his judgement that terrorism is only contemporary nonsense, however lethal. In contrast (or is it?), the other half of scholarship—exemplified, I'd say, by David J. Brown and Robert Merrill's *Violent Persuasions: The Politics and Imagery of Terrorism* (1993)—is not in the least sceptical. With zealous conviction, it insists that terrorism is only ill-defined when definitions leave out of account the greatest terrorists of all: the legitimate world states. According to *Violent Persuasions*, there are no ambiguities, and no two ways about it: the US (along with Argentina, Chile, El Salvador, and Guatemala, among others) is a terrorist state; so are 'corporate economic interests' ('there is a crucial parallelism between corporate economic interests, the definition of who the terrorists are, and our government's kind treatment of terrorist states').[6] Aptly named, *Violent Persuasions* does the kind of violence to ambiguities that double-writing does.

Were modernist artists drawn to anarchist-terrorism because of the latter's convergence with the perplexities of modern epistemology and belief? Oscar Wilde signed the petition for mercy for the Chicago Haymarket anarchists in 1886; Mallarmé testified on behalf of an anarchist friend at the Trial of the Thirty; Picasso in his youth was a fellow traveller of the Spanish anarchist-terrorists. Each of these heroes of art was caught up in the modernist ideology connecting art and lawlessness. And yet the anti-modernist, the outsider Chesterton, also is caught up in it. We remember that modernism begins in the realm of theology, in the higher criticism whereby Scripture itself was dissolved into a type of the exploded and deranged, forever ambiguous and indeterminate sentence that haunts Ossipon. Perhaps the higher criticism's latter-day episodes (*Essays and Reviews* reinforced by Darwin's impact) helped produce the anarchist-terrorist phenomenon. What stirs Chesterton is the way the anarchist-terrorist fusion models the religious believer's struggle with faith. In the same year as *The Man Who Was Thursday*, Chesterton published *Orthodoxy*. He found the figure of the anarchist-terrorist ready-to-hand as an epitome of the burdensome difficulty of faith, as well as of the romance-like revolutionary character of Christian belief. *Orthodoxy* is studded with approving references to anarchist violence—and to the lawlessness of art: 'By defining its main doctrine, the Church not only kept seemingly inconsistent things side by side, but, what was more, allowed them to break out in a sort of artistic violence otherwise possible only to anarchists.'[7]

The Man Who Was Thursday remains sympathetically responsive to the terrorist Lucian Gregory, even though Gregory is the villain of the piece. But since Thursday demonstrates that finally there are no villains—except perhaps Sunday the God—not surprisingly Gregory and Gabriel Syme are friends on *Thursday*'s last page. They are friends beyond the nightmare because they have been friends throughout the nightmare. Their friendship depends upon, and is begun by, the disclosure of their secrets to each other, and, even more importantly, by their promise not to betray each other's vulnerability. Spontaneously and arbitrarily made by both, their promise shows the opponents toy be alike, equally ruled by impulsive—and anarchistic—caprice, and yet regulated, thanks to the caprice, by a mutual betrayal of their separate ideologies. Syme insists that although Gregory is one of the anarchists, one of the dirty modern thinkers, 'I can't break my word to a modern pessimist' [i.e. to Gregory] (105). Similarly, Gregory keeps his word not to reveal Syme's detective work. The dirty pessimist-terrorist shows remarkable fidelity, shows therefore an ambiguous meaning in his doubt. But more startlingly ambiguous—and illustrative of double-writing—is Syme's final response to Gregory in the book's last episode, a masque of the quotidian powers, each of whom is a god. When Gregory breaks into the masque, to accuse the supreme gods the Ancient of Days, of never suffering, Syme's retort to Gregory asserts that the powers do suffer, that they are patients no less than agents. But Syme's retort surprisingly includes something that the finale's crowded phantasmagoria can make us forget: a blessing by Syme of the dynamiter, of the unregenerate terrorist-modernist in all the latter's explosive anger. Syme suddenly grasps a new determination of reality: 'I see everything,' he cried, 'everything that there is. Why does each thing on the earth war against each other thing? ... So that each thing that obeys law may have the glory and isolation of the anarchist. So that each man fighting for order may be as brave and good a man as the dynamiter' (182f).

'As brave and good a man as the dynamiter'? The blessing seems to confirm an undecidable nature in the terrorist figure, to confirm as well the ambiguous meaning of the agents of order or rule. By this final point in *The Man Who Was Thursday* all the anarchist-terrorists are good guys; they are on the side of law and order. Doesn't the blessing make it hard once again to tell the difference between law and order and anarchy, in a way that recapitulates the narrative's constant confusions of difference and sameness? But the confusions are not recapitulated here so much as they now produce and settle their point. What Syme sees now is not indeterminacy, but new certainty. The anarchist and the ruler are alike, not because they are each other's doubles, but because each of them separately doubles a third—and very surprising—figure: the figure of a besieged but fierce and also generous justice, itself the product of obedience to law. Justice is the law-serving energy, the passion and force which we misprise by the names *anarchism* and *terrorism*. We are wrong to think terrorism is the opposite of justice. The character of the latter is for Chesterton—and for Syme in his moment of 'seeing'—unambiguously the same as the character of the former. But the 'one burst of blazing light', the ultimate revelation (digging deeper and blowing higher)—that this is what there is to see, that justice too is terror—arrives only thanks to the proliferation of double or multiple meanings. When Syme experiences the bewildering ambiguity which results when anarchists and policemen look—and are—alike, he suffers the pain of meanings gone astray. But the product of strayed meanings is new meaning, which could not be produced prior to, or without, the wandering contradictory coalescence of established significances. Differentiations must collapse, in order to produce new differentiations. One of the new differentiations paradoxically discriminates the sameness of justice and terror.

It is characteristic of Chesterton to make writing work in this paradoxical but disambiguating way. In 1910 in his book on Shaw Chesterton sees Shaw's writing work in this manner. He does the same thing to Shaw as he does to Gregory. He treats Shaw as an enemy, then finds ways to ambiguate the enmity, and finally sees that he and Shaw are on the same side. The ambiguation that issues in disambiguation, whose very certainty is frightening (and in whose light pessimism is only a trivial scare), is what the narrative of *Thursday* identifies with terrorism. And neither faith nor history can escape submission to the double-writing, the ambiguation–disambiguation, of terrorism, if either faith or history is to see everything that there is.

It is to make some such visionary claim I think that Chesterton hazards the surrelaism of *Thursday*'s last three chapters, which begin with the police chase of Sunday, who is astride a runaway elephant he's stolen from the London Zoo for use as a get-away vehicle. *Thursday* could well end with Chapter 12, which brandishes the lantern of faith, and concludes, 'We were all a lot of silly policemen looking at each other' (150). It could well end there, because what does end with Chapter 12 is the psychological plot, in which the characters realize that ambiguity belongs to their way of knowing things but not ultimately to what there is to know. (The realization well illustrates the relation of double-writing to ambiguity.) What they know now is that they are all on the same side, and not enemies. But the last three chapters are the dynamite ones. They blow up the newly achieved knowledge, so that Syme will have to revise his view of the pieces, and come to a knowledge even more definite. How can he come to see the once-more exploded pieces, in a manner that feels not hostile, but secure about the dynamiter; in a manner that, avoiding 'that final scepticism which can find no plan to the universe' (127), trusts the way the pieces fit; or in a manner that sees the fitness even of the pieces?

The answer has been forecast mid-way through the book, when the narrator provides a descriptive formula for Syme's characteristic way of acting: 'Syme plunged into the breach with that bravado of improvisation which always came to him when he was alarmed' (100). 'Bravado of improvisation' is a leap; it plunges into the unknown by exploiting the ambiguity of the known, by heightening the unknown, the unknowable, the undecided, the unsure. Improvisation depends on the capacity I to produce double or multiple meanings, and to inhabit them. Each of Syme's improvisations depends on his being able to speak, to show, in relation to single definiteness, indefinitely. And yet improvisation is, for all its multiple meanings, single-minded: it is trying to leap into the breach in order to leap out. (Gregory also improvises in this way, by remaining faithful to his promise to Syme.) The bravado of improvisation is a model for double-writing, which uses uncertainty to gain certainty, which expresses definiteness out of indefiniteness.

This gain of expression is relevant to Chesterton's last three chapters. They astonish because, despite the apparent end of the hunt for the anarchist, the novel perversely goes on, thereby foregrounding bravado of improvisation as the narrative's alarmed mode of life, not just Syme's mode. But as the narrative's (and the author's) improvisation unfolds, so does the spectacle of Sunday's improvising. Sunday, the God, who is the anarchist-terrorist and chief of detectives in one, riding the elephant and attempting to evade his befooled cohort of outraged private eyes, throws wads of paper at his pursuers. Unfolding the wads, each pursuer finds writing which addresses himself. Each is stunned and enraged by the message he receives, because the messages implicate the detective-receiver in what appear to be stories at once bewildering and precise. For example, one message to a pursuer reads 'Fly at once. The truth about your trouser-stretchers is known—A FRIEND'; another reads, 'The word, I fancy, should be "pink"'; a third, from Sunday to a male pursuer: 'Your beauty has not left me indifferent.—From LITTLE SNOWDROP' (157, 161, 163). Now these surreal messages, these tender buttons of notes, are God's improvisations; they exhibit the bravado of meaningful meaninglessness. But they are also meaning-full. The precise specificity of the notes makes them feel as if they are intelligible particulars dropped from a comprehensive and intelligible tale no less certain than the note of certainty characteristically struck by each folded wad. It is the ability of ambiguity to strike certain notes, to issue in certainty, that enrages Sunday's pursuers. But, most significantly, it is the same ability of ambiguity to strike a certain note that leads Syme, two chapters later, to grasp the sight of everything, to know that the dynamiter is as blessed as the detective. Double-writing has its consummation here. Improvisation and ambiguity unveil a definitive apocalypse.

3

Chesterton uses the three final chapters of *The Man Who Was Thursday* to illustrate the double-writing device and, at the same time, to expound the working of religious belief, the constitutive process of orthodoxy. But why should orthodoxy bless terrorism, why strike that note? And who can believe that modernism is the companion of orthodoxy; for who finds in modernist ambiguity the power to strike any certain note whatsoever? Moreover, if the terrorist God should be in modernism and belong to it rather than be outside modernism and belong to orthodoxy, would it not be best—in order to be done with anarchism, terrorism and modernism—to believe that Great Pan is dead? Would it not be best to believe that Great Pan is dead both in orthodoxy and outside it?

These questions move me outside Chesterton, and closer to the postmodern present, in the first loop I want to make in order to situate *Thursday* in the context of the terrorist-centred tradition I propose we contemplate. I move just beyond World War Two, to 1947 and to Charles Williams's *All-Hallow's Eve*, a novel which has T.S. Eliot's word for it that it descends from *The Man Who Was Thursday*. *All Hallow's Eve* takes place in two places, two cities, at one and the same time. One place is London the worldly city; one place is a spiritual city, a penumbra-like London which houses the slowly-departing souls of the recently dead. But the doubling of London in this way creates another doubling, in time. The importance of time in this fantasy derives from Williams's coordination and counterpointing of it with the historical time of the war against fascism. Although in the novel the historical war is about to end, yet a spectral war is about to commence. We have known the spectral war under the name of the Cold War, which replays World War Two fantasmatically. But Williams's extension of spectral war forward in time also resonates with a backward extension. The dead who walk in the penumbral city perhaps are a fantasy in Williams's mind of World War One's relation to World War Two: it is as if the just-dead are ghosts of the first conflict as well as ghosts of the second. With the Great War becoming greater, there are at least two times at work in Williams's novel analogous to the novel's two places. Working across the boundaries of these separate times and places is the novel's villain, a magus, Father Simon the Clerk, a neo-fascist who prepares to rule the earth, first by cloning himself as two dictators, who are about to seize power in Russia and China (Simon himself will take the US); and secondly, by creating a female dead-alive human simulacrum, which will serve as the magus's permanent medium between the cities of the living and the dead, and between the present and the future.

The magus is this novel's version of the terrorist figure, whose association earlier in the tradition with anarchist force is shifted now to totalitarian ambition. In order to realize the magic of violence, in order to determine the world to realize his single determinate meaning solely, the magus must shift the boundaries between life and death, flesh and ghost, in a way that temporarily ambiguates them all. The ambiguation touches off the double-writing device, both in terms of what happens in the novel, and in terms of how Williams structures the narrative. What happens will include a fortunate chance. Moving in the sphere of double meanings, where life and death are indeterminate, the magus's improvisatory bravado will accidentally sweep two just-dead women's souls into the one simulacrum. But one woman's soul will thwart the other, and will thwart the terrorist magus as well. The thwarting occurs when the one soul suddenly realizes something decisively true about her conduct in life. She realizes, in a way she did not grasp when alive, her deeply culpable habit of indifference to love offered her by another woman in her circle.

This realization is a certainty that issues, paradoxically, from the terrorist-inspired ambiguation; it is a certainty described as 'a ... way of knowledge, and that knowledge perfect in its satisfaction'. As a result of her new knowledge 'she [the soul of the dead woman] was beginning to live differently'.[8] Similarly, the woman's husband, who survives her, and who momentarily rediscovers her in the simulacrum, similarly changes, coming to know for sure, with a new determination of knowledge, that he has loved his wife, and for what reasons. He arrives at this definite knowledge by meeting her when she is veiled by the magus's medium and paired with the other spirit; when she is both herself and not herself. She is in a state of ambiguous meaning. Yet this ambiguity promises a hopeful resolution. The process is pictured by Williams in terms of two paintings that figure in the narrative: one painting instances the medium of multiple meanings, the other the disambiguation of doubleness that transforms uncertainty into certainty, as when Syme sees all there is to see. Williams's narrative, we are to understand, is the double-writing that moves from one way of picturing things to the other, more certain way. It is understood that the more certain way comes to terms with reality, is a mode of realism, however fantastic the medium.

Charles Williams's work is the sign of a common link between writers who are both inside modernism and outside it: between G.K. Chesterton and Muriel Spark, for example. Williams's work also is the symptom of a thematics and of a disposition of form which we still need to account for in our history of modernism's fate. All I have been proposing is the compatibility of modernism, which we have traditionally assumed to be a word for scepticism, negative capability, agnosticism and doubt, ambiguous and multiple meanings in short, with certainty, and with the surmounting of scepticism, with what is outside it. Terrorism and the orthodoxy of faithful belief, I hypothesize, are the keys to the compatibility. Williams's magus is a figure for the terror that is encoded in modernist ambiguation and for the no less greater terror—and hallowedness—of disambiguation that is also encoded in modernism. We have been misled in thinking that disambiguation's terrorism is only encoded outside of modernism. *The Man Who Was Thursday* holds the keys to the code, but it is not the only holder. In Chesterton's light we must take a fresh look at disambiguation, belief, and terrorism in James, Gide, Williams, Spark, DeLillo—at innumerable other practitioners of double-writing—to see if we have been out of it, to see what we have been missing inside modernism.

When Gabriel Syme 'sees everything', in a burst of blazing light, he penetrates the sphere of orthodoxy, in Chesterton's terms. This means that in his vision Syme merges with the figure of the anarchist-terrorist and the artist. The merger means that Syme is enveloped in certain belief and sure knowledge. But can such envelopment be characteristic of art, whether modernist or postmodernist? Surely we do not believe that art can provide us with orthodox certainty or certain knowledge? Laqueur devotes a chapter of *The Age of Terrorism* to 'The Image of the Terrorist: Literature and the Cinema'. Having insisted on the political inefficacy of terrorism, on its pointlessness, apparently Laqueur is struck—perhaps shocked—by the proliferation of anarchist and terrorist motifs in art. 'Literature as a source for the study of terrorism is still virtually terra incognita,' he declares, as he marches towards the new land. But at the same time, he admits he expects to find nothing there to know. 'With the transition from the sciences [that is, political science] to the arts we move from a level of relative certainties to the realm of impression.'[9] Does Laqueur's diction remember impressionism? If so, Chesterton appositely describes 'the thing which the modern people call Impressionism, which is another name for that final scepticism which can find no floor to the universe' (127).

We literary critics are likely to share this judgment about art as an agnostic realm of 'impression', although we see everything to celebrate and nothing to condemn in 'that final scepticism'. Nevertheless, the very objects of our study might not be as finally sceptical, nor as finally powerless in knowledge, as the political scientist might like. The attraction of art to anarchist-terrorism suggests the novelists' desire to see everything, to produce fiction—however violently in terms of persuasion—as a form of sure knowledge. I close by outlining the role double-writing plays in a trio of characteristic fictions about anarchist-terrorist figures.

Robert M. Coates's *The Eater of Darkness*, a distinguished American first novel of 1929 (praised by Gertrude Stein, whose protégé Coates was; and published by Robert McAlmon), tells a surrealist tale about the inventor of a surreal terrorist weapon called 'the eater of darkness'.[10] The weapon, an x-ray like instrument for performing random assassinations, is a work of anarchist-terrorist art; its inventor uses it to carry out direct hits on innocent victims, who are casually chosen, and even miles away from the weapon. The inventor also uses the machine to entrance the novel's male narrator, who has fled an unhappy love affair in Paris to return to New York, the site of the story. What here is of interest is the structure Coates gives the narrative. The terrorist and his machine figure a directness and certainty of knowledge and invention that is made to appear loathsome, even if fascinating. As the narrative unfolds, as if to intermit and oppose the unambiguous certainty of knowledge and power encoded in the weapon and its artist-inventor, the form of the unfolding ambiguates the tale's elements. The identity of the terrorist and of the narrator both lose outline and coherence; the inventor is frustrated by the narrator, and the attempt to capture the inventor and to bring him to justice fissions into multiple indeterminate plots. But there is a final surprise, one that exhibits the way Coates's typically modernist experimentation resolves itself into a double-writing. The ambiguation of the narrative reverses itself. We become more and more certain that the narrator's involvement with the terrorist and his invention has displaced the narrator's aggressions towards the beloved woman he's left behind in Paris. The resolution of the displacement brings the narrative elements out of the realm of ambiguous and uncertain impressions. In this result the machine is destroyed. But in a sense it is re-built: as the new sureness of knowledge the narrator has reached concerning his desires, with which he now is directly in touch, and in which he now fully trusts. The machine was the wrong model of this certain knowledge, but it was and remains a model, nevertheless. The light of sure knowledge not surprisingly is an eater of darkness.

In Coates, then, the anarchic elements—of modernist experimental immersion in ambiguity, in Conradian cutting-up of narrative sequence and certainty—continue to lean on a will to certainty, which recalls the anarchist-terrorist fusion. We find the same leanings in Muriel Spark and DeLillo. Spark's *The Only Problem* (1984) is about a scholarly man whose obsession with Job (the celebrated victim of God's terrorism) and with suffering ('the only problem') overwhelms his life.[11] His wife drifts away from him; she herself becomes an urban terrorist, kills others, and gets killed in the process. Spark's narrative cultivates the modernist array of questions inherent in Job's story: why is there gratuitous suffering, why do friends, lovers, relatives, communities kill their own? But the questions, and the indeterminate meanings that underlie them, are not the sum of *The Only Problem*. The narrative strikes terrifying lights into its own darkness. Not the least chilling moment of certainty occurs when Spark pictures the scholar's meditation on a baroque painting of Job and his wife. The picture, serving as a double-writing device, drives home—as much as the evasive scholar can allow it to—the scholar's responsibility for his wife's final career. In the light of the picture, we see—as the scholar does—that there are no innocents. The wife's terrorism, horribly enough, gains a sad justification.

And in *Mao II*, a picture also functions as the double-writing device. The novelist in the novel, we recall from the exchange I quoted above, can not compete with the terrorist's authority and power, in the world of modern media. But as the novelist literally dies out of this novel, a friend of his, a female photographer, takes his place. The novelist's death marks the end of a career whose very success has become ambiguous, whose artistic power has been eroded by self-contradictory pressures and compromises. But the photographer has a contrastive integrity. And this makes her a match for the terrorists whom she is on assignment to shoot. Her daring intransigence among them becomes her certainty of knowledge: aided by what her camera art captures, she decides that terrorism is not worthy of belief. Of course her decision has enabled her to reach a secure belief of her own; she has discovered an orthodoxy she may trust. As in *The Eater of Darkness*, in *Mao II* one model or engine of certainty is rejected, but sure knowledge or belief is affirmed nevertheless. In modernism and outside it, the place of art is not only a realm of sceptical impressions. And inside and outside modernism, the anarchist-terrorist god continues to have his day.

Notes

1. G.K. Chesterton, *The Man Who Was Thursday* (Harmondsworth: Penguin, 1986) p. 10. First published 1908. Further page references in the text.

2. See Caserio, *The Novel in England*, Chapter One, for an account of ideas that underlie modernist ambiguity.

3. Don DeLillo, *Mao II* (New York: Viking, 1991) p. 157f.

4. Joseph Conrad, *The Secret Agent: a Simple Tale* (Harmondsworth: Penguin, 1963) p. 246.

5. Woodcock, *Anarchism*, p. 311.

6. Brown and Robert Merrill (eds), *Violent Persuasions*, p. 65.

7. G.K. Chesterton, *Orthodoxy* (New York: Image Books—Doubleday, 1990) p. 96. First published 1908.

8. Charles, Williams, *All Hallows' Eve* (New York: Pellegrini and Cudahy, 1948) p. 181.

9. Laqueur, *The Age of Terrorism*, p. 174.

10. Robert M. Coates, *The Eater of Darkness* (New York: Capricorn Books—G.P. Putnam's Sons, 1959). First published in 1929.

11. Muriel Spark, *The Only Problem* (New York: Wideview/Perigee Books—Putnam, 1984).

Chronology

1874	Gilbert Keith Chesterton is born at Campden Hill, London on May 29.
1887	Attends St. Paul's School.
1892	Publishes the "Song of the Labour" in *The Speaker*.
1892–1895	Attends Slade School of Art and University College.
1895–1901	Employed as a reader for publishers.
1900	*Greybeards at Play* and *The Wild Knights*. Meets Hilaire Belloc.
1901	Marries Frances Blogg and moves to Overstrand Mansions, Battersea, London. Begins his relationship with the *Daily News*.
1903	*Robert Browning*.
1904	*G.F. Watts* and *The Napoleon of Notting Hill*.
1905	*The Club of Queer Trades* and *Heretics*. Begins to write "Our Note-book" in the *Illustrated London News*.
1906	*Charles Dickens*.
1908	*The Man Who Was Thursday, All Things Considered*, and *Orthodoxy*.
1910	*The Ball and the Cross, What's Wrong with the World, Alarms and Discursions*, and *William Blake*.
1911	*Appreciations and Criticisms of Charles Dickens, The Innocence*

	of *Father Brown*, and *The Ballad of the White Horse*. Begins to contribute to the *Eye-Witness*.
1912	*Manalive* and *Miscellany of Men*.
1913	*The Victorian Age in Literature* and *Magic*, a play.
1914	*The Flying Inn*, the *Wisdom of Father Brown*, and *The Barbarism of Berlin*. Seriously ill and loses consciousness for three months.
1915	*Poems*.
1916	Named editor of the *New Witness*, replacing his brother.
1917	*A Short History of England*.
1918	Visits Ireland.
1919	*Irish Impressions*. Visits Palestine.
1920	Begins a lecture tour in the United States. *The Uses of Diversity* and *The New Jerusalem*.
1922	Formally received into the Catholic Church. *Eugenics and Other Evils*, *The Man Who Knew Too Much*, and *What I Saw in America*.
1923	*St. Francis Assisi*.
1925	Becomes editor of *G.K.'s Weekly* until his death. *The Everlasting Man*.
1926	Beginning of the Distributist League. *The Incredulity of Father Brown*, *The Outline of Sanity*, and *The Queen of Seven Swords*.
1927	Visits Poland. *The Return of Don Quixote*, *Collected Poems*, *The Secret of Father Brown*, *The Judgement of Dr. Johnson*, and *Robert Louis Stevenson*.
1928	Debates George Bernard Shaw, which are published as *Do We Agree?*
1929	Visits Rome. *The Poet and the Lunatics*.
1930–1931	A second lecture tour of the United States. *The Resurrection of Rome* and *Come to Think of It*.
1932	Starts to broadcast regularly on the BBC. *Chaucer* and *Sidelights on New London and Newer New York*. *All I Survey* and *St. Thomas Aquinas*.
1933	Visits Rome and Sicily. *Avowals and Denials*.
1934	*The Scandal of Father Brown* and *The Well and the Shallows*.

1935   Dies at Beaconsfield on June 14. *Autobiography.*
1936   *The Paradoxes of Mr. Pond.*

Contributors

HAROLD BLOOM is Sterling Professor of the Humanities at Yale University. He is the author of 30 books, including *Shelley's Mythmaking* (1959), *The Visionary Company* (1961), *Blake's Apocalypse* (1963), *Yeats* (1970), *A Map of Misreading* (1975), *Kabbalah and Criticism* (1975), *Agon: Toward a Theory of Revisionism* (1982), *The American Religion* (1992), *The Western Canon* (1994), and *Omens of Millennium: The Gnosis of Angels, Dreams, and Resurrection* (1996). *The Anxiety of Influence* (1973) sets forth Professor Bloom's provocative theory of the literary relationships between the great writers and their predecessors. His most recent books include *Shakespeare: The Invention of the Human* (1998), a 1998 National Book Award finalist, *How to Read and Why* (2000), *Genius: A Mosaic of One Hundred Exemplary Creative Minds* (2002), *Hamlet: Poem Unlimited* (2003), *Where Shall Wisdom be Found* (2004), and *Jesus and Yahweh: The Names Divine* (2005). In 1999, Professor Bloom received the prestigious American Academy of Arts and Letters Gold Medal for Criticism. He has also received the International Prize of Catalonia, the Alfonso Reyes Prize of Mexico, and the Hans Christian Andersen Bicentennial Prize of Denmark.

WILLIAM HUGH KENNER taught at the University of California at Santa Barbara, Johns Hopkins University, and the University of Georgia. The recipient of two Guggenheim Fellowships, Kenner is also a Fellow of the Royal Society of Literature. In addition to two works on Chesterton, Kenner is the author of over 25 books and nearly a thousand articles.

GARRY WILLS has been a regular contributor to *The New York Review of Books* and is the recipient of many awards, including two National Book Critics Circle Awards and the 1998 National Medal for the Humanities. He teaches history at Northwestern University.

LYNETTE HUNTER is a Professor of the History of Rhetoric and Performance at the University of California, Davis. Her books include *George Orwell: The Search for a Voice, Critiques of Knowing: Situated Textualities in Computing, Science and the Arts,* and *Literary Value: Critical Power.* She has also co-edited the Arden *Romeo and Juliet.*

JOHN COATS is the author of *Chesterton and the Edwardian Cultural Crisis* as well as other books on Chesterton, Kipling, and Elizabeth Bowen. He has written numerous articles about late nineteenth-century and early twentieth-century literature. He has been a lecturer in the English Department at the University of Hull.

JOHN PFORDRESHER is a Professor of English at Georgetown University. He is the author of *Variorum Edition: Tennyson's Idylls of the King* as well as miscellaneous essays on Browning, Tennyson, Dickens, D.G. Rossetti and Pre-Raphaelite art.

ELMAR SCHENKEL works as a writer and a translator. He has published works on John Cowper Powys, Hugo Kuekelhaus, and G.K. Chesterton. He has also written travel literature and a study of the relationship between literature and the natural sciences.

ED BLOCK JR. is currently an Associate Professor of English at Marquette University. He has written *Rituals of Dis-Integration: Romance and Madness in the Victorian Psychomythic Tale* and is the editor of *Critical Essays on John Henry Newman.*

JOHN McCABE has been the Chair of the Department of English at Marquette University while acting as the Director of the University Honors Program. He specializes in the medieval literature, particularly Chaucer. In 1994, he was the recipient of the Pere Marquette Award for Teaching Excellence.

MARIAN E. CROWE has written many articles on the Catholic faith and has been a regular contributor to *Crisis Magazine*. She is currently an independent scholar in Notre Dame's Program of Liberal Studies.

ROBERT L. CASERIO chairs the Department of English at Temple University. He specializes in late nineteenth-century and early twentieth-century British writers. He has written two books: *Plot, Story, and the Novel: from Dickens and Poe to the Modern Period* and *The Novel in England, 1900–1950: History and Theory.*

Bibliography

Attwater, Donald. *Modern Christian Revolutionaries: An Introduction to the Lives and Thought of Kierkegaard, Eric Gill, G.K. Chesterton, C.F. Andrews and Berdyaev*. New York: The Devin-Adair Company, 1947.

Auden, W.H. *G.K. Chesterton: A Selection from His Non-Fictional Prose*. London: Faber and Faber, 1970.

Belloc, Hilaire. *On the Place of Gilbert Chesterton in English Letters*. London: Sheed & Ward, 1940.

Block, Ed Jr. "G.K. Chesterton's Orthodoxy as Intellectual Autobiography." *Renascence* 49 (1996): 41–55.

Bogaerts, Anthony. *Chesterton and the Victorian Age*. New York: Haskell House, 1966.

Boyd, Ian. *The Novels of G.K. Chesterton*. New York: Barnes and Noble, 1975.

Canovan, Margaret. *G.K. Chesterton: Radical Populist*. New York: Harcourt, Brace, Jovanovich, 1977.

Clipper, Lawrence. *G.K. Chesterton*. New York: Twayne, 1974.

Coats, John. "Chesteron as Literary Critic." *Renascence* 50 (1998): 247–264.

———. *Chesterton and the Edwardian Cultural Crisis*. Hull, England: Hull University Press, 1984.

———. "The Return to Hugo: A Discussion of the Intellectual Context of Chesterton's View of the Grotesque." *English Literature in Transition* 25 (1982): 86–100.

Conlon, D.J., ed. *G.K. Chesterton: A Half Century of Views*. Oxford: Oxford University Press, 1987.

Corrin, Jay P. *G.K. Chesterton & Hilaire Belloc: The Battle Against Modernity*. Athens: Ohio University Press, 1981.

Crowe, Marian E. "G.K. Chesterton and the Orthodox Romance of *Pride and Prejudice*." *Renascence* 49 (1997): 209–221.

Dale, Aliza Stone. *The Outline of Sanity: A Biography of G.K. Chesterton*. Grand Rapids: Eerdmans, 1982.

Dwarakanath, K. *G.K. Chesterton: A Critical Study*. New Delhi: Classical Publishing Company, 1986.

Evans, Maurice. *G.K. Chesterton*. New York: Haskell House Publishers, 1972.

Fagerberg, David. "The Essential Chesterton." *First Things: A Monthly Journal of Religion and Public Life* 1 (2000): 23–27.

Ffinch, Michael. *G.K. Chesterton*. San Francisco: Harper & Row, 1986.

Furlong, William. *GBS/GKC: Shaw and Chesterton, the Metaphysical Jesters*. University Park: Pennsylvania State University Press, 1970.

Hollis, Christopher. *The Mind of Chesterton*. Coral Gables: University of Miami Press, 1970.

Hunter, Lynette. *G.K. Chesterton: Explorations in Allegory*. New York: St. Martin's Press, 1979.

Hynes, Samuel. "A Detective and His God; Reconsideration: G.K. Chesterton." *The New Republic* 190 (1984): 39–42.

Kenner, Hugh. *Paradox in Chesterton*. London: Sheed & Ward, 1948.

Lauer, Quentin. *G.K. Chesterton: Philosopher Without Portfolio*. New York: Fordham University Press, 1988.

McCabe, John. "On Reading Chesterton's *Chaucer*." *Renascence* 49 (1996): 79–87.

Pfordresher, John. "Chesterton on Browning's Grotesque." *English Language Notes* 24 (1987): 42–51.

Royal, Robert. "Our Curious Contemporary, G.K. Chesterton." *Wilson Quarterly* 16 (1992): 92–103.

Schwartz, Adam. "G.K.C.'s Methodical Madness: Sanity and Social Control in Chesterton." *Renascence* 49 (1996): 19–41.

Schwartz, Joseph. "Chesterton on the Idea of Christian Tragedy." *Renascence* 53 (2001): 227–238.

———. "The Theology of History in The Everlasting Man." *Renascence* 49 (1996): 56–67.

Sullivan, John. *G.K. Chesterton: A Centenary Appraisal*. New York: Barnes and Noble, 1974.

Titterton, William. *G.K. Chesterton: A Portrait*. New York: Haskell House Publishers, 1973.

Ward, Maisie. *Gilbert Keith Chesterton*. New York: Sheed & Ward, 1943

———. *Return to Chesterton*. New York: Sheed and Ward, 1952.

West, Julius. *G.K. Chesterton: A Critical Study*. Folcroft: Folcroft Library Editions, 1972.

Wills, Garry. *Chesterton: Man and Mask*. New York: Sheed and Ward, 1961.

Acknowledgments

"The Word and the World" by Hugh Kenner. From *Paradox in Chesterton*. pp. 103–156. © 1948 Sheed & Ward, Ltd. Reprinted by permission.

"Rhyme and Reason" by Garry Wills. From *Chesterton: Man and Mask*. pp. 128–144, 229. © 1961 Sheed & Ward, an imprint of Rowman & Littlefield Publishers, Inc. Reprinted by permission.

"Mapping the Artistic Terrain: 1904–1907" by Lynette Hunter. From *G.K. Chesterton: Explorations in Allegory*. pp. 54–74. © 1979 Lynette Hunter. Reprinted by permission.

"The Return to Hugo: A Discussion of the Intellectual Context of Chesterton's View of the Grotesque" by John Coats. From *English Literature in Transition: 1880–1920*, Vol. 25, No. 2. pp. 86–103. © 1982 ELT. Reprinted by permission.

"Chesterton on Browning's Grotesque" by John Pfordresher. From *English Language Notes*, Vol. XXIV, No. 3 (March 1987). pp. 42–51. © 1987 English Language Notes. Reprinted by permission.

"Visions from the Verge: Terror and Play in G.K. Chesterton's Imagination" by Elmar Schenkel. From *Twentieth-Century Fantasists: Essays on Culture,*

Society, and Belief in Twentieth-Century Mythopoeic Literature. Kath Filmer, ed. pp. 34–46. © 1992 The Macmillan Press. Reprinted by permission.

"G.K. Chesterton's *Orthodoxy* as Intellectual Autobiography" by Ed Block, Jr. From *Renascence: Essays on Values in Literature*, Vol. IL, No. 1 (Fall 1996). pp. 41–55. © 1996 Renascence. Reprinted by permission.

"On Reading Chesterton's Chaucer" by John McCabe. From *Renascence: Essays on Values in Literature*, Vol. IL, No. 1 (Fall 1996). pp. 79–87. © 1996 Renascence. Reprinted by permission.

"G.K. Chesterton and the Orthodox Romance of *Pride and Prejudice*" by Marian E. Crowe. From *Renascence: Essays on Values in Literature*, Vol. IL, No. 3 (Spring 1997). pp. 209–221. © Renascence. Reprinted by permission.

"G.K. Chesterton and the Terrorist God Outside Modernism" by Robert L. Caserio. From *Outside Modernism: In Pursuit of the English Novel, 1900–30*. Lynne Hapgood and Nancy L. Paxton, ed. pp. 63–82. © 2000 Macmillan Press Ltd. Reprinted by permission.

Every effort has been made to contact the owners of copyrighted material and secure copyright permission. Articles appearing in this volume generally appear much as they did in their original publication with little to no editorial changes. Those interested in locating the original source will find bibliographic information in the bibliography and acknowledgments sections of this volume.

Index

Characters in literary works are indexed by first name (if any), followed by the name of the work in parentheses.